Journey Through Jailhouse Jeopardy: A Good New York City Teacher Ends Up Down In Bad Rikers Island Jail

Journey Through Jailhouse Jeopardy: A Good New York City Teacher Ends Up Down In Bad Rikers Island Jail

Odimumba Kwamdela
J. Ashton Brathwaite

BOOKS

Brooklyn, New York

Copyright © 2004 J. Ashton Brathwaite

All rights reserved. No part of this publication may be reproduced or transmitted in any form or by any means, electronic or mechanical, or by information storage and retrieval system without permission in writing from the publisher.

ISBN 0-941266-31-1
Library of Congress Control Number: 2004102733

Information to:
Kibo Books, P.O.Box 021442, Cadman Plaza,
Brooklyn, New York 11202, USA
E-mail: Kibibooks@aol.com

Website: www.kibobooks.com

Manufactured in the United States of America

Author's Note

In recent years I have frequently become involved in discussions regarding the increasing public use and acceptance of profanity by youngsters as the norm, as is the same for the increasing public display of sexuality by young females, both championed by television, other media, various forms of entertainment, and glorified by most entertainers; also the continuous use of the term nigga by Black folk, used both with affection and hate – ironically.

My stand on these issues has always been one in opposition. Undoubtedly, many will readily speculate that there is some kind of religious reason for my stand against the first two, which would be strange, considering how often that charge of "non-believer" has been hurled at me. In actuality, the foundation of my opposition is something I regard as stronger than religion: my conscience.

During the years I have worked with youngsters, I sometimes asked them: Why do young comedians, for instance, use so much profanity in their acts? Why do young females so flagrantly flaunt sexuality through their manner of dressing and posturing, and like young males, consistently through their verbal communication? They saw these things as quite normal. I, on the other hand, saw the constant use of profanity by young comedians as cover for their doubt about their ability to be truly humorous. I observed that most of the laughter from their audiences come when they use profanity.

Of course, there is also the case of when youngsters are out in public or in the schools and they use profanity constantly. Therefore, there can be no doubt about the use of profanity being an integral, unavoidable, normal part of their communication.

As I was in the process of writing this book about youngsters in the New York City public schools, I found myself making a lot of references to the obsessive flaunting of sexuality by young females and much more so using profanity. I was conscious of the latter especially. While I do in fact believe that the occasional use of profanity can "spice up" creative writing and similar art forms, I also believe that its over use defeats the purpose for which it was intended by turning the "spice" unpalatably acid.

But how could I write a book about my daily dealings with adolescents in New York City and ignore the flagrant flaunting of sexuality, or play down too much their constant use of profanity and that term nigga? It would be so very unreal indeed. The references to these things herein are more that I wished to use; maybe more than you wish to read. However, as the story cried out to me to be told, I predict that you will feel it crying out to you to be read.

About the Author

In 1960, while in his early teens and still known by his given name *John A. Brathwaite*, he who would some years later change his name to **Odimumba Kwamdela**, left his native Barbados for London, England. He eventually enlisted in the British Army and served in the Mideast.

After military service, he left London for Ontario, Canada. There, he freelanced with Toronto newspapers before becoming founding publisher and editor of *Spear*, reputed to be the first Black magazine published in Canada. "I had big dreams," said he, "of making *Spear* the Ebony of Canada."

Eventually becoming disappointed with what he saw as the limitation of Spear in a nation with too small a Black population, and believing the "controversial" status the original edition of his book *Niggers This Is Canada* somehow gained made him the object of governmental harassment, he exiled himself to NewYork City. There, around the mid-1970's, he made the decision to discard the name J. Ashton Brathwaite under which he had written and was published.

At this time Kwamdela was enrolled in the City University of New York – of which he is a Literature and Journalism graduate – as a part-time night student doing full time studies and holding down full-time day employment in the graphic arts industry of Manhattan. Eventually, he also graduated from New York Institute of Technology with the Master of Science in Instructional Technology degree.

To date, Kwamdela has authored 12 books of fiction, non-fiction and poetry and a musically dubbed CD/album of poetry, listed herein under the heading *Books by the Author*.

As a New York City Board of Education high school teacher of writing and graphic arts for several years, Kwamdela taught in the roughest schools in the world; even one for adolescent inmates located in "the belly of the beast:" infamous, volatile Rikers Island Jail.

Books by the Author

Black British Soldier *
Soul in the Wilderness *
Niggers this is Canada *
Raining Ruins, Roses and Rockstones *
Back to Penny Hole Forever *
Searching Souls Down Inna Southern Africa **
Soul Surviving up in Canada *
The Small Black Book of Big Thoughts **
Journey Through Jailhouse Jeopardy ***
THE FOLLOWING TITLES ARE POETRY **
The Grassroots Philosopher
The Prophet Next Door
Blood-Boiling Black Blues
Behold the Grassroots Poet-Philosopher ***
(A musically dubbed CD/album of poetry)

INFORMATION: Any problems getting any of the above-mentioned can be easily and promptly solved by sending money order in the amount of $10 each for titles marked *, $7 each for titles marked **, $12 each for titles marked ***. Prices are in United States currency and include mailing via air-mail if foreign orders. All orders will be promptly mailed. Personal checks accepted within the continental United States only.

Kibo Books, P. O. Box 021442, Cadman Plaza, Brooklyn, New York 11201, USA.   E-mail: Kibobooks@aol.com
Website: www.kibobooks.com

ACKNOWLEDGEMENTS

Makela Amani, your computer wizardry came in so handy during the initial stages of this book.
Dr. Sheldon Taylor, not only your constant praise of the author for writing the most interesting books, but your expressed anticipation of seeing this account published, played a major role in its completion.
Malaika Brathwaite, your knack for catching those little errors in the manuscript and rewrites was much better than the author's.
Kofi Casisi (C.Cummins), your memory of events, times and places was invaluable.
Beverly and all the above, your care, concern and encouragement helped greatly in lifting the author out of the malaise caused by major surgeries to resume working on this book.

DEDICATION

Wherever they are today, this book is for those youngsters who came under my guidance and tutelage. Hopefully, those who desired to take the positive route in life did, and many of those who opted for the negative route eventually got off.

"The ruins of a nation begins in the homes of its people."
-- Old African proverb

< 1 >

Journey Through Jailhouse Jeopardy

"WELL, THE ONLY PLACE I have left that I can send you at this late date is on Rikers Island...Rikers Island Jail, that is," Mr. Thomas said to me as he sat at his desk scrutinizing my face for my reaction. Examining his facial expressions, and his fingers scratching his beard lightly – obviously not because his beard itched but as an act of pondering over the situation – I had no doubt that he had actually anticipated the negativity running through my mind.

"Nobody likes going to Rikers Island," he said, as if apologizing for suggesting that I should be the one to do so. "Reputation, you know. I'm not going to sit here and tell you that it isn't a rough experience. But there are a few who tackle it. A lot has to do with how you approach it."

It was highly unlikely that there were people in New York who had not heard of the infamous institution Rikers Island Jail, located somewhere in perhaps the most desolate spot of the borough of Queens, ostracized somewhat from the borough by the lonely and fast-flowing East River, and above which can be heard the consistent noise of low-flying international airplanes as they arrive at and depart from nearby LaGuardia Airport.

Yet these were not the things that made Rikers Island a

household word, such a well known place in New York. It was that it was home to males and females, some of whom were regarded as America's most hardened criminals, with a violent, volatile subculture of their own. Like a great majority of New York City residents, this is what I knew about Rikers Island. And this is what permeated my mind as I sat there in Mr. Thomas' eighth floor office at 65 Court Street, downtown Brooklyn. My knowledge of things such as it being besieged by enough non-stop airplane noise to eventually lead to hearing impairment and harm to the sanity would come later.

Mr. Thomas' talking about a place there where he was sending me called Island Academy rang a bell of sophistication that belied the very dubious reputation attached to the island.

Undoubtedly, this reputation was not a new one for Mr. Thomas. He set about trying to allay whatever reluctance and trepidation he thought were plaguing me. He told me that among those who were incarcerated in Rikers Island jail was a large population of adolescent offenders 16 to 18 years of age, an age group that the law had determined education had to be made accessible to no matter what their predicament. In the case of Rikers Island Jail, for instance, facilities had to be set aside there so the Board of Education of the City of New York could conduct school. Such schools, operating outside of the traditional school system, are called Alternative High Schools.

In spite of the negativity running through my mind, Mr. Thomas did not have much convincing to do. Though I harbored much negativity about the idea of going to Rikers Island in the short period of time, practicality dominated the situation.

For one, I had then been teaching for only three years, meaning that I was not yet an appointed teacher. In those three years my performance had been graded satisfactory officially; unofficially, I had, in my enthusiasm, often taken my performance above and beyond the call of duty. But I must admit that by now I had already recognized that putting in all this extra enthusiasm meant nothing to the Board of Education. Without being an appointed teacher at least, a teacher was susceptible to being mistreated for whatever reasons that could be used to justify the meting out of the mistreatment – Including being discarded at any given time. And their status would not be regarded by the teachers' union to have reached that stage to warrant spending too much time in defense of. For another, my present predicament was a classic example.

My most recent teaching assignment was at Thomas Jefferson High School, in the dilapidated East New York section of Brooklyn. The administration there had suddenly decided that that the state of the school's budget was such that they had to excess another teacher, a Board of Education euphemism simply meaning to "get rid of." I was that final victim. And it was done at a time in February when the staffing of the schools was already completed. In fact, I would learn later that the decision to excess me was actually made after the normal time of the semester to end this act had expired. At this time it was unusual to find schools still not fully staffed. Making matters worst was that license area had to be considered. Teachers caught in this bind were left to seek a position elsewhere or place their hopes in the coming September semester. Whatever the case, the bureaucracy not only had its justification to excess me but left no one directly responsible for carrying out the act with any guilt over the nasty situation they had so suddenly created for another human being.

Faced with the dilemma of taking on the challenge of Rikers Island or placing hopes in the system somehow rescuing me from the predicament it had thrown me into, I concluded that taking on Rikers Island was a wiser move.

It was past mid-February of 1987.

As instructed, I drove across the BQE (Brooklyn-Queens Expressway), took the Astoria Boulevard East exit to East Elmhurst, without getting lost, thinking of course of what was ahead in store for me. Ironically, my time to get lost came during the relatively shorter distance to Hazen Street that ran straight ahead into the mile-or-so-long bridge that would take me over the East River and to the gates that would allow me entry into the actual Rikers Island Jail – "the belly of the beast," as labeled by some.

Being the conscientious person I am, I wanted to create a good impression by being early for my interview with the principal. It was not to be. In the past three years I had walked freely into Thomas Jefferson High and High School of Graphic Communication Arts, where I taught until the decision to excess me and I ended up at TJH, as it was for my very short stint at Eastern District High school. But now, it already seemed obvious that getting to a school located in Rikers Island Jail was going to be, as the popular saying goes, "a horse of a different color."

There were three major D.O.C. (Department of Correction) checkpoints to get through before making it to the school building. One to get from one side of the bridge to the next at the Control Building, then getting beyond the Control Building into the jail grounds where the actual jail buildings are located, then there was the third set of monstrous gates to get through before getting to the school. And the barbed wire and razor wire decorating these checkpoints, as was the case with the overall surroundings, certainly wasn't a good case for easy access. Getting to the school didn't mean getting into the school. There were two sets of steel doors on the building to get beyond. While not having as formidable an appearance as the others, getting beyond these doors, it would turn out, could be a more time consuming accomplishment.

Not having the Board of Education pass required for this special school, and not having the required D.O.C. pass, either, certainly did not help. One of the correction officers directed me to the little security building. There I learned that I would have to phone the school to verify the need for my presence there before I could be issued a temporary pass. This pass would not allow me to cross over the bridge driving or walking. Instead, I was to park my car in the nearby D.O.C. parking lot, if I could find a space, and await transportation to take me to the other side of the bridge. There I would have to disembark, go into a second security building, known as the Control Building, exchange my bridge pass for an inside-the-jail pass and await transportation – whenever it became available – to take me to the school building located in C.I.F.M. 76 (Correctional Institution For Men).

After much delay, I made it out of the miserably cold February air into the small vestibule of the building. After a second delay the second set of gates, right there leading into the school from the vestibule, was opened. Quite ironic, it seemed. But how was the "new guy on the block" to know how much power-tripping some correction officers attached to being in control of these doors and the keys to them, how much bad blood they generated, how very well a few C.O. (correction officer) bullies saw them as tools of punishment against teachers who dared not to display to them the subservient traits they expected from them.

So finally I was at Island Academy Alternative High School.

Inmates-students were still lined up in the hallway, meaning that they, too, were quite late for classes, for a long line of them stretched from one end of the hall to the next and another line formed in the middle passageway that turned to the right and extended beyond another pair of internal steel doors. . A Hispanic captain was issuing them orders in a no-nonsense manner. About five C.O.'s listened and tried to maintain quiet.

The C.O. who had opened the doors leading from the vestibule into the school for me was locking the doors back and simultaneously talking to me when some of the inmates noticed the new face, and assuming that I had to be a new teacher, commenced having their say quite noisily and humorously, they obviously thought:

"Damn! We getting' a new teacher!"
"Let's see how long the nigga is gonna last."
"We gonna run the nigga outta here before the end o' the month."

"The nigga, he done look scared to death, in shit."

"Word-up! He ain't gonna be here too long!"

As I made my way past these youngsters to get to the principal's office, they kept up their comments. The C.O. with me told me not to pay "those damn animalescents" – a description he thought more appropriate than adolescents – any attention.

Hearing the commotion, those youngsters on the line that extended beyond the doors to the right obviously wanted to know what was going on and were pushing forward to get a firsthand look, not content to settle for the descriptions that were shouted out by those who were in a position to have a good look at me, causing hilarious laughter:

"He's an afro-headed nigga."

"We gonna hold him down and cut that Afro to fuck off."

"Don't he look like one of those black power niggas from outta the nineteen sixties?"

" Yeah, man, he musta been down wit' the Black Panther Party."

"A Michael Jackson nigga."

I knew what their comments were all about. It had been a few years now since the popularity of the Afro had dwindled away significantly and most Black youngsters had resorted to the down-to-the scalp haircut which they brushed constantly to achieve the "waves" look. To them, anyone wearing an Afro as big as mine was so very old-fashioned. They had also turned the epithet "nigger," like their use of profanity, into an integral part of their vocabulary. I knew from my teaching at TJH and HSGCA over the last three years that trying to dissuade them from constantly indulging in these habits was a waste of time.

I also understood the reason for their "Michael Jackson nigga" comment. Even though Michael Jackson by now was well into his shameful racial metamorphosis of slowly changing his skin color from black to white, they still thought my Afro reminded them of the huge one sported by Michael and his brothers of the Jackson Five era – 1970's. I really thought it to be quite funny that the moment this Michael Jackson comment was uttered how so many of the youngsters automatically broke into a song-and-dance routine: "...pa pah pah pa paaaaah...oh, baby, gimme one more chance, oh, baby gimme one more chance...pa pah pah pa paaaaah," a very catchy phrasing from an early Jackson Five hit that remained still popular.

True, I understood the young inmates' reaction to the presence of the new teacher, as they saw me, not knowing that I was not yet hired. However, being ushered into the principal's office was like being offered some form of sanctuary from them no matter how brief.

The principal, Mrs. Gee, proceeded to instruct me as to her expectations. She told me over and over that a school in a penal setting was different in many ways. Knowing that I had just come from Thomas Jefferson, and having heard quite a bit about its dubious reputation at the very top of the list of New York City's "bad schools," she assured me that even the experience of teaching at TJH did not prepare a teacher for some of the differences at a school located in a penal setting.

One of the things she insisted on from all her teachers, she said, was that in spite of the fact that Island Academy was located in Rikers Island Jail, that the youngsters were in jail for committing crimes, teachers were yet to refrain from addressing them as inmates. "They are inmates to the D.O.C. To the B.O.E. (Board of Education), they are students." And though subtly said, I had no doubt that she wanted me to know of the resentment some D.O.C. personnel had for the presence of the B.O.E. on their turf, seeing the bringing of education into jail as senseless and doing more bad than good as far as doing their job was concerned.

After her lengthy instructions – all delivered in a stern manner, without any facial expression resembling a smile – Mrs. Gee wanted to know if there was anything I might want to get off my mind. I thanked her for offering me the position. I then told her that I was aware that I was being hired off the strength of my graphic arts license, a vocational teaching category, but unlike most vocational teachers who were qualified to teach only in their vocational area, I also had an academic background that qualified me to teach creative writing and journalism and would like to have this incorporated into my program, though I understood very well that part of her instructions that the B.O.E. had invested several thousand dollars on state of the art graphic arts-printing equipment, believing that if the youngsters could learn a skill some of them, upon release, could become gainfully employed and save themselves from getting caught up in the losing cycle of recidivism, a predicament that follows so many of them into adulthood or is taken there by them.

She agreed that this was a good idea. For one, many of the students did very poorly in grammar and writing. For another, she said, surprising me, "Mister Brathwaite, I know of your strong writing ability. I have read some of your writings in publications you were responsible for editing and producing. They were given to me by a gentleman with some connection to Island Academy at a time when I was speaking of the school's need for a teacher with your versatility to replace Mister Crown, who was here for the past six months and was just let go because he got absolutely nothing done. The gentleman's name is Mister Speigel. He said you both taught together at the same high school in Manhattan some time ago. Believe it or not, but once Mister Crown left I intended to contact you. They beat me to it at Court Street."

Yes, I knew Mr. Speigel. We did teach at Graphic Communication Arts High School at the same time until one semester he suddenly disappeared. For those few months we had conversed frequently, mainly because he was trying to get a city-wide high school publication off the ground, so to speak. He was also into writing. Also, judging from the position I was now hired for at Island Academy, and from which Mr. Crown was recently sent into excess, I felt almost certain that he had to be the same Mr. Crown, a late

fiftyish Black American guy who was also teaching at HSGCA during my time there and was given his excess the summer before I was in typical Board of Education style.
Something else I had to say to Mrs. Gee regarding part of her instructions, it being characteristic of me to approach my job conscientiously and efficiently. I just had this thing in me about trying to do the very best I could. And it required no one watching over me to bring out these qualities.
I was shown to what would now be my classroom. There was a teacher of science who was temporarily and hastily assigned there as a result of the sudden decision not to rehire Mr. Crown. It was a situation somewhat like my first assignment when I was hurriedly sent to Eastern District High School to assume the position of graphic arts teacher because that teacher had suddenly taken ill. But not long after a graphic arts teacher from another school with seniority decided he wanted the position and I was unceremoniously let go to accommodate him, or "bumped," a euphemism used within the Board of Education in such cases. I was then trying to make the change from the graphic arts industry in Manhattan to the B.O.E. It was wise indeed that I was trying to make this change without letting my employer know, for there were no more teaching positions available and I was able to somehow put enough credible twists to incredible excuses to return to my job of 12 years. But while the adventure at E.D.H. was short, I could still say that as second on the city's "worst schools" list, my subsequent position at TJH meant that I taught at what were regarded as the two worst schools in New York City.
I wasn't sure if being bumped out was awaiting the science teacher. But I thought so later that day when the C.O. who had let me in from the vestibule, an Italian-American, came to the classroom to caution me not to let "these damn inmates" con me into getting started on "the wrong foot" by forcing me into succumbing to their value system. I told him that while I had never taught at a school in jail, this was my fourth school in three years. Suddenly, he seemed to have more confidence in me.

The teachers who come here usually don't last long, he told me. He told me also that they were almost all new to the profession and came to Rikers Island not ever having a taste of "the shit youngsters can dish out." The science teacher, an Italian-American, he told me, was a new teacher and was having a lot of problems with the youngsters just like the teacher before him.

I had no reason to doubt his observation in regards to the new teachers. In the short time of three years with the Board, I had observed that much of the idealism espoused from B.O.E. offices didn't translate into reality. Take all that talk about making sure new teachers were given a lot of help in getting started, I had seen none of that.

I had no doubt that the issue of too many new teachers at Island Academy had nothing to do with them wanting to be there, but that they had no choice. The experienced teachers with seniority and tenure wouldn't accept such an assignment, so "throw" the new ones in, like throwing a novice gladiator into the arena to fight the lions. More about this situation is forthcoming.

I soon learned also that the Mr. Crown, whose position I now had, was indeed the same Mr. Crown who had taught at HSGCA during the time I taught there. I should, in actuality, say that when I went there I found him there.

By my third day at Island Academy, when it was generally accepted that I had made a positive start, the jokes about Mr. Crown's get-nothing-done method of teaching were being told to me hilariously and disappointingly. What they all found so funny was that "Uptown Crown," as Mr. Crown was also know at HSGCA – in fact, he was given the name there by his students – was a man who was always professing to know so much about everything. I listened to the humorous stories about Mr. Crown but volunteered no opinions. By now, the story tellers knew that I knew of him as they described him.

Mr. Crown would soon return to Island Academy to pick up the last check owed to him. He came to the classroom to see me and asked me several times, what it was that I knew and could do that he didn't and couldn't that led the principal to excess him in favor of me. I avoided the issue. But knowing him as well as I did from at HGGCA, I thought it quite possible that he actually was serious, not even taking into consideration that whenever I went to his classroom to relieve him for one period, his students were so totally in control of his class to be, as such do-as-I-please behavior is described, "crawling all over the ceiling." Equipment that was whole one day was sure to be broken the next. When we taught adult night classes at HSGCA, before long the word would circulate among the adult students that there was another teacher two floors below also teaching graphic arts and his students would search me out and ask to have their class change to mine.

As to the science teacher, he now had no science class and it was a bit too late to excess him, so he was told to assist me until something could be worked out for him. I knew this would soon be done because the class had an assigned teacher's helper (paraprofessional or para for short) in the person of Dwain Martin, a Black American in his mid-20s. He was hired by the Board only a year earlier – after just finishing six years of army service – and sent to Island Academy on his first BOE assignment.

In time, I felt fortunate to have Martin as my helper. He was, by the way, the first para ever assigned to me.

With such incorrigible students' behavior, it's imperative that teachers should have some help. Martin's help would prove more valuable than that of other paras. For one, students who give the teacher a hard time are sure to give the para a much harder time because, to them, the para is "not a real teacher, as the same is true about their attitude about a substitute teacher. Also, these students are fully aware that paras and substitute teachers generally fear them. Fortunately, Martin was one of the few paras who did not harbor this fear. I attributed it to his military experience.

Since I was one of those "old fashioned" enough to be of the firm conviction that students should not be given the green light to behave as they pleased, the class was Progressing quite well, enough so to be conspicuous to others. By quite well I don't mean to insinuate that there was a problem-free situation, for this cannot be accomplished in any public school in New York City.

The problems that I was told the science teacher was having with the students made themselves manifest almost immediately. I wasn't trying to determine which side was responsible for initiating the problems. I had come into contact with some teachers whose methods I thought helped in creating such problems, and I certainly had come into contact with students who consistently exhibited downright mean spirited and disrespectful attitudes toward teachers, said and did whatever they pleased, whenever and wherever they pleased, with threats of physical violence, all backed by that ever-present ally: loud profanity. This was the prevailing situation here.

Teachers know that the system expects them to possess that special brand of tolerance to be able to withstand from students hurt-to-the-bones disrespect, on-going stressed out, blood-pressure-raising volatile behavior in the same manner attributed to Jesus of Nazareth's handling of the temptation of Satan during his 40 days and 40 nights in the wilderness. There are some teachers, however, who at times feel that they have been mistreated just too much – often by students young enough to be their children – and feel compelled to resort to a verbal defense not conducive with the passivity suggested by psychologists, demanded by the system, and internalized by the students as weakness.

The teacher in question here was new but had perhaps perceived of this unfair equation that rather than solving problems exacerbates them more often than not. This is the speculation here because when he could no longer tolerate the name-calling and cursing hurled at him – along with the rolled up paper and pencils thrown at him whenever his back was turned – he would resort to defending himself in a manner the Board of Education regards as unprofessional. Those unaware of these situations will undoubtedly question why a teacher faced with this kind of behavior from students don't report the offenders to the administration. This would be the right course of action to take if the administration – or the broader system, for that matter – had a policy capable of deterring such behavior.

In the traditional schools it is customary for students engaging in incorrigible behavior to be expelled from school for but a few days. Then they are welcomed back to continue from where they left off. In most cases, they are not expelled at all but given one of the "oh-you-poor-kid" lectures by principal, assistant principal, psychologist or social worker and returned to the classroom to posture triumphantly to their peers and thumb their noses with impunity at the teacher. In fact, they know so well of the teacher being almost vulnerable in student-teacher disputes that in these cases a common student's threat is often made to the teacher: "I'll get your ass fired."

As to the case of a school like Island Academy, located in a penal setting, one would naturally assume that there would not be much of a behavioral problem. Indeed, when I first arrived and saw the correction officers, I felt a great deal of relief. I told myself that I would now be free from the daily students' confrontations, disruptions and disrespectful tirades of the past three years. After all, these were real law officers, not the ordinary school guards in New York City schools that students saw as totally powerless and therefore treated as such.

In responding to the constant harassment of the students, the science teacher in question here would at times use some racial epithets under his breath, often audible enough to be clearly heard: "Black sonufabitch" and "nigger" for the Blacks, and "gawddamn spicks" for the Hispanics.

What was I to do? I was relatively new to the school. I also had not an iota of doubt that the students were being downright nasty to him. Added to this was that I had been the object of similar behavior in the past – also knew others who had been – and knew how it felt, and how it could pound away at the worst side of the persecuted being Subjected to such wanton taunts and disrespect, much of it precipitated foolishly by the need of youngsters to impress their peers. For it must be understood that doing good is not the thing that normally impresses in this circle. On the contrary, it is regarded as a sign of weakness, a characteristic that when detected leads to youngsters being ridiculed and beaten up by their peers. I must also confess, from a teacher's perspective, I, too, did not take kindly to the Board of Education's – the system's – philosophy that teacher's were to accept this kind of attack from youngsters under the pretext that it was their way of showing Professionalism.

It was common knowledge throughout the system that an inordinate number of new teachers suddenly quit the system within three semesters, mostly those who were full of this professionalism the system demanded. The majority came into the Board brimming over with enthusiasm as to the positive mark they were going to make. But very soon, students perceived of their "by-the-book" method of doing things and concluded that it was just the weakness that they could exploit to make themselves look tough to their peers.

I was doubtful that the science teacher would be one of the early "walk-away-from-it" casualties. However, it was very likely that he would fall into that other "casualty" category, the one strengthened by financial commitments to tolerate the disrespect, the harassment and stress primarily to collect a check every two weeks, known as "take the money and run."

Martin, having served as teacher's helper to both Mr. Crown and the science teacher before serving in the same capacity with me, was convinced that Mr. Crown had elected to be in the "take the money and run category," for he assured me that the students were no less severe in their attitudes toward Mr. Crown than toward the science teacher. And while he complained about their disrespect and the impossibility of any teacher being able to teach such "bad-ass kids," he didn't seem to let stress take him over the way it obviously did other teachers. This confirmed to me that

Martin had observed in Mr. Crown exactly what I did back at HSGCA. And while it might not say much for teacher's professionalism, I must admit to my understanding of why Martin couldn't help himself laughing when telling of how the students usually took Mr. Crown to task and his reaction to them doing so.

Eventually the administration did work out something for the science teacher. He was even given a letter for his file commending him for the good job he did in trying to hold together the graphic arts class in the absence of a qualified graphic arts teacher and despite not having knowledge of the subject area. If it seems that I was defending him, then it must come as a surprise to be told that I wasn't at all endeared to him. Maybe subconsciously those under-the-breath racial comments had something to do with this. I remember, though, his constant saying that the students gave him a lot of problems because of his white skin.

When these youngsters got into their nasty moods – especially when, it seemed, it was as a result of their wants and whims not being catered to immediately – race definitely wasn't the precipitous factor for the unleashing of these nasty moods. As a matter of fact, in the inner city schools, with which the account is primarily concerned, and student population is overwhelmingly Black and Hispanic, it is not unusual to hear the complaint from Black teachers how many Black students display a better attitude toward white teachers, even asking questions of one another as to the reason for this despicable action. And my observation over the last three years told me that their disappointment and questioning were justified.

White teachers didn't believe that this situation actually existed. And while many would deny its existence, they yet used it to their advantage. For even though remaining the great majority of the teaching force, they still exhibited this fear of being threatened by the recruitment of more Black teachers, at a rate still slower than theirs.

As to the question of those Black teachers regarding Black students' better attitudes to White teachers, I heard many reasons given, including the lack of self-respect legacy of slavery of which I have no doubt. But I saw another side in White teachers being more willing than Black and Hispanic teachers to ignore students' disrespectful behavior that would lead to them being liked and therefore contributing to their happiness. I must also state that while to a much lesser degree, I have heard the complaint from Hispanic teachers of a lack of respect from Hispanic students. This came especially from females, claiming that Hispanic males, raised with such chauvinistic values, resulted in male Hispanic students not respecting them as Hispanic teachers.

< 2 >

It didn't take long to discover some major differences in this school in a penal setting and the traditional schools. It also differed significantly from the alternative school not in a penal setting, but created for students whose behavioral problems were also such that the system concluded they couldn't be taught with students with supposedly normal behavioral traits.
   Within a few weeks of being at Island Academy, I had seen enough to have decided it would be a good idea for me to make June of that year the end of my time there, if that wasn't decided for me by the administration through the excess method. For one of the things I heard frequently in those few weeks was that Mrs. Gee was a woman with quite a mean streak, which she used to make decisions capriciously, that she wasn't a person to be easily pleased, that she made demands of teachers that were impossible to be fulfilled by anyone – including herself – especially in a

school where the students had some very unique problems, especially that of operating around an obvious subculture of on-going volatility, where surviving their predicament in one piece was their major concern. That the student population was much smaller than that of the traditional schools didn't make for an easier task. Seven months from now, September 1987, the beginning of the next school year, I would surely join the many other teachers at 65 Court Street looking for a new assignment elsewhere.

Of course, there were no female students at Island Academy. The school for adolescent females wasn't far away but out of sight. A damn wise idea indeed, considering that conversations about sex among the youngsters were endless and couldn't be curtailed by anyone.

I can't say what percentage, but in time I was quite surprised at the number of these students who were fathers, many with more than one child. Another big surprise along this line was the ages of some of the mothers of their children. Most were young teenagers, but there were those in their mid-20's, meaning that they had a few years on their teenage lovers.

If the mention of no female students at Island Academy seems to indicate some kind of regret, not quite so. On those occasions when I heard the issue of "for or against" coeducational high schools discussed, on the one hand, I had no doubt that some of the boisterous behavior in the schools could be attributed to the mixing of the genders and it inevitably leading to each side consistently trying to impress the other. And as already stated about this age group, as I saw it, engaging in negative behavior was considered a very effective way to accomplish this. On the other hand, I saw a good side. I had heard the idea often espoused by female teachers especially, that they had experienced the worst behavior from female students. True, there were some female students who tried extra hard to "out-nasty" their male counterparts. However, I feel justified in saying that in the face of many bad situations, if there were to be a voice to eventually say, "Homeboy (or homegirl), yo, you shouldn't do that no more," it would always be the voice of a female student. The males always seemed bent on doing all in their power to exacerbate the bad situation. I likened their role in such a situation to seeing a dangerous fire and rather than thinking about dousing it with some water, the pyromaniac thought of how much excitement it would generate to douse the fire with gasoline instead takes over.

So now faced with all these adolescent males, constantly hearing correction officers refer to them as "animalescents" and the "worst" group of inmates to have to deal with, even worst than the hardened adult criminals, who themselves were known to wish not to have any contact with adolescent inmates, not wanting to have meals at the same time as they did, not wanting to come to evening classes if some adolescents would be brought back to the school floor then, and personally experiencing how demanding, defiant, disruptive and destructive some of them were, my desire not to "hang around" for too long should be understood.

Seeing the C.O.'s some weeks ago when I came to Island Academy, I was very much under the impression, that the continued presence of those assigned to the school floor was certain to keep students' behavior in check, they wouldn't be able to do as they pleased, as they did in the traditional schools or those alternative schools not located in a penal setting. I soon learned that this was wishful thinking.

This was the 1980's, not the old era of chain gangs, when discipline could be meted out as wardens saw fit, and as correction officers knew they could get away with far more often than not. These youngsters, many of them junior high school and early high school dropouts, were constantly talking about going to the jail's law library to check up on their rights, about initiating law suits against those who violated their rights. Those who could hardly read were never at lost for a smarter inmate who would do the reading and explaining for them for an agreed upon number of cigarettes or a specified amount of commissary goodies.

Whenever a teacher would dare to admonish them a little too harshly about their unacceptable behavior, they would want to know from the teacher, "So what you gonna do? You gonna expel me? Where you gonna expel me to? I'm already in jail; ain't shit more they can do to me now."

And indeed, this was true; a truth that made teachers' life hell. No matter how disrespectful and disruptive the students, they couldn't get them out of the classroom so teaching could take place. An inordinate amount of teachers' time was spent trying to correct behavioral problems – every day. A few of us had that I-mean-it tone in our voice that at times would succeed short of a showdown in getting an offending student to decide, "Yo, lemme get to fuck outta this nigga's class before I get myself into trouble for punching him in his snot-box (nose)." But true to the folly of so many administrators, Mrs. Gee insisted that no students, no matter the depth of his transgressions, was to be put out of the classroom. There was this brilliant solution of hers: "Write out a report and give it to administration."

Writing a report during class, when a teacher must be teaching and dealing with behavioral problems simultaneously can't be an easy task. Hence, the report should be written when the teacher had a short class break. Then the problem would be addressed the next day at the earliest, meaning that the teacher was left to somehow continue to tolerate not just the disruption of this student but that of his homeboys who came to his defense.

Why not let the C.O.'s assigned to the school floor remove the worst offenders from the classroom for even two hours, not the two or three days they would be expelled for in New York? No, this couldn't be done because the D.O.C. had this policy of keeping their inmates together. Why not have a "time out" break for these students so they could be taken to a room and kept there under the guidance of a C.O. until they calmed down? No, this wasn't feasible as far as C.O.'s were concerned. Once inmates reached the school floor, they would claim, it was the responsibility of B.O.E. personnel to deal with them. The duty of the C.O.'s was to bring them to the school floor and take them back. The only time they were to intervene was for reasons of safety, if there was a fight, or threats to anyone, part of the many schemes devised so they wouldn't be bothered too often.

One of Mrs. Gee's brilliant solutions to one of the pervasive classroom problems – as she thought it to be – that I observed with much skepticism in my very first days was for teachers to constantly walk around the classrooms waking sleeping students. The sleeping problem was a result of the students getting little or no sleep at night. Their lack of sleep resulted from fear and distrust.

For those who don't know, it will come as a big surprise to learn that the worst case of fear and distrust plaguing inmates in jail is for each other, not for C.O.'s (guards), as is popularly assumed, for there is a tremendous amount of bad-blood existing among inmates. This situation led to these youngsters having to, as they put it, "sleep with your eyes open." It was only after coming to the school floor that they felt safe enough to obey the dictates of their bodies to go into a strong sleep, many snoring loudly.

It didn't matter to Mrs. Gee that the students would often become very angry when their sleep was repeatedly interrupted by the teacher or para, causing them to become verbally abusive, issuing their profanity-laced threats. This was a common occurrence in all classes, particularly during periods one and two and to a lesser degree three.

Some of the youngsters were not content to sit in their chairs and put their heads down on the desks; they wanted to sleep comfortably and would wage long arguments about their rights to go in a corner and lie down on the floor or pull up a few chairs together and stretch out on them. Some teachers grew so fed up having to spend so much time waking the youngsters – and being abused for doing so – that at times they would pluck up the courage and go against the dictates of Mrs. Gee and let the sleepers sleep on.

A bad habit that almost always came with their sleeping was the pushing of their hands down inside their pants and holding on to their penises. It certainly was a strange sight to at times walk the hallway and look into classrooms and see several students sleeping, others with their heads falling from side to side and bopping up and down, eyes opening and closing slowly and uncontrollably, and the faces of the bewildered teachers saying as clearly as words, "Lord, I hope this class is over before Mrs. Gee comes by," as they continued to teach those few who had their eyes open, those with their eyes in a state of not knowing what to do, those with their heads falling from side to side and bopping up and down.

Mrs. Gee certainly couldn't be accused of not wanting to stamp out this sleeping mania and the bad habit of penis caressing that invariably went with it. Trying to stop the latter didn't generate near as much verbal abuse as did the act of trying to stop the sleeping. Their reaction to this was almost unanimous: "So what? It's my dick, I can hold on to it if I want to." Speaking and acting in ways that would shock you was undoubtedly inculcated into their culture.

In any event, Mrs. Gee walking up and down the hallway and looking into classrooms went on unceasingly. She could often be seen or heard having a dispute with a teacher for their inability to quell the sleeping. "Why are your students sleeping?" One thing was obvious, though, she wasn't always eager to use her position of power to personally intervene and show that "this is the way it's done." There were assistant principals to take on this embarrassing task of failed intervention by administrator with power.

Over a period of time, there were different assistant principals under Mrs. Gee, generally two. I remember them very well but can't quite remember in what order each came and went. I am sure that Mr. Roker, Mrs. Shore and Mr. Brines were among the first ones I met. They would be followed by Mrs. Sitro and Mrs. Elders. I can't remember that Mrs. Gee ever got much out of Mr. Roker, who was Jewish, outside of his readiness to introduce games into any classroom whenever he thought there was a need to get students involved in something. He would be gone at the end of the semester to take up a less involved position at the district superintendent's office in midtown Manhattan. Taking over from Mr. Roker would be Mrs. Shore.

When the task of solving the sleeping problem fell on Mrs. Shore, she often got started on it with the rolling of the eyes and that help-me-Jesus look up to the ceiling. It soon became clear to me that it wasn't a simple task of her wishing she didn't have to do it, for she certainly wasn't one who feared a confrontation with students – or teachers, for that matter. Clearly, too, I think her anger resulted from her wondering why Mrs. Gee couldn't do more to help solve a problem she truly didn't like in a more substantive way other than identifying it and writing bad reports daily for the files of teachers who could neither magically nor miraculously find a prognosis for problems that were mostly jail-mentality-oriented, an issue to be addressed later.

I saw in Mrs. Shore a streak of that "old fashioned" disciplinarian characteristic I heretofore attributed to myself. As a result of possessing this characteristic, she wasn't going to take kindly to youngsters who could be her children – not even those who viewed themselves as tough Rikers Island prisoners – disrespecting her. I don't know how many times I heard the warning issued to her by students, "Yo, you crazy little lady, I'm tellin' you, you had better get outta my face. " Sometimes as she would approach them, they made sure they spoke loudly enough for her to hear, though pretending it wasn't meant to be so: "Here comes that little pain in the ass agen." But no matter how argumentative and confrontational they would become, Mrs. Shore would not be deterred.

I had left my native Barbados several years ago while still a young teenager. I still saw the "old fashioned" values of respect for teachers, parents and elders, as they were instilled in children there during that time, as very important. I guess Mrs. Shore, a Black American, must have come from the South, for it seemed that these old fashioned values were more so a part of the cultural upbringing of Southern Blacks than of Blacks from the supposedly more sophisticated big cities of the North where disciplinary transgressions of youngsters were accepted as the norm.

I would be remised if I didn't mention how some teachers perceived of Mrs. Shore at times, as if forgetting that they were not the students. I must say, however, the resentment for her from both students and teachers was in no way of the same magnitude as that for Mrs. Gee. For Mrs. Shore, it seemed a case against what was seen as this attitude in her mannerisms that was just too maternal. With Mrs. Gee, on the other hand, both teachers and students were sure that there was this characteristic of tyranny in her that often made itself manifest.

In time, I would see teachers shed tears because of unsatisfactory reports by Mrs. Gee about their classroom management that would be placed in their files. They felt they were doubly punished; punished by perhaps the roughest students to be found anywhere, then by the principal after they had tried so hard to do their very best to please her.

I observed that the overall attitude toward Mrs. Gee was a bad one. I must say, though, that I took into consideration it not being unusual for the person in charge to be often spoken ill of by subordinates. Admittedly, after being at the school for almost a semester my relationship with Mrs. Gee was still in good standing. Some teachers had even been teasing me that "she likes you...and she's divorced too. That's why she's so miserable...she's made it up the career ladder but has no man to go home to. You should get in there and make her happy so she'll stop making us unhappy."

She had not yet said anything negative about my classroom performance. I must admit that the students' sleeping problem hadn't quite pass me by. Compared with other classes, though, the number of sleepers in mine were few. I always made every effort to wake the few but when they adamantly refused, particularly when the cursing was involved – in fact when I had reason to anticipate it happening – I would conclude that I had done my best and it was senseless to wake, say, two or three sleepers and be faced with major class disruption because of the certainty of others jumping on the bad bandwagon as invariably was the case under such circumstances. Worse than this, I didn't have a lot of tolerance for being cursed at – especially by youngsters who were young enough to be my children.

Working in my favor, too, was that periods two, three and four were my periods for teaching graphic arts-printing, which other than including some graphic arts-related math, textbook reading and spelling – areas in which many of these students were very weak – was mostly a hands-on vocational subject. From past experience, I knew that many students preferred vocational subjects, often to the point of wanting to ignore academic subjects, which they would do if only allowed to. And so it was here also. As a result, during these periods, motivating my students, getting them involved wasn't much of a problem. Of course, when the time came to get them involved with the math, spelling and reading, in spite of the give-it-to-them-in-small-doses tact I utilized, their motivation would diminish significantly. They would be unanimous in their reason for being reluctant to cooperate: "This ain't no math class." Why is it dat you be teaching English in this class anyway?" "I don't wanna be reading dat shit." This kind of defiance was also exhibited when a lesson had to be copied from the green "blackboard," and discussed, or when a quiz/test was to be taken, in spite of the fact that I would have prepared them psychologically for it from the day before.

One thing they always demanded to know about copying lessons from the chalkboard: "why do we have to write all this shit when all you had to do was to make enough copies from your copy and hand the shits out to us?"

This readiness to "act-up" was mostly prevalent during my evening periods when there was more emphasis on writing, even though they knew of the structure of the classes prior to their first attendance and had it reinforced in them during the first days of their attendance. Knowing what took place during the morning periods, they tried all they could to have it reenacted during the evening periods. Working in my favor was that I would threaten to never let them come to my graphic arts periods if they insisted on not cooperating with the program. In my no-nonsense way, I sometimes confronted them with the alternative of "throwing you out of the class." A popular response would be, "just who this nigga be thinking he is anyway? He can't be throwing niggas outta their class. He gets paid to teach us."

I must admit that I was more fortunate than those teachers who taught academic subjects only and therefore almost always had their "backs up against the wall" because of the major absence of students' interest. Thinking of the possibility of not being allowed into the classroom during graphic arts periods, or not being allowed to get involved in graphic arts activities on those occasions when I gave them the chance to do so, they would often opt to dispose of the books and pencils across the floor along with the many pieces of rolled up paper that they threw at each other, purposely dragging the desks and chairs around, and as I was known to reprimand them for their regular use of profanity and the term nigga, they would increase their usage until it was found not to change anything in their favor.

There were also vocational classes in tailoring and computers, followed in time by carpentry, barbering and culinary arts. The teachers of these subjects were not as hard-pressed by the students, either, as were the academics-only teachers. But it must be reiterated that we, too, were faced with some bad behavioral problems.

For one, instructions must be structured so classes can be conducted in a manner conducive to learning taking place. And there was no doubt whatsoever that the tolerance level of these youngsters for following structure, accepting discipline was extremely low. Many came to classes with their minds made up as to what they were going to do. The teacher rejecting this was a sure harbinger for endless complaints, arguments and dissatisfaction. Then there was the stress-engendering need youngsters would consistently unleash when things were not done the way they were sure they should: instant gratification. Each one's wishes were to be catered to immediately or their demented, spoiled-brats' behavior would be showered upon the source from where they expected and demanded that instant catering to come from.

Looking back to Mrs. Gee's dealings with her assistant principals, when in the long run Mrs. Shore surprised everyone and suddenly left Island Academy for a less stressful position within the Board, Mr. Brines assumed her role.

Mr. Brines, a Black American, about 40, over six feet tall and a bit on the heavyset side, was generally regarded by teachers as a nice guy. I concurred with this assessment. Mrs. Gee utilized him in a manner similar to the way she utilized Mrs. Shore. The obvious difference was that she, as the saying goes, "gave him a ride for his money." He was always hurrying up and down the hallway, rushing to classrooms to address behavioral problems.

Students obviously didn't take Mr. Brines as seriously as they did little Mrs. Shore. Undoubtedly, they saw in him a man with the kind of sexual preference attitude that told their homophobic minds to "give him a hard time; he ain't a real man." So the speculation here is that their extra hassling of Mr. Brines had much to do with the homophobic attitudes so many of them possessed. By the same token, it might have been an unconscious thing with Mrs. Gee, too, that she always had him running up and down like the proverbial chicken that just had its head chopped off. Her chance to show her ability to control a man.

I have no doubt, either, that at times Mr. Brines felt compelled to put on a tough guy act to convey the message to the youngsters that their assumption of him being a softy wasn't so.

I recall a bad confrontation in the making between Mr. Brines and one of my students. Mr. Brines had some no-nonsense words for the student, and deservedly so, I felt, because the attitude of the student was no less than nasty to Mr. Brines after he insisted on seeing his ID card, which

Mr. Brines had initially asked for in a pleasant manner. Next, the student was up in a real fighting mood, threatening Mr. Brines, "I ain't playin' wit' you, nigga. You come in my class and harassing me 'n' shit 'cause you know I'm an inmate. But you better step off before I lump you up...before I snuff yo ass out."

I reminded the student that Mr. Brines was the assistant principal, that he had a right to ask to see his ID, and that he had even asked to see it nicely. Being rational with him was a waste of time. Nothing new.

I wasn't one who was often in a rush to get the youngsters in trouble with the D.O.C. and have them sent to the Bing or given additional time in jail. But when I thought a situation was getting too far out of hand I would do what I thought best to curtail the problem. In this case I called a C.O. because I was really convinced that the youngster was going to hit Mr. Brines: "lump him up" or "snuff him out," as was their popular sayings.

I witnessed a few such confrontations with Mr. Brines. I must say, though, that Mrs. Gee used to really get it from the students. Teachers would tell of times when she came to their classrooms and the students would automatically start defending them against her, as though they were so sure she was there to give them – the very teachers the students were confrontational with – a hard time, criticizing them for one reason or another. Their favorite descriptions for her were used so often – and to her face at that – that the shock they were meant to generate was losing its potency: "Here she comes agen, dat miserable old fart." "Dat bitch-ass nigga."

Really, she wasn't old, but middle-aged and attractive. But to the age group these youngsters belonged a middle-aged person was old, especially if the person had a few gray hairs showing.

As to my statement about not always trying to get the youngsters in trouble, it must be borne in mind that I have also emphasized my "old fashioned" value system. Hence, when I thought a situation required the taking of a stand, I took the stand without regards to the criticism to be hurled at me by the students. I took the stand especially if it was because of a developing bad situation that I had several times warned the to be sufferer of the consequences about, then the situation really got out of hand because he had chosen to ignore me. I knew the criticism against me would be as certain to come as the sun rises in the east and sets in the west: "Snitch-ass nigga;" "snitches get stitches;" "hate that nigga, man;" "see you in New York you'll get yours."

I knew why, as principal, Mrs. Gee would want to see her students in their classes not sleeping, even though I, like other teachers, sometimes questioned the wisdom of waking the sleepers to invariably throw the class into pandemonium. And as already stated, in the worst case scenario, I left them alone with their heads down on the desks. When I did get into confrontations with students regarding this issue it would be primarily because my old fashioned value system wouldn't allow me to ignore students in a classroom stretched out on chairs, desks, on the floor in a corner. In this case, I took a stand against it no matter the depth of the confrontation that would almost inevitably come.

A "little" bad habit that was a big bad habit to me was that of students sitting on the teacher's desk or pulling up a chair next to the desk – any desk, but especially the teacher's, and sometimes right in his face – reclining in it with feet stretched across the desk. So many students couldn't understand why I made such a "big deal" over such a "little thing" that didn't bother other teachers. I guess some of these teachers, being in the habit of sitting on their desks, felt that the students should be allowed to do the same. In fact, I knew of some who didn't think it mattered. I believed, though, that the major reason for them not taking a stand against it was because they didn't want to incur the anger of the students. But when students displayed their intent to sit on my desk, I would initially *ask* them not to. When they insisted on doing so, I would tell them *not* to.

"You don't ever see me sitting on the desk, do you?" I always asked the defiant ones. And indeed, I never did sit on my own desk, in part possibly – though not likely so – because the demand for my help always kept me moving around my classroom. Whatever the case, it was a policy of equality with me, which I thought to be helpful when students observed that when teachers came to my classroom and went to sit on my desk, I would ask them not to and offer them a chair. Admittedly, though, it might not have been the equal situation I thought it to be, because I thought teachers sat on the desk because it made them feel comfortable while students were driven to do so by a macho feeling which incorporated some disrespect for the teacher. The bottom line to it, though, as I saw it, was that chairs were made for sitting on, not desks.

This wasn't, as the youngsters always put it to me, "back in the olden days" when youngsters generally adhered to that philosophy of authority, "Do as I say not as I do." It was clear to anyone about 40 years old that the value system of today's youngsters had changed a billion times over since what they referred to as the "olden days."

Another issue on which I took a firm stand was that of students coming to the class and immediately deciding what they would do and wouldn't do. If this was allowed in even one case, it bred other such cases. And in this case I could see no logical grounds on which I could stand in accepting that some could do as they pleased but others couldn't.

I constantly reminded them of my philosophy about disrespect in the classroom, even had it posted on the wall in large words: They could disrespect me if I disrespected them. Also posted on the wall was my aversion to their non-stop profanity no matter who was the object of it, but I especially resented being cursed at. I more often told them that I was a proud Black man, proud of my African ancestry and did not at all like being referred to as nigger. I realized that their constant use of profanity was such an integral part of the youth vocabulary that even the system had decided to accept it as the norm.

I had spent three years teaching at two major schools, each with a student population of almost 3,000. So inexorable was the students' use of profanity and that nigga epithet, most knowing of it would no doubt think me crazy to think I could change it. But in truth, it wasn't unusual for even some of the very "tuff guys," when in my classroom and became conscious of the profanity and the term nigga flying out of their mouths, to say, "Sorry, Brathwaite, man," even as they would back up their apology with a comment to let me know that it was a natural thing.

Hispanics, no matter their color, used the word nigga with the same frequency as Blacks. The conflict was that it was used with both affection and in anger. Moreover, they called everybody nigga regardless of their race, color or nationality. And they would try to rationalize away their embracing of the term to me by telling me, "A nigga is an ignorant person." I would tell them that the term nigger was conceived by White people during the African slave trade and used against people of African ancestry in a demeaning manner, to set them aside as inferior sub-humans. They were fully aware of this derivation; hence, it strengthened my belief that Black youngsters, who were responsible for transforming the word nigger into what it now was and gave its usage unprecedented popularity, did so to rescue themselves from the ugly, racist stigma it was created to be. I would tell them, furthermore, no matter how hard they tried to obliterate the stigma, to destroy its original intent, to even make it an affectionate term, at the end of all this evasiveness, the term will still be recognized as – and used as – a sub-human description aimed at people of African ancestry. I would explain to them that similar derogatory names were given to other nonwhites by Whites as they went around the world intent on conquering these people and taking their lands: Chinese, chinks; East Indians, coolies; more recently Hispanics, spicks. In retaliation, around the 1950's, Blacks started calling Whites honkies. None of these people embraced "their" derogatory names and used them so often to the point of giving them national – and even international – credibility.

I also consistently warned them against their proclivity for fighting in the classroom, for quite often nasty brawls would just break out. Then there was the unhygienic act of spitting on the floor. There was also the embarrassing act of sneakily masturbating in some corner or under desks, generally after they had been eye-raping one of the female B.O.E. personnel. On the school floor, this act was often precipitated by prolonged visits to the offices of female clinical staff members who supposedly looked "so fly." It wasn't an unusual thing, for it was said that many of these youngsters were punished with extra days for engaging in the act back in the dorms where female C.O.'s would be the objects of their excitement.

About fighting in the classroom, I would remind them of what I shouldn't have to. It got them sent to the Bing, to solitary, and prolonged their time in jail. It is not an act of trying to pat myself on the back by my saying that I had a success rate of preventing classroom fights much better than that of other teachers, as I observed, and as C.O.'s did also.

Student arguments were many and boisterous, about sex, girls, fast cars, and drugs. These arguments were difficult to put an end to – often impossible. Then they got into "snapping" on one another, which involved personal verbal attacks (harsh ridicule), but attacks of the most harsh kind were made against the character of sisters, girlfriends and mothers. The latter two – and the components of weakness and inability to deal well enough with these attacks – were what constituted the main cause for tempers raging out of control. Strangely, even as an argument would reach a ready-to-explode stage those in the midst of it would continue to give their assurance: "We ain't about to fight...we just playin' wit' each other."

I had witnessed this kind of situation many times before, heard this "we ain't about to fight" claim only to witness a sudden degeneration of the situation into a vicious intent to-inflict bodily-harm clash between the same claimants.

So it was my habit whenever I heard this claim of peaceful intent, while the argument still resembled a pit bull attack, to stop wasting my time saying, "That's enough, you guys...stop it." I called in whoever was paid to stop it from happening. I would be called names, castigated for not minding my own business, for "making a big deal out of little shit like dat." I was as sure of this as I was of having just prevented a fight. If they would have taken their business out of the classroom, I might have minded my own business. This not being done, and what was done already having been done, I would remind them that I had just saved them from D.O.C. punishment and saved myself from having to write out reports as to what happened. The Board of Education already had me doing a lot of unnecessary paperwork.

As to the issue of them sneakily masturbating, I knew the act was nothing new among adolescents, but take it to the washroom, I kept telling them.

It was nearing the end of June; hence, the end of the school year. Within a few days I would start to fulfill the obligation I had signed for rather than going on my eight-week summer vacation: teaching six weeks of summer school. I was coerced into doing it by Mrs. Gee, for I certainly didn't want to continue working into the middle of August.

I was told that the summer heat brought out the worst in the behavior of the students. It turned out to be true.

There was no air conditioning in the dorms. In the school, the air conditioning system apparently had a mind of its own and therefore worked when it felt like and wouldn't work when it didn't feel like. Students still wore their beige clothing – as opposed to the adult inmates who wore dark-greens – but now they were issued short pants or they simply cut the pants legs off and wore no socks with their sneakers. Since their beiges were almost always a few sizes too big, they now had a more rag-tag look than they did during the cold weather months.

There was a weather-related problem back then too. The heating system was no more reliable than the cooling system and apparently only the tougher guys were able to get their hands on long sleeves shirts or long sleeves thermal vests. The others wore short sleeves shirts. Those winter mornings when the heating system took leave of its duty, as angry as the students might have made you, you couldn't help but emphasize with the ones in short sleeves drawing on every bit of initiative to keep their exposed hands warm. Undoubtedly this was part of the reason for that hands-inside-the-pants obsession. Whatever the case, it seemed an inhuman condition to subject them to – jail or no jail.

I gathered that more than the summer heat, the thought of being "locked down" – not locked up as far as they were concerned – during the beautiful summertime, with the noise of airplanes arriving at and departing from nearby LaGuardia Airport all day and all night nonstop, and the countless gulls shitting all over the place in amounts unimaginable, they felt homesick more so than during the cold somber winter. And the fact that they so often blamed others for their predicament rather than themselves, could not have been helpful.

I can't say if the summer heat exacerbated their bad attitudes, but yes, their behavior was more intolerable for those six weeks. There were more fights, keeping them in the classrooms was more difficult. They got smacked around and written up more often by C.O.'s. That captain who would punish them by making them all strip naked and stand in a line against the wall in the hallway with their hands on their heads obviously increased this punishment now. And as to the issue of not being able to keep them in the classroom, there was something about that hallway that grabbed their attention. If occasionally the presence of a C.O. in the hallway seemed to make their going out there a little dangerous, they would take turns in twos, threes and fours to congregate at doorways and look up and down the hallway. When they saw their homeboys from another class they would engage in loud conversations. If they saw some enemies they would exchange threats. If they saw a female staff member they would alert others who were not in the doorway about her presence and there would be a dash to the door, followed by the exchange of their views about what they thought about parts of her anatomy. This happened a lot more frequently now with the warm weather dictating the wearing of lighter clothing. Even on the rare occasions when there was nobody in the hallway, there were those who still insisted on taking up watch of the hallway from the doorways, seemingly anticipating – or praying for – the period of hallway inactivity to end soon.

Finding themselves locked down in jail, so many students find that urge to prove themselves great lovers and constantly write poems and create art about love.

< 3 >

After what seemed much longer than six weeks, the summer school session eventually ended.

As I headed home to East Flatbush, Brooklyn, I reflected on the period of February to mid-August. To put it bluntly, it was one hell of an experience from the first day of the inmates having a great time making fun of my big Afro and one other thing I didn't mention earlier, my unusual beard, sparsely grown but hanging six inches down from my chin. And my long "mustache" similarly grown, no hair on the top of my upper lip but starting a little above where the upper and lower lips part, they thought gave them the justification for referring to me as "the Chinese-ass-looking nigga." In fact the beard and mustache were of such growth that when I was eating, say, a doughnut, the ends of my mustache usually got pushed into my mouth, as it was true that if I bent over to partake of some soup and forgot about my beard, I would sometimes see the end of it in the bowl. The youngsters were simply viewing my beard and mustache curiously as so many other people always did: unusual for a person of Black African ancestry.

I had allowed the youngsters to have their fun of my hair until the novelty of it faded away within a few weeks. I even chided them sometimes about being jealous because they couldn't grow a beard and mustache like mine.

Their fun ended when the weather warmed up and I relieved myself of wearing long sleeves shirts, sweaters and jackets for stretchable polyester skin-tight short sleeves shirts and my biceps, twice the size of most of theirs, were exposed to them. Though not a tall man, suddenly they were lavishing praise on the way I was built: "tuff guy," "little-big man." So many of them wanted to be "like Brathwaite." One had even circulated the rumor that wouldn't go away, that he had witnessed Brathwaite do 500 push-ups in the gym without stopping to take a breather. It had students demanding to see me repeat the feat, a good enough reason for me not to give credence to the lie as he who circulated the rumor pleaded with me to do in the interest of his reputation.

I had completed the semester and summer session with another name from the students: "Mister Perfect." They had started much earlier to lay their accusations against me: "Damn, he don't expect niggas to make a mistake;" "he thinks he's perfect; " "just watch, the nigga gonna catch a heart attack wit' all dat perfectionist shit he be into."

I always countered these charges with the actual facts: "As long as you're a human being you'll make mistakes. I don't think I am perfect and I don't want to be. I don't think I know everything, either. People who think they're perfect and know everything are some of the biggest fools you'll ever meet because they listen only to themselves. What you guys really mean about me is that I don't want you to start doing things unless you intend to do the best you can. If while you're doing the best you can you make mistakes, I have no problems with that; it's when you make mistakes because you didn't try to do your best that I have big problems with."

I thought of Island Academy youngsters. Board of Education personnel were to see them only as students, not inmates. As far as Department of Correction personnel were concerned, on the other hand, they were not students at all but inmates (criminals). And to make matters worst from a B.O.E. perspective, our students viewed themselves not as students at all but as inmates. They had internalized this to the point of constantly saying of Island Academy: "This ain't no school; this is a damn jail."

I would often tell them that school is not all about a building, or where that building is located, but about learning taking place. I would also tell them of the opportunity they had to get something good out of a bad situation. Imagine coming to jail and having the chance to improve yourself to be able to fit into the job market when you are released. Maybe, despite the obvious evidence, in a case such as this the conflict in the paradox was too strong to reign true. If the negative students' sentiment "this is jail, not school;" "we're inmates, not students" wasn't unanimous, then it was very close to being so.

Six months at Island Academy wasn't a long time, yet long enough for significant observations to be made and many opinions formulated. These youngsters – most of them incarcerated for drug-related crimes, but some for armed robbery, gun possession and shootings, attempted murder, and rape – were mostly also school dropouts. Free in New York, many had, a long time before being arrested, exercised their right to do as they pleased and not go to that dreaded place called school. Then they found themselves locked up on Rikers Island and *made* to go to school – in jail of all places. Their complaints about this were so many to show beyond a doubt that the disappointment and anger they felt over being *made* to go to school in jail outweighed that they felt over their actual imprisonment. They couldn't wait for the time to come when they would be declared "adults" and therefore be eligible to join the adult population and be able to chose to not attend school. True, there was a minority that wanted to attend school because, according to them, it made the time go faster. It seems fair also to mention here that many of the youngsters usually expressed their desire to be transferred to the adult population because they wanted so badly to get away from their fellow adolescents whose behavior, by popular Rrikers Island repute, was far more volatile than that of the adults prisoners.

A disturbing observation was that the inmate population was primarily made up of Blacks and Hispanics, far fewer Whites and fewer Orientals.

Black and Hispanics were always angrily taking the system to task for sentencing them to jail for crimes Whites were given probation for. They were also far less likely than Whites to get bail. The leniency toward Whites was especially strong in cases involving adolescent offenders. One well known rationale for this disparity in sentencing along racial lines was the admitted belief of some judges that Blacks and Hispanics were tough enough to survive the rough conditions in jail and in general Whites lacked that prison mentality necessary to survive with these rough Black and Hispanics prisoners.

I gave a lot of thought to this and realized that I had seen many Blacks and Hispanics who were just not tough enough to mix with the general population (GP) of other Blacks and Hispanics, some having to be placed in protective custody (PC). If the system was so concerned about the well being of the not-so-tough, why jail these guys? Or why not jail those guilty Whites thought not tough enough to survive the tough guys and place them in PC also?

True, there wasn't a strong White inmate presence. But from what I saw, I can honestly say that they were not singled out to be set upon. I can't even say that they were showered with racial epithets, unless being called "white boy" or "mighty whitey" can be so categorized.

An on-going accusation attached to this disparity in sentencing was that White inmates were so sure that it did indeed exist that in the scheme of inmates' excuse-making toward shortening of jail time, they were known to frequently use this vulnerable-white-boy-ganged-up-on thing as a major reason why they should be released ahead of time.

In the six months I had been at Island Academy I was constantly warned by C.O.'s to "never trust any of these inmates." Initially, I didn't take the warning too seriously, believing part of it had to do with some prejudice C.O.'s had to have for inmates. I wish I could say this was the case. But I learned that it was a wise warning. Many of the youngsters did possess some devious con-artist ways that belied their youthful looks and super-innocent posturing. They were adept at winning your trust then taking such ruthless advantage of that trust to create paranoia in you as to what they would do next.

Since their major concern was to survive, there was always this absolute need of theirs to have weapons (contraband) for protection. They generally operated in little deceptive groups that allowed them to break off dangerous pieces from chairs, desks, lockers, and very expensive equipment, and other unimaginable sources, under the ever-vigilant eyes of the teacher and para without being detected. For they operated in that con-artist manner known among them as "I got your back." And since their motto "snitches get stitches" meant for each other had proven itself to be a serious threat and not some kind of nursery rhyme joke, deceptive practices were seen but not seen. I would be remised if I didn't mention here that they were geniuses at creating little but harmful weapons from the most unlikely things, deception that must be seen to be believed.

Teachers and paras knew that it was an important part of their job in the classroom to constantly keep their eyes on their students. Another thing they knew was that students meticulously checked their every move. As they did this collectively, the two pairs of eyes of teacher and para provided no match at all for the many pairs of theirs. This situation wasn't helped by what the D.O.C. thought was such a great policy against contraband: "time back" to inmates who found and handed in contraband. True, it looked good on the surface. But knowing that handing in contraband would cut down on their time in jail added to the need for them to get their hands on this important commodity and lay claims to having found it some-where.

And so everything always had to be locked away in lockers or in little rooms. Whenever students said "gimme," and "I want," locks had to be unlocked and locked back. And these calls to "gimme," and "I want" were continuous, to the point where teacher and para would occasionally not lock something back, an example of the intent of con-artists to create the kind of confusion beneficial to their needs.

Those things small enough for students to easily abscond with, they had to sign for. All of this was a job unto itself that got on the nerves. This was where it was worse for the teachers of vocational subjects than for those teaching only academics, for while they, too, were faced with the contraband problem, it was not near as serious a problem in their classes as in the vocational ones. This meant that I had somewhat of a double problem: this contraband one with vocational classes and with the academic subject where it was so much more difficult to motivate these students.

B.O.E. personnel were also constantly warned by the D.O.C. to not bring anything into the jail for inmates. Their specialties were cigarettes and Snicker candy bars. They served the bartering business so popular in jail. Though threatened with being arrested if caught doing so. B.O.E. personnel still took chances and did it. I wouldn't say that my old fashioned ways were such that I never contravened this rule.

I certainly didn't make it the habit I knew others did in their efforts to get the students to like them. I was too dictated to by old fashioned ways to give students things to get them to like me. And I never gave a single cigarette because of my conviction of it being a drug. But I plead guilty here to having given Snicker candy bars, and only to the few who felt they were tough enough to go against the penal code and openly help out – even cooperate with – the teacher. Those who lived by the code that helping out or cooperating with the teacher made them look like a "dolgier" (a weak person) couldn't get from me even a piece of the nuts contained in a Snicker.

Refusing these youngsters wasn't a simple thing for those not endowed with the old fashioned value system I speak of. These youngsters didn't know what *no* meant in this case. The more they were told *"no,"* the greater grew their determination to defeat your resolve, to prove they had what it took to make you change your mind. Knowing so well that they wouldn't accept no because of having mothers and others capitulate to their demands since early childhood, and not caring to be pestered inexorably with the same issue, I came up with a certain solution to take over where no failed: To their pestering for cigarettes, Snickers – and the other things they also wanted brought for them – I told them to "see me tomorrow." Come tomorrow and I told them to "see me tomorrow." When this went on for three or four days they would angrily demand to know, "How comes every day you be telling me you gonna bring it tomorrow but you never do?" I would remind them that I never said a thing about bringing them anything tomorrow; I said to see me tomorrow. Even now, some would still persist, "So you gonna bring it tomorrow then?" And I would again respond, "See me tomorrow."

Those who now got the message would make their disappointment known through the usual use of profanity. Those taking a bit longer to get the message would soon give up in the same manner.

Why did this method succeed when the method of open refusal did not? To them it was tantamount to making a damn fool of them. As much as they hated being told no, they hated being made a fool of more.

I had survived from February through mid-August with Mrs. Gee, even got a satisfactory rating when others didn't fare that well. Undoubtedly, this thing about her liking me so much was meant as more than a little joke; it was still being said.

Within a few weeks of my being at Island Academy, Mrs. Gee had made this statement to me twice: "Mr. Brathwaite, you do know of course that I expect your support," in her usual manner of stressing her point and her impeccable way of speaking, perhaps not expected of her by some, she being a Black American from whom they perceived it normal to hear some ebonics. I didn't quite know what she meant, but my reading between the lines led to my interpretation that she expected me to be looking out for her interest, to work with her against her detractors, of which I eventually found out there were several.

If my perception was right, she was definitely looking to the wrong person. I was never one to get too close to people in authority, no more than that I was that sociable that I mixed with others a lot. I mostly withdrew into my solitude where I even talked to myself, meaning that I couldn't be so privy to much of what her foes – or her friends – thought and said about her. Until now, I didn't even know the names of all my colleagues. And I certainly wasn't a cut-throat. So on both occasions my response to Mrs. Gee's probing was, if she meant that she wanted me to perform my job efficiently and conscientiously – and not act maliciously against her – she was assured.

Other than running a very popular class – though under trying and adverse conditions – from February through August, three issues of a school newspaper, Academy News, were produced entirely in my classroom, and quite professionally, as was the unanimous opinion of all – Academy staff, personnel of other schools, others connected and not connected to the Board of Education, and the D.O.C.

Other schools generally had their newspapers done outside the school setting and had to pay to have them produced. Not many of these eight to ten pagers, printed only in black and white, were that professionally produced.

Even the newspaper at HSGCA, where they had many of the big state-of-the-art equipment for this purpose which Island Academy didn't have, did not have that professional look Academy News had. And at this time there were only two computers and one laser printer in my classroom, along with the printing presses, cameras and other relevant equipment, in good condition but no match for those at HSGCA, New York City's giant major graphic arts school. Academy news was even produced using color for some of its 20 pages.

Already Mrs. Gee was being praised by her superiors and fellow principals regarding Academy News. She was also getting praise from sources outside the B.O.E. Academy News was widely praised as the best School newspaper. Mrs. Gee even made sure she sent copies to corporations. Some of Mrs. Gee's fellow principals were already making plans for having their schools newspapers produced through my classes.

Was it me she liked, or was it what I was doing that made her look so important?

Really, I wasn't too concerned with pats of adulation on the back, for I often thought I saw hypocrisy behind this action. I liked the fact that students felt so good about the newspaper. This was especially the case with those who contributed writing and art. They went around reading their articles and showing off their art – with their names at that – to everyone and giving high fives to each others. They mailed out copies to family and friends – particularly girlfriends – for them to see

At any rate, as I made plans for what little was left of my summer vacation, I also thought of my change of plans that would see me back at Island Academy instead.

Something important – along with a few things not so important – that I wanted to do forced the change: I was appointed to Island Academy, where after completing the probationary period, my uncertain status of *per diem* teacher would change to certain status of *tenured* teacher.

< 4 >

Before Jailhouse Jeopardy: Manhattan

True, this story is primarily about my teaching experience in Rikers Island Jail. However, there was my prior teaching experience in the traditional public school system where such interesting and shocking events would often unfold, that some of them deserve more than being superficially addressed. So while much more will be detailed about the Rikers Island experience, there must be a diversion here to tell of my initial teaching experience at Manhattan's High School of Graphic Communication Arts, followed by that at Brooklyn's Thomas Jefferson High School, then the reconnection with the Rikers Island experience.

Being aware of the generally curiosity held for goings-on in jail settings, there is this anticipation of the desire to bypass these other experiences and jump forward to the rest of the Rikers Island experience, a personal prerogative, but one that will result in missing so much.

In any case, as stated earlier, I was in and out of Eastern District High quite speedily, though in this brief time I thought I observed enough to no more question its second place spot on the "worst schools in New York City" list – told to me later – as I could prove otherwise. Students were engaged in that kind of behavior referred to as "crawling all over the ceiling." Their profanity bounced off the walls.

This being as it may, that morning on February 2, 1984 I went to the High School Staffing Unit and was informed by Mr. Thomas that he had a sure position for me at the High School of Graphic Communication Arts on Fiftieth Street and Ninth Avenue in Manhattan. I was elated.

I had visited this school some months earlier regarding getting my graphic arts teaching license and was told by the man I spoke to that it would be a good thing if I would one day returned there as a teacher because of my graphic arts experience, having a Bachelor's degree in journalism – just what the school was about – and was studying for a Master's degree in creative writing and literature . So this morning I reminded Mr. Thomas of my desire to teach creative writing. He advised me to take the graphic arts position because with my experience in this area I would be immediately ready for good differential raises. But if I was registered in the computer as teaching in an English area, differential raises for my degrees wouldn't be near as much. But I could be registered in the computer in the area of graphic arts, get paid as such and still teach English.

I went to HSGCA to see the principal. A White woman in the office told me he wasn't there. Then a White man came, and without having been told why I was there she told him that I was there to see the Principal about a teaching position. The man told me to follow him. We ended up in a little office about four floors down. There, he not only told me that the principal wasn't in but that he wouldn't be back until the next day and that there were no positions available. He wished me luck elsewhere.

Dejectedly, I went back to 65 Court Street. As I entered the staffing office Mr. Thomas looked up right into my eyes.

He wanted to know why I was back there. I told him of my visit to HSGCA and that I was told that there were no available positions.

He had spoken to the principal that very morning on my behalf, he told me, and he knew I would soon be there to see him. The school had the position and wanted it filled urgently.

Mr. Thomas grabbed up the phone angrily, declaring, "I'm so sick and tired of all the politics they play at that school. The position is available and they have to give it to you." The principal was in his office, had been almost without break all morning. The position was also still there. The man I saw was an assistant principal, one so closely attached to the graphic arts department that it was impossible for him not to have known of the open position.

Mr. Thomas stuck the necessary papers back in my hand and told me if I wasn't in the mood then I should go back to HSGCA the next morning. I was in the mood and took off back to the school.

The principal, Mr. DeMarco, told me that what he had heard about me from Mr. Thomas, I had the potential to fit into the school well. It was an ATR (Absent Teachers' Relief) position. I would start out teaching as a substitute teacher, covering the classes of teachers who were absent, which was a big problem the school system faced. Then I would go on to substituting half of the day and teaching my own classes the other half. If my performance was satisfactory, I would move up to full classes schedule. Having the enthusiasm most new teachers usually start out with, I was disappointed in not having my own classes right away. But I wasn't going to refuse the position. For one, I wanted to get a start; for another, substituting was usually a temporary thing and even if the substitutes lasted out the semester they were not paid for the June to September summer vacation like regular teachers, while as the ATR I would be registered in the computer as a regular substitute and be paid as were the regular teachers.

In an eight-week period I might have covered classes

five periods every day. I understood then what the principal meant that morning when he hired me and said under his breath, "They are absent so often, I might soon have to hire as many substitutes as regulars." I understood, too, why serving as a substitute was regarded as a very trying task. It was so deeply engrained in the minds of the students that substitutes were "not real teachers" and were at the school for them to give a hard time to conclude that it was a part of their cultural upbringing. When they arrived at the class and saw a substitute, they moaned and rejoiced at the same time; moaning because the substitute wasn't a real teacher and rejoicing because as such they were free to engage in behavior worse than they did for their "real teachers," but that was the reason for much of their absenteeism. Those who dared to cooperate with the substitutes were constantly denigrated as "nerds."

Covering classes meant that I often had to go from floor to floor. So I saw the extent to which students roamed the hallways in their little groups avoiding going to classes. They regularly had nasty confrontations with the school guards. Of course, the stream of profanity was inextricably bound to these confrontations. And of course, too, there were the same kind of confrontations among themselves. The days that I didn't hear boys telling girls to "such my dick, bitch" and girls giving the response "you lick my pussy, nigga," had to have been very few.

At times when this repulsive behavior was played out in the classroom and I showed my disgust or said something like, "Do you have to use that language?" I was sure to hear their favorite responses aimed at me, "So if you don't wanna hear, nigga, you shouldn't listen." "So you shouldn't be all up in our business then."

The conversations about sex, using graphic details, never ended. There were times my opinion was even asked for, to which I would respond that I not only thought their language was unsuitable for the classroom but that I was old enough to be their father and wouldn't get involved in their lewd and debased conversations. Boyfriends and girlfriends manipulated the system so they could be in the same classes together, at times holding hands and kissing. When I took steps to put an end to this behavior, I would hear that I was "just jealous and want her for himself."

I recall covering a special education class for two periods each day for over a week.

As for any class I knew I would be covering for more than a short time, I prepared lessons. Being a special ed class, it was comprised of much less students than the overcrowded numbers usually found in other classes. There were about ten boys and only two girls. One girl and her boyfriend were inseparable. They would often try to test me by attempting to get down on the floor or go into the darkroom to carry out their lovey-dovey activities. On a few occasions I called in a guard when I thought they were getting out of hand and the other students were giving them support. The guards would issue the usual warnings and threats, then leave me there to be ridiculed by the students. On one occasion, obviously feeling helpless to correct the situation, one guard asked me what I expected him to do with these "damn crazy kids." He then removed the two offenders from the classroom. But they were soon returned by an assistant principal who assured me they would now behave themselves. It wasn't long after he departed that they were back to doing what they were doing.

The other girl was much more quiet and subdued. While she said very little, she was always physically in the midst of the goings-on. One day when the first girl was absent this one became the object of the attention of a few of the boys, physically well developed youngsters. They kept up a tirade of sexual commentaries directed at her. As usual, she listened but said nothing. It was said over and over that if only "dat teacher would leave the class" they would take her into the darkroom and "rape the ass" off her. When one of the boys wrapped his arms around her in quite a rough manner, I decided the situation had gone too far and called a guard. I told him the reason why and that I thought it best if the girl was removed from the classroom. He wasn't at all eager to do so but did eventually.

As far as I was concerned, I had rescued a nice, quiet young lady from being harassed by boys with very foul mouths. Within a few minutes the guard brought the girl back to the class. He told me she wanted to stay in her class. The girl surprised me by attacking my decision: "You can't be puttin' me outta my class like dat. They wasn't even doin' me nothin'. I was havin' fun, but you don't wanna see me have no fun."

The guard ushered me outside and told me somewhat apologetically and sympathetically, "You're new; you don't know them yet. When you get to know 'em, you'll know that you can't let 'em make you jump too much. Don't think that the guards don't want to help you. But there aren't enough of us to deal with the problems in this damn school. This group you got here is a real pain in the ass, dat's why their teacher be always out absent."

That darkroom was a major attraction to the students, always running into it to carry out their activities, to witness the activities of each other, to be mischievous with the chemicals. I had kept telling the assistant principal that the problem could be solved by putting a lock on the door. He would agree and promise to. It was never done.

What if I had ignored the situation with that boy and girl and it was taken too far? I wanted to know from Mr. Cator, a Black American teacher who had been teaching at the school almost 10 years and who voluntarily acted as my mentor. He told me emphatically that the very students who criticized me for not letting them behave as they pleased would blame me for not controlling the class. The guards who don't want to be bothered would say it could have been avoided only I had called on them to do their job. The administration that insisted on keeping problem students in the classroom would tell the parents of the students it wasn't because of a school problem but that the teacher of the class was inept, by which time I would already have been dismissed. "Mister Brathwaite, you did the right thing," he assured me. You did CYOA," a term he had mentioned to me from the very beginning and told me everyone in the school system utilized it and so should I, or I was sure to regret not having done so. "Mister Brathwaite, as long as you are in this school system make damn sure that you never neglect to do it: Cover Your Own Ass."

There was another class I covered frequently which I wished I didn't have to. It was a class of mostly 17-year-old seniors, not far from graduation. As with this kind of class, once it was known that "the real teacher" was absent, other than turning up to sign the attendance sheet, very few of the students – sometimes none – remained in the class. The news of the real teacher's absence had a way of reaching them way ahead of time.

There was a Black girl in this group whose presence was conspicuous from the day of my very first seeing her. Many of these girls had the obsession with flaunting sex appeal and obviously dressed to perpetuate it, so much so that I often wondered, particularly in the case of the younger ones, why parents would let their daughters come to school dressed like this. This girl had taken it to a level above the others, clad in skin-tight (-est of all) jeans and body-hugging tops.

Sometimes she took it to another level by wearing those spandex bottoms. Made of stretchable fabrics. They could be bought in sizes smaller than the size and shape of the anatomy they were meant for, but capable of being stretched to hug the anatomy so tightly, and have everything meant to be covered so conspicuously impressed out, to be as close to having these parts nakedly exposed could ever be. And she certainly was one of so many Black and Hispanic females with very curvaceous hips and posteriors.

All her fellow students could disappear from the classroom, but from the very beginning she remained behind and initiated conversations with me as if we knew each other for some time. The problem was that her conversations would always get very personal and her language was very flowery. And she showed not a sign of embarrassment as she asked me about: wife, children, cheating on my wife, what I would do if I caught my wife cheating on me, what I thought about her, how did I think she looked, older men pursuing her since she was thirteen, the first time she and a boy set out to "do it" on her fourteenth birthday and it never happened because "that fool couldn't find what he was searching for" and blamed her, how soon after that his much older brother "cornered" her and he "found it just like that," how she was exposed to sex before she was a teen because her mother and her boyfriend made the mistake of leaving the key in the lock of the cabinet where they used to hide their pornographic films and she and her sister found it and had a key of their own cut so when her mother and boyfriend left them home thinking their "stash" was locked away safely from them they were watching the men and women "doing it."

    Ironically, I was the embarrassed one and kept trying to dissuade her from raising such conversations. I told her of having two children her age and how badly I would think of it if I knew they were doing as she was now doing. Once, when I was a bit more severe in my criticism of her than before, she responded with laughter but obviously disappointed, "You know how many men out there wish they had a beautiful young woman like me to talk to 'em like I talk to you?" And she promptly stood up and started to strike some modeling poses for me, meaning to show even more clearly what she had to offer.

    I told Mr. Cator about this and how uncomfortable it made me. He suggested that I not make any complaint against her as this could lead not only to her resented feeling over what she perceived as the nerve to reject her but also the embarrassment to cause her to think she had to defend herself against me. "The school system is never gonna believe you over a student, Mister Brathwaite. Always cover your own ass." When only one to a few students turned up for class, he informed me, I could take them upstairs to the school library where there were always others present. The very next time I had to cover the class and only this student turned up, I told her of the change to the library. She insisted on going into the classroom. I insisted that I had go the library.

"You know, Mista Brathwaite, I don't think you have to go to no damn library," she said. "I think you just tryin' to avoid me. I think you're nice guy, but, man, you be acting' so scared of me, I wonder if you ain't a faggot or something." Then she quickly covered her anger with a smile as she walked away and shouted back, "See ya tomorrow – if dat stupid teacher don't turn up."

It was out of character for me to shout back at her what I had in mind: "Not if I see you first."

Naturally, I had no way of knowing that there was nothing aberrant about this kind of behavior; in time, it would be done by others. I would hear of it happening to others.

Shyness not being a prevalent characteristic among these youngsters, I would eventually learn that a surprising number of the girls were mothers, through them proudly volunteering the information. Very seldom were the fathers of their children around to help them out; the responsibility fell on the girls and their mothers. And why? Once the "no-good nigga" knew of the pregnancy he disappeared out of their lives. "The nigga" he sez "it ain't" his. "The nigga, he in jail."

I was aware of the teenage pregnancy problem before now, for it was a regular media item. I heard it was a problem among teenage White girls too. It wasn't easy to discern how badly, though, as in such a case considered negative, the media mostly focused on Black girls, then Hispanic girls, not much on White girls, knowing of the proclivity of much of White society toward this way of dealing with such situations. I wondered, though, if Black teenagers didn't help in focusing attention on themselves as the major culprits in this moral erosion because so many of them often demonstrated a greater willingness than others to publicly spill their personal business for a few moments of attention.

I must admit that the more familiar the students became with me, the more they eased up on their bad attitudes. I guess it had something to do with my being a regular staff member and feeling obligated to have at least some kind of educational quiz for them when I covered a class, as opposed to others covering classes who were not on the regular staff list and didn't bother much about doing this. It didn't help the situation, however, that the regular teachers, when knowing they would be absent, would deliberately lock away from the covering teachers everything meant for running the class in that "this-is-my-class" manner. And whenever they returned to their classes they would have a litany of complaints about the wrong things the covering teachers had done – not only for the students but for the assistant principal in charge. Undoubtedly, this was a "cover your own ass" tactic because it made them look like better teachers than they actually were. Some of them even created bad situations for this reason.

There was an Italian-American teacher who was regularly absent. Two of his classes always fell into my coverage schedule. He was the consummate complainer. When he returned to school I always found myself having to answer to the assistant principal about problems I had supposedly caused. One day he came to school late, after I had covered his class. Very soon after the assistant principal came looking for me to resolve another of his complaints that I had left the classroom in disarray. I denied it because I knew such wasn't the case. The assistant principal took me to the classroom and indeed there were newspapers, other kinds of paper and some books all over the floor, along with a few chairs and desks turned upside down. I assured him that I was the last one to leave the room, had locked the door and that the classroom wasn't in the state it was now in.

The AP told me to stay there as he hurried out the door to find the complainer at my request to let him make the complaint to my face. He was surprised that the complainer had so quickly disappeared and couldn't be found in any of the few places he was sure to be. He was also surprised that he had disappeared from the scene when he had set out to find me, instructing him to stay there until he returned. The AP, also Italian-American, then figured it out. "That cry-baby sonufabitch," he said. "he never stops complaining. There's always something with that man. No wonder the kids can't stand him."

I didn't think the students couldn't stand him because of his complaining but because of the way he carried himself. A book should not be judged by its cover, true. That to stereotype others is wrong, also true. But I thought the students couldn't stand him because of the disheveled way he carried himself. Everything about his appearance made him look like he was among the ranks of the homeless who slept around anywhere. That wherever you saw him and whatever he was doing he was also ravenously consuming a doughnut and a cup of coffee did nothing to enhance his image.

The morning, about a week later, when I saw him engaged in a shouting match with a Hispanic student, I stopped my rush for the elevator to observe. He was insisting that the student wasn't to get on the elevator. The student, not as big as he, pleaded with him to give him a break because he was going to the top floor and didn't want to walk all the way up there, plus there were no other students to cause a scene. He wouldn't hear of it, carrying on loudly to get attention and show others how tough he was. The shouting continued. The student soon made the accusation that "you ain't got no right to be puttin' ya hands on me, muthafucka," and with that he let go with a haymaker of a right hand which caused the complaining teacher to automatically drop his coffee and doughnut to grab for his extra protruding nose where the haymaker had landed and resulted in a gush of blood. He called out to me to stop the fleeing student. I turned away and headed up the stairs for my intended destination. At least it gave him an excuse to leave school and go to the hospital, I thought next day when I saw him with his nose so nicely bandaged.

Another thing I didn't like about that man was his habit of squeezing on his female students in that supposedly paternalistic way. I was convinced it was just his way of getting that "cheap thrill" from these physically well endowed young Black and Hispanic girls, as I believed to be the same with some other White male teachers I observed doing the same.

The girls didn't seem to mind this attention. I guess it made them feel like the adults they wanted so badly to be. Maybe their mothers had never warned them against falling victim to this cheap thrill thing. Maybe they did. But these were youngsters who had grown up on the TV culture. Along with its shameless glorification of random violence and sex, TV encouraged them to rebel against anything their parents stood for. All the shows with child stars in them showed these child stars almost always arguing with and mouthing off their parents, as they did other adult authority. It didn't matter if the shows were comedy or drama. And of course, kids watching TV internalized what they saw as the "real world" and emulated it quite well.

< 5 >

Well, eventually one Mr. Siwel moved on to another position and three of his periods were given to me. I became, as the youngsters would say, "a real teacher," even though I was still classified as an ATR because having only three regular periods a day didn't make up a full schedule. I could still be called upon to cover at least two other classes when not occupied with the regular three.

Once told that Mr. Siwel was the graphic arts teacher who was moving on, and knowing that the three periods given to me were his, I made it my business on about three occasions when I had no classes to cover to go to his classroom – with his permission, of course – to see what I was about to get myself into. He couldn't have been one of those caught up in the teachers' absenteeism habit, for in the weeks I had been at the school I had not covered any of his classes, although I had met a few of his students in other classes I did cover.

Mr. Siwell, a white man I assumed to be in his mid-50's, had a stern look about him. His students, a mixture of 15 to 17-year-olds, consistently did and said things they obviously knew would upset him. If they wanted his attention and called out his name without using the "Mister," he wouldn't even look at them until they did. Some, rather than cooperating, would simply forget about addressing him at all. Even if they called out "Mister Siwel" without first raising a hand, he wouldn't respond. Some just simply refused to raise a hand. When he proceeded to discuss the lesson on the chalkboard. Not one student got involved. His calling out names individually and directing questions to an individual student at a time either got a very long delayed response or no response at all. They consistently called him names, which though murmured under their breath could yet be deciphered: "dat man," "dat crazy man," "dat weirdo." It couldn't have been more obvious that there was a breakdown in normal communication between teacher and students.

Mr. Siwell took it upon himself to prepare me to run his class. He regularly characterized the students to me in whispers inaudible to them, identifying them by the clothes they were wearing. By the end of my second visit I knew who I was supposed to give a grade of barely passing, a little better than barely passing, or one of failure. The barely passing and little better than barely passing grades were to be given to a very few; failing grades were overwhelming.

Mr. Siwel told me that being Black I should get along with the students, a mixture of Blacks and Hispanics, a lot better than he did. Strangely, he also told me that the one thing he abhorred about them most was that constant use of the word nigger. Hearing it all day, he said, really got him upset.

Though I knew that my old fashioned value system found not much tolerance within the youth culture, I yet got the feeling that Mr. Siwel's teaching methods were emanating from a foundation of failure. Hence, if he really thought he was preparing me to take over his classes, he was very wrong. Of the many things he told me, I initially took only that advice not to let the students know that I was new to the teaching profession. If they knew this, he assured me, I would have to go through an extra hard time being "put to the test." So having previously helped out in tutoring adults to pass GED exams through a Crown Heights, Brooklyn neighborhood program, when they ask if I was a new teacher, as I anticipated they would, knowing now how very much they liked to ask personal questions, I would tell them I taught adult education.

Once the news got out that I would soon be taking over Mr. Siwel's three morning periods, the teachers in that department – all of whose classes I had covered – would make comments in this regard to me when they saw me in the teachers' room.

Mr. DiVito, an Italian American, wished me "good luck with the sonufabitches." I had covered his classes many times and he had told me he was eligible for early retirement in less than a year and he intended to do so for sure. His students were a hard-headed lot. With the windows of his classroom overlooking Ninth Avenue, I witnessed that he spent a lot of time trying to keep them from opening the windows and throwing things down at unsuspecting pedestrians walking on the pavement. It wasn't unusual to hear a victorious shout such as "I just hit the bitch in the red dress." There was a small group of about four boys who always attempted to fly their hurriedly made little kites from the windows. "Real teacher" Mr. DiVito couldn't get them to curtail their behavior and when I covered the class they saw no reason to do it for me either.

Mr. Pietro, Italian American, one of the old guards at the school, couldn't see how I could succeed where Mr. Siwel had failed. "Good for him that he's moving on to something else and not letting the little monsters drive him crazy." I didn't pay him any attention. I never had the rapport with him that I had with Mr. DiVito. Whenever I covered a class of his he would return to school and lay claims to missing things from his classroom. And he would do it in a manner meaning to make me look like a thief. He definitely had an ownership of space and things mentality.

Assistant Principal Mr. Pesquito, too, another Italian-American, the very one who had usurped authority and refused me the position, now with a number of his pals present, offerred his subtle pessimism about "we'll just have to wait and see if a new boy like you can make it where an experienced teacher like Mr. Siwel had such a hard time." Then he followed this up by making reference to the liberty he took that day in refusing me the position and the fact that it wasn't only turned around but I was still at the school. Smirking, and trying to be humorous, he commented, "Well, I see you got some friends in high places down at Sixty-Five Court Street, but I don't know if they can help you here."

He had a reputation around the school as an obnoxious fellow. Part of his duties covered the area of teachers' punctuality, and like so many other teachers, I, too, was late on a few occasions, leading to the crossing of our paths and my witnessing his sour face and hearing his unpleasant manner of speaking.

Mr. Solomon, a Jewish man, seemingly in his late-50s, was my assistant principal. After telling me of all those things expected of me, he gave me a pile of manuals and booklets that I was supposed to read and would lead to making me into a competent teacher. And on the first day I was to take over from Mr. Siwell he went with me to the classroom to introduce me to the students.

When it was thought that no more students would be

turning up, he announced to those present that Mr. Siwel had accepted another position and I was their new teacher. The moment they heard of Mr. Siwel's departure, they cheered loudly and started giving each other those multi-part handshakes common among Blacks folk.

Mr. Solomon went back to his hiding place and I was left there to fend for myself with the 25 or so students who turned up that morning.

I told them some things about myself, that I was from the island of Barbados, that I had left there as a young teenager and lived in London, England for some years, then moved to Ontario, Canada and lived there for about the same length of time, then moved to New York City in the early 1970's. I also told them of other places I had been while serving in the British Army, starting when I was only a few months older than some of them. I asked if they knew where England was, where Canada was. Not knowing then that students in America were very poor on geography, I was surprised that few knew that Canada was a nation to their north and actually shared a common border with the United States. I told them of ending up in Canada as a youngster and finding that I was lacking in education and skills I made up my mind to return to school to improve my education and learn lithography/graphic arts/printing. Then when I moved to the United States I took my education to the university level in spite of the fact that my skills were serving me quite well.

I went on to tell them that in every country there was an emphasis on education. It was important that youngsters at least graduate from high school. After high school and they were able to handle college, they should make every effort to go to college also. But if for whatever reason they couldn't take on college, there were trade skills they could acquire, some of which could actually make them more money than a college education. If they had neither education nor skills, they would end up always doing dead-end jobs with a very dull future.

They were very impressed with my military and traveling experiences. About education and skills, not so much. Only wanting to know "how much money that makes." Hearing that they had to work their way up from the bottom didn't impress them, either. So in regards to these two issues some countered with "so boring," how much more money they could make in a short period of time selling drugs.

I had to get discipline into the discussion. I mentioned how disgusting it was to disrespect those "who were not disrespecting you." I emphasized even more that to disrespect without being disrespected meant that you had to have first "disrespected yourself."

There were many attempts at disparaging Mr. Siwel as "no kinda teacher at all." I had a fair degree of success in trying to dissuade them from doing so. All in all, though, having the discussion was a wise idea; it got me off to a wonderful start. And with a bit of humor I concluded on the issue: "Your teacher is very deep into self-respect, that means that I will never disrespect you, so you should never have any reason to disrespect me."

Mr. Cator had suggested to me that I never give the students too much work in a lesson: not too many pages to read, not too much to write, not too much math. This was, he assured me, the best way to get them agitated and talking about "boring." Mr. Siwel had given me a similar suggestion about this situation, perhaps the second of only two suggestions he gave me that I applied credibility to: Give them no more than two blackboard lessons, two sessions each of reading and writing, one session of math and one quiz each week, and hands-on activities the remainder or they were sure to start "acting up." In time, combining these two methods would prove to be a feasible formula. The tolerance of youngsters for what they perceived as being given an overload – especially of what they didn't like – was very low indeed.

When the periods ended around the third day of my being "the real teacher" and after the students had rushed out to go to lunch, one didn't join the rush, A 16-year-old Black girl from the Bronx, very attractive.

"Hi, Mista Brathwaite," she approached me. "My name is

Nikki. I just want you to know that I want to help you. I know it ain't easy for you dealing with all these students alone – especially the way some of 'em be acting. When you need a little help here and there you can call on me."

The word had gone around that Mr. Siwel was gone and there was a new teacher so some of those who had habitually avoided coming to classes turned up, increasing the number of students I had to deal with.

I was overwhelmed by Nikki's offer, for she did it so assuredly to tell me that she was serious. She came to the classroom first period next morning – when I didn't have a class to cover or a regular one, either, because my regular three periods were two, three and four – as I was writing a lesson on the blackboard. She sat down and started to write the lesson in her book as she talked with me. Then when she was through writing, she wanted to know if I was sure what was on the blackboard was the end to what I intended to write. I assured her it was. She promptly took the eraser and wiped every word from the blackboard. Somewhat exasperated, I asked, "Girl what on earth are you doing?"

She let out a beautiful giggle, then explained: "Mista. Brathwaite, did you know that there are some people who can write real good on paper but they write so crooked when it comes to writing on a blackboard? I ain't trying to put you down, but your writing goes uphill and downhill like crazy. So I'm gonna rewrite this lesson from my book for you 'cause I don't want your students to be laughin' and downin' on your writin'." And she rewrote the lesson – better than I did, I had to admit.

She wanted to know if I had a home-room class. I did. In what room was it held? I gave her the number. There was no need to ask about time, home-room classes being all conducted at the same time, for about 15 minutes, for the major attendance taking that would determine how many students attended school each day, and for other services such as issuing travel and lunch passes, also for "touching base" with some students for one reason or another. Because the time for conducting home-room was so short in leading up to a normal period for many home-room teachers, they usually had one of their home-room students to go to the major office for the attendance book and have it there in their home-room classes, then return it to the office so they would be able to rush off to start their normal classes. Nikki voluntarily assumed the responsibility of doing this for me. After she so willingly did this chore for me for some time and realizing it took her to the very top floor both for bringing and returning, hence, doubly cutting into her class time, I told her of having another girl in my home-room who would take over the returning of the register so she wouldn't be so inconvenienced. She didn't want to hear of it. She had given me her word of being my helper and here I was "trying to get rid" of her. Not long after, without any pressure from me, she agreed that it wasn't a bad idea at all that the student in my home-room class should do the chore of returning the attendance book to the office. She didn't even believe that I was "trying to get rid" of her. Now I had my second volunteer helper in Maria, another 16-year-old, of Puerto Rican descent, also quite pleasant and attractive. She even relieved me of taking the attendance myself, and couldn't see the sense in another girl from another home-room having to take my attendance book back the office and then having to rush off to her class when she was in the class and could easily get it – and take it back too. Logical as it seemed, I wasn't about to do something that would convince Nikki that I really wanted to get rid of her. This was especially helpful because home-room period was a time of much confusion among the students; homeboys and homegirls, many perhaps seeing each other for the first time in that very long time since just yesterday morning at home-room time. And the noise in all home-room classes was excessive to the point of students not hearing their names called out for four or five times. And when it was a morning for the issuing of lunch and transportation passes – particularly the latter – the confusion increased with male students in particular engaging in all kinds of devious efforts to rob the teacher of passes.

Nikki could not be in such a hurry, or nobody could be waiting on her eagerly enough that at the end of my periods she wouldn't at least give me some hurried help to straighten up the classroom. When students directed unacceptable behavior at me, she wouldn't neglect to admonish them for their "disrespect" of me when I "never disrespect" them. It wasn't too long before her peers (males in particular) were calling her "Brathwaite's main squeeze ." She never let the teasing bother her. To a much lesser degree. It was the same thing with Maria. She never let it bother her, either.

Yes, Nikki engaged in little transgressions; for instance, that bad habit of students to find excuses to leave the classroom and wander around for a while. But she never did it in that I-don't-give-a-shit manner which many students showed to the teacher. She would, instead, be pleasantly devious. Well, I had to tolerate it being disrespectfully done by many in her age group, so why should I expect perfection from her?

In time, I got to know the students better, and they me. I learned that a simple thing as getting to know and call them by their names was an act so personal that it helped tremendously in creating a bond. I learned now that I had my own classroom, when I had a class to cover to take the students to my classroom and not go to theirs. Covering classes in their classrooms had them believing that you were on their territory as opposed to when you took them to your classroom and they felt they were on your territory and were a bit inclined not to act-up as much.

Some days behavior wasn't so bad at all, when students somehow unanimously decided to adopt a laid back attitude and mind their own business – until the next day. Big, tough-looking Scotty was such a type. He just couldn't seem to be able to refrain from putting on displays of strength, using other students to be his victims. He usually came to classes late and left ahead of time. He didn't act like a tough guy, insisting on being disrespectful to the teacher while doing so. He didn't ask if he could leave, either; simply said, "See ya, Brathwaite." "See all o' y'all niggas tomorrow." I knew of no one – not even the ones thinking they could challenge him in the tough guy department – who were sorry about his habit of being last to come and first to depart.

I certainly had much less tolerance for Benjamin. Unlike many of the male students who didn't carry book bags, just stuck their books away somewhere, he always carried a big one. There were never any books in it, though. It was packed with an assortment of chocolate bars, M&M candies and cookies which he was unrelentingly loud in trying to force others to buy at the store prices, a real rip-off if it was true, as was popularly believed, that they were stolen. I had previously met Benjamin while covering a class he was in. He told me several times that I couldn't stop him from selling his goods in the class because it was his class, and I wasn't even "the real teacher," and that the real teacher didn't mind it, so why should I? I discussed the issue with his teacher, who rather than deny or say something against it, simply laughed it off.

It was different now; Benjamin was in my classes. One day as he was arguing me down about his right to sell in the classroom, which caused much disruption. Scotty, for whatever reason, came rushing back into the classroom. What I thought was bad luck turned out to be good luck. "Mista Brathwaite, man, what kinda teacher is you, taking so much lip from dat nigga ?"

Benjamin was no softy but it ended up with Scotty proving to be tougher as he made good on his threat to Benjamin to "bodyslam yo' black ass outta this class and taking away all dat shit you be haivin' in dat bag." For he did bodyslam him, threw him out the classroom door into the hallway to fall on the floor, then threw his bag behind him. It wasn't closed properly so the candies spilled out on the floor. In very little time a number of students from different classrooms were all over the floor snatching up candies and cookies.

I then learned from Scotty that "that boy don't even belong in here." I knew very little about him, how then was I to know that he wasn't the real Benjamin? The real Benjamin was another student who had been absent from school for a long time and this youngster had assumed his identity for his own reasons. Next morning he came to me pleading – and demanding – to be allowed back in. My decision had already been made: good riddance; go to the teacher who thinks your actions are funny.

I should say, though, that he ended the episode on what I thought to be quite a funny note, no doubt hoping to strengthen his position. A few of the other students had joined the fracas late to help Scotty in the final moment of depositing him into the hallway. He told me of them, "Mista Brathwaite, see those niggas, they be in the lunchroom talking some bad shit 'bout ya." Without giving it even the briefest of thought, Scotty countered, "So what, nigga? Brathwaite is our teacher; we can treat him as bad as we want; you can't. Ain't that right, Brathwaite?" I wasn't about to give credence to his absurd philosophy. The others who jumped in late immediately did so, however, and in unison like they had practiced it: "That's right, ain't that so, Mista Brathwaite?"

I had learned to be diplomatic in words and actions. When students would sneak into the classroom, I no longer started making demands that they leave immediately. They felt that readily complying made them look not at all tough so they would go into their defiant act to impress their peers. I would simply ask them to go to their classes. Much more often than not they would either try to con me into letting them stay "for a little while," which I knew wouldn't be little, and they would linger briefly and then disappear. It certainly beat getting into a confrontation.

One of the rules and regulations was that students shouldn't be allowed to eat in the classroom. They insisted on doing so anyway. Bringing in big sandwiches for breakfast wasn't unusual. Once they made it into the building with their breakfast meals it was impossible to stop them from dining. Before lunchtime the talk of hunger would start circulating. They would start collecting money so one or two could ease out of the building to buy their cheeseburgers and French fries to be sneaked back into the school and finally into the classrooms. At first I used to tell them they couldn't leave the classroom. I soon found out that they interpreted the popular American motto "Land of the free and home of the brave" to mean that they were free to do as they pleased and no damn teacher was brave enough to stop them. I made a change. Insist on leaving the classroom and I won't wage an argument trying to stop you, but I had a right to stop you from turning my classroom into a fast-food joint. Those who felt free to leave did so. However, after I kept calling the guards for them, they stopped arguing with me for the right to eat meals in the classroom and did it somewhere in the hallways or stairways.

I didn't have Nikki's support on this issue. She was nice enough to tell me privately that I "shouldn't make such a big deal" about it because other teachers didn't get themselves upset trying to stop it.

It was almost impossible to go to any floor and not see bits of food on the steps and in the hallways.

Inexperienced as I was, seeing some food stuff scattered on the floor outside my classroom door one evening, I notified one of the men from the from the clean-up crew and asked if he could clean it up. He adamantly refused and told me today wasn't the day for doing that on this floor. It would have to wait until tomorrow or the teacher could clean it up. I was unaware at the time that these guys belonged to a strong union and that they actually earned more money than many teachers. The City thought teachers should see their job as a civic obligation for which they were paid less than other city workers as if they got groceries, housing, rides on public transportation at a reduced rate.

The boombox culture was in full swing. Youngsters took them everywhere and liked to hear them blaring out music. In school was no exception. The popularity of rap music was rapidly escalating. Students wanted to hear Run-DMC, Public Enemy, The Fat Boys and others even while in school. Teachers were to stop them from playing these big boomboxes in the classrooms or be accused by administrators of not being able to control their students. With their administrative power behind them, they couldn't do what would have been most effective against the problem: stop the students from bringing these music boxes into the school in the first place. Needless to say, parents couldn't stop their children from leaving the house for school carrying them.

HSGCA was a structurally sound building, not too many years old. But it had no air conditioning. When the weather started to get quite warm teachers were constantly reminded to keep the students away from the windows. Administrators went around checking. Once it became uncomfortably hot keeping students away from the windows became a full-time job – one that didn't work. It didn't help the situation that some of them were immature enough to spit out the windows at others outside and carry out shouting conversations with any of their homeboys and homegirls seen out there. They might even see staff members who they thought they should harass and did so.

Included in the rules and regulations was that the habit of some of the female students to wear rather skimpy and skin-tight clothing during the summer wasn't to be allowed in the school. These girls insisted on "flaunting it" anyway. When they found it difficult to get into the school dressed in that manner, some came acceptably dressed but with their skimpy dresses and skin-tight shorts either under the acceptable wear or hidden in their bags. All that was left to do when they got into the school was to go to the washrooms and relieve themselves of the acceptable wear for the unacceptable, giving teachers another problem to deal with.

Having just briefly addressed the issue of students' bad attitudes toward administrative power, I must document here a happening that serves as a classic example of this:

The day before Mr. Solomon was to come to my class to observe for the first time my teaching ability, I informed my students of the impending observation. I told them when he

came in the morning I was depending on them to display their best behavior, be cooperative, ask relevant questions, and don't be mean to Mr. Solomon or me.
When Mr. Solomon came the next morning everything was set for him. I commenced the lesson, knowing that if the students did as they promised me they would the observation would go off without a hitch and I would come across looking better than Mr. Siwel perhaps ever looked. But I never even got pass the first part of the observation, discussing the lesson on the blackboard and giving the occasional practical demonstration pertaining to the theory. I already knew of Mr. Solomon as an AP much nicer than Mr. Pesquito but with a very inflated ego as to how much he knew. I couldn't finish more than a few words before he would interrupt to tell me what I was doing wrong and to demonstrate how it should be done. I had no doubt whatsoever that I was doing very well but his inflated ego told him that he had to prove to my students that while I was their teacher he was in charge.

Marlene, the often mouthy girl from Brooklyn who sat in the back constantly discussing boyfriend issues with Shirley, started to murmur her displeasure. She wanted to know when she was going to get a chance to ask a few questions and why the teacher wasn't given a chance to finish anything he started to say or do. Very soon dissatisfaction was being widely expressed. It would seem that the sensible thing for Mr. Solomon to do was let me finish, but his giant ego still wouldn't let him. Then addressing Marlene's dissatisfaction, he made a little statement that "you kids have to understand that Mister Brathwaite is the teacher but I am Mister Brathwaite's boss." It was a much bigger statement than he thought. The foremost cheeseburger consumer Darnel injected himself angrily: "What you mean 'bout you's Brathwaite's boss? What you think this is, slavery? You come in this class thinkin' you's a redneck slavemaster and dissin' Brathwaite in front o' his students."

After this, the observation was doomed because the students kept shouting down Mr. Solomon and calling him unflattering names, particularly "redneck racist." Embarrassed, he tried to save himself from the verbal onslaught by accusing them of disrespecting their teacher. They vehemently denied that they were disrespecting me, that it was he who was disrespecting me and since I wasn't "dissing" him back they were doing it for me. He elected to leave the classroom, instructing me to give him a list of their names. Scotty got in the last words as Mr. Solomon hurried out the door: "Good. Get outta here before we throw your ass out the window."

I had not seen students become quiet so quickly. For a few minutes I sat at my desk looking at them as they looked back at me, nothing being said. They sensed that I was disappointed. I eventually confirmed my disappointment to them. Why could they not let me get through my first Board of Education observation? They were unanimous in their belief that the real problem was caused by "nobody but that redneck-ass nigga," and that they did what they did for me.

The last period ended and as Nikki helped me to straighten up the classroom, she suddenly broke the existing silence. "You're angry, right, Mista Brathwaite? I wish it didn't have to happen like dat. But that man wasn't right. I believe he was dissin' you and the students defended you."

After thinking it over for a while, I concluded that there was much justification for my students feeling the way they did.

Only a few days later Mr. Solomon summoned me to his office pertaining to a few of my students he saw acting up outside of my classroom door. He gave me a little lecture on what to do to avoid this. I must say he did it nicely and I felt sure it was just to remind me that he was still an expert on student and classroom management. Now, describing for the first time with Mr. Cator what transpired during the observation, I also mentioned this little lecture.

Mr. Cator gave me a classroom number and told me of the period he wanted me to go there and check out "what an expert" Mr. Solomon was at classroom management. He insisted that I should go because I was "sure to learn something very important." I did so. Mr. Solomon, with only two teaching periods a day because of his AP status, was teaching his students. Some were chasing each other around the classroom, others were running in and out of the classroom, yet others were throwing around their paper airplanes. Not one was paying attention to what he was teaching or the orders he gave to sit down.

I told Mr. Cator later of what I saw. "He's the expert who tells all of us in this department how it should be done. And that's the way it always is in his classes. And would ya believe that he's one of those typical AP bullshitters that makes sure the real bad kids don't get programmed to their classes?"

Assistant Principal Haney, one of many White teachers who wasn't of Italian or Jewish heritage, was one I considered to be an excellent administrator. I had often covered classes in his department. He was always ready to listen, give honest advice and help out. He never tried to prove how competent he was by making the new teacher look incompetent. When students got the word that their teacher was absent and a substitute would be covering the class and they did their disappearing act, Mr. Haney let me know that they usually did this under the circumstances, not make me think that there was some kind of incompetence I exuded that caused them to disappear.

Mr. Pesquito had given me no reason so far to change those bad feelings I had for him. Even if it was true, as was widely said, that his bad attitudes was a result of a postwar syndrome thing developed from his involvement in the Korean War, that still couldn't excuse him being consistently obnoxious, to the point where he was well avoided – "like the plague," so to speak. He also had this habit which male teachers often gossiped about in a joking manner, but I, like the few Black and Hispanic teachers, thought to be very "tacky." He often locked himself away in his congested little ground floor office with one of those physically well endowed Black or Hispanic female students, under the pretext of them doing chores for him. Knock on that door at times when it was obvious that he was in that little room with company and he would be reluctant to answer, or would display a nasty attitude when he did. Why did he have to lock the door? Surely, he had to have been aware of his colleagues' criticism of him for this habit, not to mention the endless students' gossip. Surely, the principal was aware of it also. Why did he not put an end to such unprofessional behavior?

And mentioning the principal, he obviously thought being principal made him so very important that he was entitled to subservience from the teachers. No matter the situation, he never spoke first, this was for teachers to do and they did. I observed that at times when we did so he didn't even reciprocate. He had showed me this side of him several times. Then I made the decision, job or no job, "fuck that snob;" I would speak to no one who didn't speak to me.

There was a morning in my home-room while I was sitting at my desk tending to the confused business of issuing transportation passes and barely escaped becoming a casualty of school violence. Within a split second of moving my head to the right an object flew within an inch past my left eye with such velocity that when it struck the wall it broke into a few pieces. After Maria assured me that she was okay, I inspected the pieces on the floor and realized the object was a new bar of soap. It was a malicious act that was meant to cause hurt. That thing could have taken my left eye out. The fact that I wore glasses could have made it worse. All the students looked on in sudden silence. None would say who was the culprit that tried to hurt me. I felt sure that it came from a group of boys who were always occupying the back row making excessive noise. Now they were uncharacteristically quiet, with their faces displaying what I thought to be a devious feigning of innocence. It told me that I was to never be off guard where there existed such lawless deception.

Not long after, I had a similar experience while covering an afternoon senior class on the second floor. We were deeply involved in a writing assignment when suddenly there was a shattering of glass caused by a brick hurled at the window from outside. The students frightfully ducked for cover as the brick fell right at my feet. Then they got up, took their belongings and disappeared from the room. I noticed that a group of students who were outside with their boomboxes blaring out rap music and dancing had just as suddenly disappeared. As with the case of the bar of soap, the man in charge had me write out a report. I never heard a word about either.

Well, it was seldom that one could walk through the school without being hit in the nostrils by the pungent smell of marijuana. Was there a link between incidents such as these and the marijuana?

One morning as I rushed for the elevator, Mr. Clair was getting off. He had a white towel holding to his nose and forehead. He lifted the towel briefly to show me the blood coming from his nose and a lump on his forehead. He was on his way to the hospital. Mr. Haney was with him and asked me to go upstairs and cover Mr. Clair's class until he could find a substitute.

Out of the bad habit of foodstuff being thrown on the floor, Mr. Clair had fallen victim to a banana peel right outside his classroom door. Defying the supposed norm attached to this situation, he somehow fell forward – instead of backward – flat on his face.

When I got to the classroom, I witnessed a shameful scene. There were several of Mr. Clair's students gathered around the bloody spot where he had fallen, laughing and making fun over what had happened to him: "The nigga , he got his shit busted open;" "he done got fucked up real bad;" "he ain't gonna be back any time soon;" "ain't nobody be missin' him no how 'cause he was such a boring-ass teacher;" and other insensitive remarks.

I wish there was no need for me to say this, but most of those constituting this shameful scene were Black, primarily male.

Mr. Clair was a Black man from Barbados. I wasn't as close to him as with Mr. Cator, but there were times when he did give me the kind of information and encouragement I thought very helpful for a new teacher to get.

I had covered Mr. Clair's classes on a few occasions. The thought that he would be out for the remainder of the school year, though not far off, and I would be covering his evening classes at times, did nothing for my happiness. He had a few students who were unpleasant. In fact, when he was about to go absent for the first time after I became part of the staff, anticipating that I might be the covering teacher, he gave me tips on how to deal with his students. One of these tips was to "sometimes you got to hear them and don't hear them when they get too rude." He was a caring and dedicated teacher.

One of the problems I had run into in his class was a slim-built, though sinewy-looking 17-year-old, not less than six feet tall, who was always demonstrating his pugilistic skills against unwilling students. The one he picked on most was perhaps five inches shorter but with a stocky build. The slim sinewy one always got the better of the stocky one, causing him to do everything to avoid him. I asked the stocky one one day why he, such a tough-looking guy, was so afraid of the slim sinewy one. He told me that he wasn't afraid but he was a good boxer and he knew he was no match for him. But why did he have to box with him, I wanted to know. He could wrestle him instead. But the kids didn't want to see wrestling, he told me. I told him that when people fight wars they do what they think will help them to win, not what their enemies think they should do.

I might have seen the slim sinewy one in two after-school fights on the pavement outside the school, and indeed he had used his fists quite potently while being cheered on by the crowd. Then one evening as I walked out the school I was greeted by a commotion on the pavement. The slim sinewy one and the stocky one were going at each other. The stocky one was taking some good punches. But then he managed to grab the slim sinewy around his neck, lifted him off the ground while still giving his neck a rough time, threw him down hard on the concrete while still wringing away at that neck, dragged him around while treating that neck as if he truly wanted to break it and rip it off his shoulders. It took three guards to get the stocky one off the slim sinewy one. The coughing along with the concern the slim sinewy one showed for the condition of his neck made it obvious that he had been put through a very rough time.

The stocky one searched me out to eagerly tell me of his victory over the slim sinewy one. I told him I had seen it. I also told him I hoped they wouldn't get into other fights. He assured me there would be no more fights between them because he "didn't go around lookin' for no drama. And besides, dat boy knows that I might not be able to outbox him, but I'll sure as hell break his neck or his legs." I was convinced that theirs was one class disruption I wouldn't have to put up with again.

I recall also covering a class to which a little fellow and a much bigger fellow came with a dispute between them in progress. Their threats and insults aimed at each other quickly escalated as other students urged them on. I warned them of my intent to call the guard if they insisted on pursuing their dispute. Guards not taken too seriously, they ignored me. What was so strange about the situation was that the much bigger fellow was being urged on by most of the other students to "kick dat little nigga's ass," "how you be lettin' dat little punk talk you down like dat?" And indeed, for such a little fellow, he was taking a brave stand. Suddenly the big fellow rushed the little fellow with bad intentions on his face and in his words. But the little fellow was quite elusive. He dragged desks and chairs between them, dodged around classroom equipment, obviously intent on making his way to the door safely. As he did so he kept shouting out, "Yo, you ain't fair, you and your homies gangin' up on me. If you ain't a coward, gimme a chance to go and get my niggas too.'"

He managed to escape out the door, which I had pushed wide open to get rid of him and avoid the problem reaching a head. He still had a chair in his hands and actually threw it over my head at his adversary. Yet I was relieved because I was sure it was his last brave stand and he wouldn't be back. I was so wrong. Several minutes later I heard a commotion out in the hallway. I looked out and there heading for the classroom was the little fellow with about six other students. "Teacher, open the door," he demanded. "Now, I got my niggas too." The students in the classroom were encouraging me to open it. I stood by the door. I asked that one of them get on the emergency classroom phone and get help. Not one did. But the little fellow and his homeboys were making so much noise that it attracted the attention of a guard who intervened. As for the emergency phone on the wall, I subsequently picked it up and like the majority of them in the classrooms, it was out of order.

At this stage I was already strongly inclined to believe that the Board of Education's espoused philosophy of the "kid-gloves" treatment approach to solving students' behavioral problems played a significant role in these problems continuing and getting wore. I must say, though, that I learned on my own that total rigidity wasn't the answer. Teachers had to be able to make a joke with their students, so should it be in the reverse, in spite of the latent danger in the interpretation of some students that this was a sign of weakness to be exploited. It was therefore absolutely necessary for teachers to have that intuitive feeling as to where the stopping point was to be. This wasn't easy for some to determine. I will be audacious enough to state my belief that this I-shall-not-be-removed old fashioned stand of teachers like Mr. Siwel and Mr. Crown contributed to the great problem they had reaching students.

Almost from the very beginning, I was opposed to this thing called "cafeteria duties," a period teachers had to help in the supervision of students in the lunchroom. Firstly, the yearly budget for the schools ran into the billions of dollars and it should allow for the hiring of people to do this job. Secondly, after putting up with the problems in the classroom, why should a teacher have to deal with the lunchroom where students often got into their "food fights," throwing food at each other until it was all over the floor and on the walls?

Of course, as a new teacher I didn't know that some of the billions of dollars never got used for the intended purpose, that there were crooks at every stage throughout the system – starting big-time at the top – who took their share; hence, that unfair situation of teachers often having to use their own money to buy supplies for the functioning of their classrooms.

Within close proximity to HSGCA was Westside High School. What was the motive for building them so close to each other, I couldn't say. I can say for sure, though, that it contributed to problems among students, for the students at both schools thought there should exist an adversarial relationship. And so they had their frequent "wars" in the area. Sometimes they even infiltrated the other school.

As the days to the end of the school year dwindled significantly, I found myself faced with another annoying problem. Those students who had elected to do a disappearing act from classes for a long time were now doing a reappearing act for the end of term finals. Their disappearing act meant that they had learned little or nothing from the class, that they had not taken any of the other tests or quizzes. Now they were pestering me nonstop about: "you not goin' to fail me, right?" "I know that I'm gonna pass, right?," "I be doin' my work so you better not fail me." I wouldn't give a direct reply but would tell them that I fail no one; those who got a failing grade failed themselves. I certainly didn't believe that rewards should be given for no accomplishment. Even if they did pass the final test it wasn't accomplishment enough.

I anticipated the non-stop annoying complaints to during test time when they would be confronted with questions they had not a clue about: "He didn't teach us none o' this shit;" "Why the nigga givin' us shit we ain't never heard nothin' about?" This wasn't the case with only those who did the disappearing act; there were those who attended regularly who showed no interest in anything related to school and reacted similarly.

My tests were never difficult, though not as ridiculously simple as test samples I had seen shown around the teachers' rooms. I didn't believe in trick questions. I believed tests were to prove what you knew, how much you maintained. Also, before handing out the test, I would repeat to my students several times that it was very important that they "read the test before doing it" because I structured some questions in such a way that they helped in giving the answer to others.

Now, there were grades to be entered, report cards to be prepared, and the yearly attendance book to be straightened out. As I went over the grade cards from the beginning of the school year, I noticed that Mr. Siwel had been extremely conservative with grades. Almost all the students had failing grades. The few with passing grades were graded at the minimum level. I can't recall if there was a single positive citizenship report. I discussed the issue with Mr. Cator. He advised me against this. Principals don't say or do things to imply to teachers that they expect them not to be too conservative in their grading, he told me, but they are not known to be lenient with teachers who habitually give too many failing grades, either. It made the school look bad and therefore the principal, who would find some other reason to rid the school of the offending teacher. He thought there was some justification to Mr. Siwel's grading because of the don't-care attitude of so many of the students. But he reminded me of his tenured teacher status as opposed to my per-diem status. Getting rid of a tenured teacher was a difficult thing to do; getting rid of a per-diem teacher was "as simple as spitting."

Mr. Solomon – and even Mr. Pesquito – concluded that I had put in a very good performance for those few months, especially considering that I was a new teacher. They even listed me on the school's short list of teachers deserving of a choice of a free lunch. They obviously had noticed that while I had my bad days, many of my students were often involved.

Even when covering classes, I made every effort to get them involved. With both vocational and academic backgrounds, I was more versatile than covering teachers with a background in only one area. I would engage students in journalism and English classes, whereas a covering teacher with only the vocational background couldn't, or engage students in the vocational classes, whereas the academic-only covering teacher wasn't even allowed to go into these classes. It was of tremendous help to me that at the time I was editing and publishing a pocket size magazine called *Root*. I showed copies to journalism/writing students. They were impressed that I was the driving force behind a publication with a professional look that made the publications of their giant graphic arts school look quite amateurish. They then took me more seriously than they did their regular teacher. A good thing that wasn't such a good thing.

And I must note here that there were some older teachers in the vocational area who were just bullshitting their way along to retirement, doing very little. They couldn't if they wanted to because they came into the system with the much older equipment and couldn't be bothered to go out and learn about the contemporary equipment that replaced the old in their classrooms.

True, I was pleased that I was judged to have done well by the administration. I didn't care about their free lunch of my choice, though. I cared a lot more that students who had been attending the school sometime before I came and were ready for graduation, sought me out to sign their graduation book even though I was never their regular teacher.

I gave Nikki and Maria their well deserved thank you gifts, Nikki a bit better because she did more. She would be graduating June of the next year. And as the school year came to an end, she repeated it again: "Mista Brathwaite, I just hope that you don't leave this school before I graduate." Seemingly, I would be around, for I was assured by administration that, unlike some of the new teachers who were given that dreaded excess letter and wouldn't be back for the new school year, I would be.

< 6 >

Come September and I was back at High School of Graphic Communication Arts, happy to be back but not happy with my schedule. I had to share a classroom with a senior teacher. It smelled of problems, knowing of their propensity for acting as if the classroom was a room in their home.

Then came the time for the adult evening classes for which I was selected as one of the instructors and was happy to be. But again, it required that I use a classroom shared by two senior teachers in the mornings. They were both complainers of the kind to be justifiably labeled "pain in the ass." One complained in the manner of I-am-boss-in-this-classroom, the other in a manner often given the "sissy" label. Whatever the differences in complaining by these two (both Italian-American), I just couldn't help but contemplate that great threat Whites (male especially) seem to feel by the presence of a Black male invading "their space."

Not only did I have to share a classroom with the first teacher while teaching the kids in the mornings, but he was also one of the instructors with the adults' evening training programs which required us to share some of the same equipment every other evening.

He did whatever he could to make my using them impossible. When, for instance, I was ready to use the graphic arts camera in the darkroom to make negatives, I would discover that the fuse and lens were removed. Sometimes even the chemicals would have disappeared. In the case of the presses, the safety mechanisms, customarily used in high schools to prevent accidents, would have been tampered with to render them inoperative. The glasses for the light tables would have been removed. How do you explain this to adults whose unions were paying the Board of Education to conduct these programs?

My discussions with the AP in charge of the program often didn't solve anything. I just couldn't resort to teaching too much theory to adults who were primarily concerned with hands-on training. I had to be constantly calling on my initiative. As I was still the ATR teacher, I had a master key which opened most of the classrooms. So I would slip into one of the classrooms and borrow for my needs, and do whatever was necessary not to let the teacher come in the morning and discover that someone had dared to violate his space.

There was a complete difference between teaching kids and adults. With the adults there were no disruptions, no cursing or other acts of disrespect, no demands to be helped right on demand. They could be separated to work in little groups in an orderly manner.

Although after a stressful day of dealing with the kids I longed to go home, it still wasn't unusual when teaching the adults and was notified by someone that the 9:00pm finishing time was up for me to feel that the time had slipped away so fast and not allowed me time so I could have finished what I was doing. With the kids, on the other hand, even a two-period teaching session could seem like a much longer time. This was a sentiment held by all teachers involved with the evening program.

I should steal that "same ol', same 'ol" phrase popularly used by the kids when things remain almost the same. Doing so will save me from the monotony of being redundant.

For other than being involved with the adult program, generally speaking, the same things were happening at the school this new school year as had happened the last. Also, I did set out primarily to document my teaching experience in Rikers Island Jail. Such being the case, I see no reason not to accelerate the documenting of my teaching experience at HSGCA.

I continued my teaching at this school through the ending of September 1986 when I was informed that that there wasn't enough money in the school budget to rehire me for the new school year beginning in September.

I was, to say the least, surprised and disappointed. Following a trait in me to look beyond that told to me, I started to look for what might be the real reason.

I thought of the teacher who made it so difficult for me to conduct my adult evening classes. Not long ago I had gone to his morning classroom to ask him about his constant removing and hiding the camera lens. Apparently he thought it presumptuous of me to do so, leading me to remind him that the equipment were the property of the B.O.E. not his. He started to raise his voice at me in a manner I didn't appreciate. True, I didn't want to jeopardize retaining my position at the school. I could have walked away like many would have done under the circumstances, but I was never good at allowing people to get away with stepping on my pride. And seeing that there were several Black students in his class, I jumped back on him and told him, perhaps louder than he did, that he was never again to ever shout at me like that. Knowing that these guys liked to run to the principal with that you-are-the-godfather attitude, I had no doubt that my telling him off would also reach the principal's ears.

I thought of having sold copies of a book authored by me to a few individuals in the school. Much of my writing reflected socio-political issues regarded by the dominant culture as "Black power" and had little tolerance for. I saw validity in Mr. Cator's assumption that "one of our Negroes into whose hands you put that book must have run to the man with it, knowing that the man don't like progressive-

thinking adult Blacks like you influencing Black kids."
 .   I thought of the issue regarding Reesa, an afrocentric Black American young woman about 15 years my junior, from Union City, New Jersey, but residing in Brooklyn. She was employed as a teacher's helper at the school. We became very close, mainly, I guess, because of our views being so similar. In any case, she had told me how "pissed off" she was with Mr. Pesquito constantly "getting' too damn fresh" with her. After he took his freshness too far, ignoring her rejections, she said, she filed a grievance against him.

What made this an issue to be considered as a possible undercover reason for my excess goes back to the time Reesa was sick and I had to go to the office to pick up her check and take it to Brooklyn for her. Mr. Pesquito was there in the office and the secretary thought it necessary to tell him that I was there to pick up the check of "that young woman you had the problem with." She even told him how friendly Reesa told her over the phone she was with me. He replied with sarcasm, "So I was told...heard when she doesn't know which class to find him in, she goes from floor to floor asking for him. Isn't that so, Mister Brathwaite?"

I theorized that Mr. Pesquito believed that Reesa was my woman, that I, being so quiet and unassuming, might have had something to do with her filing a grievance against him. More importantly, though, it might have been too embarrassing for him to face me every day. So railroad me out of the way. It set me to thinking that I might not have had to look for a new position come September 1986 had I not gone to that office on Reesa's behalf. But what the hell! Not doing so might not have changed a damn thing; the wheels of "good riddance " must have already been set in motion.

Let me state here that Reesa wasn't the only one to paint such a picture of Mr. Pesquito to me. There was another young woman, White, a new per diem teacher who had previously told me, with teary eyes, that he always gave her a hard time, that she didn't get an excess letter but that she wouldn't return in September because she "couldn't stand that sex maniac bastard."

I had no doubt that I had done a relatively good job at HSGCA. Believe it or not, I was again listed by the administration as one of those teachers deserving to get another free end-of-school-year lunch of my choice, could be partly to obscure the real reason for my excess. Whatever the case, I wouldn't have it.

The adult evening students must have been very pleased with my instructing, for they constantly brought me little gifts. Even from my high school students came several nice Christmas cards. There certainly were many students so incorrigible to sometimes conjure up in my mind the worst thoughts of them. But I also gave thought to the fact that the bad elements tend to stand out so strongly above the good because of the way their behavior is constantly trampled into your mind, and how they succeed in doing so by getting the uncertain elements on the periphery to join in, and that the good elements even if more than the bad can't seem to change the bad in any significant way. Consequently, I would be remised not to say that there were good students also. Already I had the feeling that so many people had suddenly walked into my life and took over.

I was sorry that Mr. Clair, after losing his wife suddenly, a nice woman from Philadelphia, seemed to lose the will to carry on and soon followed her.

I couldn't say the same about the teacher who got his nose busted by the student and was given a black eye sometime later by another student. After I refused to go to his assistance when he was socked in the nose by the student, he had tried so hard one morning to set me up for an argument in the presence of the principal to create the feeling that I was not professional. He epitomized the bullshit teachers who talked a good game about "professionalism" but were more like the proverbial drunken sailor in a bar.

What can I say against a principal who gave me my start? I recall when I heard that two of the journalism teachers were leaving HSGCA, I went to him and suggested myself as the regular competent replacement rather than having to look elsewhere, not yet knowing of the politics of the B.O.E. He said he would keep it in mind. However, I soon heard it said in the teachers' room in a put-down manner that I thought I was going to be the new journalism teacher, but that the remaining journalism teacher had already suggested one of his buddies from another school.

I had covered this man's classes quite often. Initially he preferred me to do so over others. After his students started to give me some adulations about me being a publisher and editor of a "fly magazine," his attitude changed drastically.

Being able to decode hypocritical situations, I wasn't at all surprised that even those teachers who tried to make things difficult for me from the beginning were now meeting me, and like those who gave me no problems, wishing me well, telling me what a great job I was doing, wanting to know if I had anything lined up yet, and what school I would be going to.

For those who I felt had done me no harm, I told them as they knew it to be: I was still a per diem teacher; there was nothing certain at this level. For those who tried to make the going hard for me, I gave them the same sarcastic response: There was this great high school in the jungle in the Congo and I got a position there. There were canoes already waiting to transport me down the river on my arrival.

I was witness to Nikki graduating. She had always said she couldn't wait to be finished with the "crazy" high school scene and enroll in college. I wished the beautiful, excited young lady well and encouraged her not to give up. She assured me that she would not, but if such a thought ever entered her mind she would think of having made me the promise not to and the thought was sure to disappear. I couldn't tell her then what I can tell her here: that she is at the very top of my list of Good, Pleasant, Respectful Students.

< 7 >

Brooklyn Before Jailhouse Jeopardy

Even before the first day of the new school year started in September 1986 I was dreading the thought of having to go to the High School Staffing place at 65 Court Street. The new teachers there at this time looking for positions would be so many to emit feelings of discouragement.

In any event, the day came and I did what I had to do. I was very fortunate that the regular graphic arts teacher at Thomas Jefferson High School had taken ill and couldn't return at this time so I was sent there to fill the position.

I got off the number 2 train at Pennsylvania train station, walked down from the elevated platform to the street and commenced walking along Pennsylvania Avenue. Of course, being sent to fill the position was no assurance that it would be given to me. So as I walked along the thought of getting or not getting it occupied my mind.

The boarded up houses, the few spaces where houses used to be, their surroundings now taken over by wildly growing weeds and other foliage, with empty cans and bottles that once held beer and soda strewn around, and parts of the pavements badly in need of repair along the short route didn't make for a pleasant sight or for creating an encouraging mood. I wasn't surprised, though; very unflattering things were so often reported about the East New York section of Brooklyn. Whatever the situation, I was sure that if the position was offered to me the sight would no longer appear so forlorn and any discouragement in my mood would improve significantly.

I was ushered into the principal's office to be interviewed by the principal, Mrs. Lorde, and the assistant principal, Mr. Hookes, who was AP of the department I hoped to be hired for. They both seemed to be pleasant people, especially the very soft spoken Mrs. Lorde.

I showed them samples of my work, some I had done at HSGCA and some of those I had done outside the school system. They were highly impressed and said that they had never seen work of that quality produced in the school.

There was no journalism class and the English department was adequately staffed. However, since I would be producing the school's newspaper, when the time for doing this came I could employ my journalistic skills. I was shown a copy of the school's newspaper, The Thomas Jefferson Star, and as I looked over it, I hoped they wouldn't ask for my opinion. Everything about it was carelessly and unprofessionally "thrown together," telling me the teacher was either a careless person without pride, or being one of those from several years back, got into the system not so much because of what he knew about the subject area but who he knew. I had heard this often said of other White vocational teachers who got into the system several years earlier when Blacks were unofficially locked out of so many places. And to be honest, I was convinced from some instances at HSGCA that there was validity to the accusation.

I was given the position.

I thought the classroom could have had some more equipment, maybe because it was quite big and because of the wide assortment of equipment I had been around at HSGCA. There was enough, though, for good production and to keep busy. In fact, thinking of it later, I would realize that Thomas Jefferson wasn't a graphic arts school but an academic one with a graphic arts class and two other vocational classes being offered. And there were two good things about this situation: Not a lot of vocational teachers in the same skills area to pull against one another, and the great chance that the AP wouldn't have a clue about the skill being taught by the teacher under him and therefore would be in no position to play the I-am-boss card too often. Mr. Hookes was a commercial artist who knew nothing about graphic arts.

Of course, the student population at TJH was overwhelmingly Black and Hispanic.

Within a few days I learned that my program would be changed. I would have only two periods of graphic arts, two periods of arts and one period of writing – also a home-room period. The change suited me fine. I knew of, and had no doubts about, my writing ability. I didn't possess the paper qualification to teach art, an area, that like writing, I had also gravitated toward for as far back as I could remember, but admittedly never thought I was able to handle as I did writing.

I anticipated from the beginning that my students would be ready for me, ready to put me to the test. If they were not, it would have been a little miracle. There was no miracle.

They were 15 to 18-year-olds, some left back from other classes. As usual, several of the males were caught up in the act of flaunting their toughness, and several of the girls with flaunting their sexuality. I disliked both acts as they both inevitably led to classroom disruptions.

In all my classes there were a number of students who thought they were tough, engaging in a lot of those childish pranks such as throwing around objects, play-fighting of the kind rougher than playing, running around the classroom, interfering with equipment, lighting up cigarettes to smoke, engaging in the constant use of profanity, and any other acts they felt sure would annoy the teacher and lead to a confrontation with him, for it was by taking him on that they best proved their toughness. But there being varying degrees of acting-up, as there are with other situations, there were some students in my second period art class who might as well had observed the behavior of their counterparts in my other classes and decided that the degree of their bad behavior would be the worst. They, in fact, took it to such a degree that I concluded that the bad behavior in the other classes, and even that among some of the others in my second period class, wasn't so bad after all.

Maybe I should not have initially had the audacity to give them that little lecture of mine about self-respect and respect of others, respecting the teacher, and the teacher respecting them. Maybe they were bent on proving to me that all that was nonsense I believed in but they did not.

There were about six males who sat together in the back whose ages ranged from 16 to 18. They often got started by directing sexually explicit conversations at four girls, 16-year-olds, who sat together in the front. The girls would immediately reciprocate. Very often the conversation led to the physical between them, touching, grabbing, pushing, shoving, and some other students though not as bad behaved would yet contribute to the already noisy situation by making their opinions heard. It certainly didn't help that there were so many students to each class and there was no teacher's helper.

I set about learning their names that would enable me to address them in that personal way that would help in narrowing the gap of unfamiliarity. It helped some, but they were obviously not ready to close that gap. They were still having a hard time addressing me by my name. They preferred "hey," "hey, you," "dat teacher, what's his name?" "Mista Afrohead." They were wasting their time; not only would I not answer but wouldn't even acknowledge that I heard them.

My second art class fell on the last period. Initially several of the students elected to act-up. I found it so strange, though, that eventually they started to accept me while the pandemonium in the first art period persisted almost unchanged. Part of the strangeness about this situation was that there were thirty-six students crammed into the last period class compared to the 26 in the first art period. The last period students, exhibiting behavior still not handled well by my tolerance, also exhibited a love for their art. The majority of them when they came to the class acted as if they truly couldn't wait to "get down" on drawing their specialties: cartoon characters. They constantly complained about the one period being so short they never got to do what they wanted to. So when they came to the classroom, in their noisy manner, they demanded their folders immediately. The day there was to be a blackboard lesson to be copied and discussed, that was when their worst behavior surfaced.

This was a clear case of my being helped by the graffiti culture so loved by the youngsters but found to be so annoying by the great majority of adults – including me. This wasn't the youths' most loved version of graffiti – the one that so desecrated public places and things – but the private version. If they couldn't be creating a public nuisance that brought them such euphoria, they could certainly experience some of that euphoria by engaging in a major element of graffiti: cartoon characters. Children throughout the United States grew up with an infatuation for cartoon characters.

One day in the teacher's lunchroom I found myself engaged in a conversation with a Black American teacher. In response to his question about how I was making out in my new position, I mentioned the different situations in these two classes. He mentioned the inevitability of a teacher having a hard time starting in a new school. Then he assured me that the same way the situation improved in my first art class, it could be done in the second, but it wouldn't be done until some changes were made. He asked me to listen as he called out the names of some students and tell him if they were in the class. Every student he mentioned was indeed in the class.

"That's your major problem there," he assured me. "See, those are the baddest-ass kids in this school. No teacher wants them in their class. Plus they like each other's company. And since you are the new teacher, they threw them all into your class. But you don't have to take it. Tell Mister Hookes they have to be broken up. Believe me, he knows all about it."

Admittedly, being in a new position, I was reluctant to complain too soon. But I had discussed the situation with Mister Hookes on about three occasions. And he did come to my classroom on two occasions to help in solving problems caused by these students. Each time he did his paperwork solution thing, leaving the way clear for the problems to get started again. I also got the feeling that the perpetrators didn't take Mr. Hookes' authority seriously.

By now, I was getting some help from two students, Melissa and Serena. Melissa took care of the all matters pertaining to attendance, like marking the register and attendance cards and returning the relevant documents to the main office. Serena took care of folders, handing out and collecting supplies. At the end of the period she would bring all these things back to my regular graphic arts classroom after we had straighten up the arts classroom. Once Melisa was through with attendance she retained that seat there by my desk and did all her class work right there. She was there when Mr. Hookes came in, in response to my most recent complaint about the disruptive behavior from the students in the back. He assured me that he would break up the bad union. As soon as he left Melisa whispered to me: "Mista Brathwaite, I don't think you're gonna get help from dat sad-ass excuse for a man. All he cares about is lockin' himself up in his little office with that Jewish boyfriend of his. Let him put some of these nigga's in that man's class."

I was sure no one but me heard her, or I would have been convinced that Serena had, when as soon as she put the materials down on the desk in my regular room, she had almost the same observation about this issue.

Melisa was an 18-year-old who didn't manage to graduate on time but was aiming hard to do so at the end of the semester in February 1987, not go into June 1987, the date Serena, 17, aimed to graduate. They were both attractive girls. It was no surprise to me that the "tough guys" in the back inserted into their conversations what they thought these two girls were privately "doin' with the teacher, an old dude" that they should be doing with them instead. Then they would give their unflattering descriptions of the teacher.

If there was a semblance of solace for me here, it was that as these disruptive students fell into that do-as-I-damn-please category, after lunch period they often did what such students generally did: find somewhere to go that pleased them more so than staying in school.

By exercising this right, my having to see any of them in an afternoon class was highly unlikely.

As the days crept by not one of these students was yet removed from the class though Mr. Hooks had promised to have the situation "straightened out soon."

There was time for a test for which all the disruptive ones and their "gal pals" were given what they deserved: a very poor grade. No sooner were the grades handed out that as I sat at my desk some paper-made missiles started coming from the back in my direction. I issued the warning that if I was struck I intended to go outside and lay a complaint with the law and have them arrested for assault. Soon, about four of them made their way to my desk and surrounded me, using the usual profanity and demanding to know why I had failed them. I didn't fail anyone, I assured them. If anyone failed it was either because they did very poorly or didn't do anything at all.

As I got to my feet, one brushed against me in a strong enough manner to tell me that it was done deliberately and with bad intentions. "Son," I said, staring at him, "you are never to touch me again. Don't ever do that again. I mean it."

"So what you gonna do, nigga?" one asked, stretching himself up to appear taller. "So you be thinkin' you so tough 'cause them niggas in yo' other classes be rubbin' it into yo' head 'bout yo' big muscles? You might got muscles 'n' shit, but you too damn short to hit me on the chin."

Melisa was still sitting there, having not even attempted to move an inch out of the way. She suddenly came to my assistance. "Mista Brathwaite, don't let these motor mouths be scaring you. If they was so tough they won't be actin' like a gang." This led them to verbally turn on her, using those favorite words "bitch" and " 'ho." Using these terms didn't warrant the calling of anyone to stop them from using them; such terms were used so often to seem normal. However, I was ready to do so when one of the taunters stepped on Melisa's foot. With cheetah-like agility, she jumped up angrily, grabbed his shirt and proceeded to be so physically rough to belie her usual demeanor. "Nigga, I'll slap you so silly, you'll stop thinkin' dat I'm a girl."

Melisa would soon stop, but she would tell me later, "I stopped only because with my luck the trouble makers would get to stay in school and I would be the one to get suspended. And I really have to graduate in February."

Strangely, after the fracas ended, everyone reverted to their seats. The disruptive ones huddled together and spoke in whispers among themselves like true conspirators. I thought of the dangerous situation that was brewing, dangerous because there was no doubt that the two ring leaders were drunk. I previously had a premonition that they were drinking beer before coming to school and told Mr. Hookes about my belief. On this morning, there was no believing, the smell of beer coming from their breath was unmistakably strong.

A few minutes before the class would be over, I was leaning over a desk suggesting to a student how he could improve on the project he was working on so diligently. For though not a trained artist, I was of the opinion that I had the ability to offer helpful critique nonetheless. Suddenly I felt a hard object slammed into the back of my head. Instinctively,

I grabbed for the spot, then looked at the palm of my hand. It was covered with my blood. I next looked in the direction where I believed the object had come from. Most of the disruptive ones were making a dash for the door, leaving a trail of noise behind them. I rushed for the door and ignoring the wound, I managed to get a hold of the last student attempting to flee down the stairs. They had taken off in different directions. The youngster was taller than me by a few inches but his struggling to break away from my grip was to no avail. He kept proclaiming his innocence, and that he knew not who the guilty one was.

The teacher who had enlightened me about the disruptive students happened to appear on the scene and when I told him about what had transpired he took the student's ID particulars then suggested that I should let him go. He said I had a justifiable reason for restraining him but that I was to bear in mind that the school system and the law were "so gawddamn screwed up," it wouldn't be surprising if they came to the conclusion that I was in the wrong for physically restraining and trying to force information out of a student who was part of an attack against me.

While this was going on, Serena had gone to Mr. Hooks. When I went back into the classroom he was there with his note pad ready to write. Of course, no one had seen who threw that hard clay cup that hit me in the back of the head. Using napkins, Melisa and Serena were attending to my wound like they were nurses. "You awright, Mista Brathwaite?" Melisa kept asking. "You should go home."

"You should sue the damn school, Mista Brathwaite," Serena said, looking at Mr. Hookes with blame in her eyes. 'Cause, see, there was no kinda reason at all why all them bad-ass niggas should be in this class."

A Hispanic youngster, who had excellent artistic potential, said, "Mista Brathwaite, I told you not to be turn yo' back on these thugs in this school. You should know better. In truth, he did say so to me one morning when a student was being nasty. I was surprised at the reaction of the leading girl among that disruptive group of girls. Liking that loud-mouth girl, obviously obsessed with what she thought was her great sexual appeal, who was always trying to generate a sexual atmosphere in the classroom, wasn't an easy thing for me to do. She repeated a few times, "damn, man, them niggas didn't have to take their shit dat far". I actually thought I heard sincerity in her tone.

The class was over and I headed downstairs for the first aid room with Mr. Hookes. In that short time the news was already out. Some students, Black and male primarily, were pointing at me and making insensitive remarks: "There goes the nigga dat got his head busted open," "they fucked up homeboy," "the nigga shoulda had ducked faster." These and other similar comments were made with and to laughter.

To me, it was despicable. I thought back to Mr. Clair's fall at HSGCA and the same despicable reaction of some students there. I couldn't help but seriously wonder as to *what* – not ***who*** – had raised such youngsters.

I was showered with words of sympathy from Mrs. Lorde. It wouldn't be until years later that I would realize I wasn't as wise as Melisa and Serena or I would have gone home and bring some kind of legal action "to whom it may concern" for subjecting me to such danger and making no effort to change it. Instead, I foolishly remained at school that day to complete my program.

Of course, by the end of the lunch periods the news had spread all over the school. There were students in the graphic arts classes and the English class who had become quite comfortable with having me as their teacher, and especially so with those students in the last period art class. Some of them came to classes later prepared with an array of ideas as to how I should get even with those responsible for assaulting me.

The two main instigators especially, Lionel and Paterson, were bent on controlling my class. My old fashioned value system told me it wasn't to be so unless over my dead body.

I spent the rest of the day predisposed as to what was going to be done starting the next day should Lionel and Paterson and their followers attempt to pull off anything

similar to that day's stunt. I even went to sleep thinking about them. I woke up in the morning and there was still no change. I was still thinking of some very bad plans I had conjured up in my mind for them from the evening before should they ever physically threaten me as they did when surrounding me in their intoxicated state, even though Cummins, a friend of mine who was teaching at another Brooklyn school, admonished me against the thought. I took his advice to take a day off and calm down instead.

The day off might have calmed me down more than I knew. But when I headed back to Jeff, as the students popularly referred to their school, I knew I still had bad intentions in mind for Lionel and Paterson especially. As the train stopped at each station, I reassured myself that this was the day their behavior in my classroom would be ended come what may. Strangely, my mind kept focusing several years back to when I was a teenager in London and sat in a West London cinema and watched a tense western drama, *High Noon,* starring Garry Cooper. Cooper had rode out of the town to avoid a shootout with the bad men only to decide that he had to go back to the town and engage in that shootout that would prove he wasn't afraid of the bad men and would save the town. I, too, felt I had my honor to defend against a group of punks.

Fortunately for the town's people, Cooper did return and rid the town of the lawless bad men. Fortunately for me, Lionel and Paterson and two of their most ardent supporters were expelled from the school not to return until a guardian of each came to the school on their behalf. I had no doubt that if it was known to the B.O.E. what I had in mind for Lionel and Paterson if they repeated their actions against me, I would have been fired on the spot.

On this morning the remainder of the gang turned up – late as usual and making their noisy attention-seeking entrance. I was ready with my little no-nonsense speech as Mrs. Lorde looked on: The habit of constantly disrupting the class had come to an end. Constantly opening and closing the doors to go and come and to let friends in would no longer be accepted. For the disruptive who sat in the back, I had new seating plans which were to be adhered to. Whoever saw Lionel and Paterson before I did should inform them that I no longer wanted to have them in my class.

The defiance of the disruptive was made known. They insisted on being given their folders. I insisted on cooperation. They never had anything in their folders other than attempted drawings of lewd pornography. When the new leader stood up and announced his intention to "get the hell outta this nigga's class right now" and two others followed him, they could not have known how happy they made me, so much so that I didn't even give thought to their threats to "wait for him after school and give him what he has coming to him."

They would never return to the class for the remainder of the semester, though I did see them occasionally in and around the school being themselves: loud and obnoxious. They would occasionally aim a few smart comments at me which I ignored, knowing it would make their day if only I would respond. The class ran so much better after their departure.

I had some problems in other classes too, though certainly not to the extent that necessitated much complaining from me. Most of them were the kind of annoying problems that were not so bad to be in that sure-to-drive-me-crazy category. Problems in the English class usually were centered around the lack of motivation to read and write so prevalent among students, which often led to the discarding of books and papers in a manner they were not meant to. Most students in the graphic arts classes were usually quite busy designing and producing, others liked to be printing, often talking of perfecting it so they would eventually be able to "print a whole lotta money," something they could never understand why I wasn't doing instead of teaching for "no kinda money at all." The problems coming from this group were mostly about their desire to get into rapping in the classroom, childish misuse of the chemicals against each other, and lack of motivation when taught the basic fractions required of the subject area. I sometimes even had some problems with my most enthusiastic class, last period art.

One of the very few major problems I had with this class came from the Palomino Brothers. The two seemed to have a perfect siblings relationship. They were always together, even insisting on sitting next to each other in the classroom. So naturally, when one started throwing rolled up paper, pencils, crayons, markers, brushes and clay, the other joined in the "fun." And stopping them was impossible. When my tolerance reached a dead-end I told them that they were two young men behaving like little kids and they both jumped up at me together, the older one threatening as the other gave his "yeah, dat's right" agreement." The threat was, "Think we're little kids? Little kids, hun. Well, we got some plans for your ass. When we done with you, you ain't never gonna believe two little kids could coulda mess you up so damn bad." It was at this juncture that I wrote them up and they were suspended from school for a few days, something I really neither set out to have done nor expected would be done. Their behavior wasn't of the disrespectful magnitude as that displayed daily by the disruptive ones in the earlier art class.

The number of students had actually reached 40. Two girls who regularly helped me out were Luz and Leeanne, two very opposite personalities. Luz was New York born of Dominican Republic heritage. She could, as the saying goes, "talk you to death." On those rare occasions when I wasn't engaged in my habit of walking around the classroom observing and helping but sat at my desk instead, where she had stationed herself after earlier taking the attendance, she would be ready to continue with stories of her life.

One memorable story she told me was about the time a man tried to rob her mother on the subway platform "in broad daylight." She had walked ahead of her mother who had stopped to buy tokens. She looked back to see her being cornered by the man. She ran back to her mother, shouting to the man, "Let go of my mother." She was told to "shut to hell up or I'll throw your ass onto the tracks." He still had her mother cornered. She then stuck her hand into her bag in which there was a brown paper bag containing something belonging to her mother's brother that she, only 14 years old at the time, had secretly brought along because of a rapist reportedly roaming their neighborhood. She pulled out the brown bag, and with all the courage she could muster, cocked the gun in it, stuck it in the man's face and warned him, "I'm telling' you one last time, mista, you get away from my mother or I'm gonna blow yo' fuckin' brains out." Shocked, the man said to her, "Little bitch, you ain't got no right carryin' dat gawddamn thing aroun'." And he fled.

Her mother got over the shock of the man trying to mug her but not the shock of her daughter carrying a gun and pulling it on someone.

Luz' conversations usually contained curse words. She didn't use them in a manner of showing disrespect. It was just a habit. I would often tell her that she needed to wash her mouth out with laundry detergent and bleach. She would promise to stop using the curse words around me. She didn't succeed. When she realized she was still using the words, she would apologize. It was for this reason that I stopped her from taking the attendance in favor of Leeanne.

For another thing, there were a number of other Hispanic girls in the class, some of whom were Luz' friends, and when she was taking care of the attendance and there was no response to one of their names being called because of absence or tardiness in answering, Luz would think it ever so funny to call out, "Where dat 'ho'e at? She be late or the bitch stayed home to be in bed wit' some man?" This would lead to other similar "humorous" responses from the class, especially in the case of the student not being late coming to class or wasn't out, was present but didn't answer in a timely manner and now felt the need to defend her honor. On one such occasion Luz marked one of her friends absent. I brought it to her attention that the student was present. She called out to her in Spanish that elicited much laughter from the Hispanic students, including the one she marked absent. I insisted that she divulge to me what she had said. She wouldn't but kept laughing. Out of curiosity, I decided I would pry it out of the student she marked absent. She finally announced, laughing, and against the wishes of Luz, "Mister Brathwaite, she said she marked me absent 'cause she knows you like me better than her just 'cause my ass is bigger than hers."

There was no aberration about Luz' frequent use of saucy language; it was done all day in and around the schools. What's more, the crazy psychologists had given their stamp of approval to all forms of free expression, and the legal system thought there were to be no boundaries to freedom of speech.

Leeanne was a 17-year-old light skinned Black American. She was very quiet, cooperative and respectful, which led me to conclude that there was more beauty to her than what was so obvious. There was a strong fixation on her from the males, from the Black ones especially. Many of them often wanted to discuss her with me. It wasn't unusual that they would try to cover up their admiration for her with the "bitch think she's all dat" accusation. I did not entertain these discussions, although when they would come up with that suggestion of her having a light-skinned, long-hair, fine features superiority, I would respond that I did not see this side of her. As a person born in British colonial Barbados and lived the last several years in England, Canada and the United States, I had no doubt that I had a much better perception than most of attitudes based on race, color, caste and class. They couldn't be played out so subtly for me to not detect them.

One youngster took his fixation on Leeanne so far as to implore me to say some good things about him to her. I told him each time, in no uncertain manner, that I was an adult and their teacher, old enough to be their father; hence, I thought it inappropriate to get myself involved in such an issue. He and Leenne should sort that out between them. He finally told me that he didn't know how to approach her. I told him that only a woman who had no kind of class would be ill-mannered and obnoxious to a guy who approached her in a nice and calm manner and said something nice to her.

"Something nice like what?" he wanted to know.

"Tell her how very nicely she dresses. Tell her you like her hair style. Tell her she is beautiful."

He huffed and puffed and said to me, "Brathwaite, man, you gots to be crazy, ain't no way I would ever say nothin' like dat to that bitch. Then she be getting' a swell head and be thinkin' she be all dat."

"You know, Mister Medford," I said to him, "I think it's you who has the problem. Your problem is that you're one of these Black guys who thinks the best way to approach a woman is by standing on the corner whistling at her and making crude sexual remarks. And if she doesn't like being approached like that, then curse her out. But the same guys would kill other guys if they dared to do the same to their mothers and sisters."

I knew I had cornered him the way he said after a slight pause, "Word! Word-up, man!"

Leeanne did spring an out of character surprise on me one day. It came about as a result of that bad habit some students had of not answering when their names were called for the attendance. And of course, she was well abreast of this habit, knowing that they would wait until she was through with the attendance and started to do her class work, then to come to her complaining about "how comes y'all didn't call my name?" As teacher, I knew of the importance of getting the attendance right, even if it meant calling some names four or five times. It wasn't the same with a student taking care of the attendance.

So it was that on this day when a few students started the complaint about not having heard their names called that I asked Leeanne if she had called out their names two or three time to make sure they were not absent.

"Mista Brathwaite, I only got one period in this class and I got a lot of work to do in dat short time. I don't be callin' no names more than twice. You gotta stop all this nice guy thing about beggin' them to answer to their own names. Give 'em a break the first time, but if the muthafuckas insist on their childish game of acting cute, let 'em go down to the office and get their names entered.

I didn't say a word but stood over her as she sat at the desk correcting the attendance book. Suddenly she looked up and her eyes caught mine staring at her with a mixed look of exasperation and surprise. She placed her hands over her mouth, gasped and giggled somewhat embarrassingly, then said, "Oh, Mista Brathwaite, what did I say? Did I really say that? Sorry. When my mother comes to the school and ask how I be doin', please don't tell her about this."

Sometime later I would see Leeanne in the corridor heading for her class and there by her side was was Medford. Clearly, he was happy that I had seen him with her. The next time I saw him I was heading to my graphic arts class with Serena. He wanted to "have a few words" with me. Serena proceeded to the class when I stopped to hear what he had to say. Almost immediately he started to tell me how beautiful Leeanne was. I looked in the direction of Serena and told him, "That's a beautiful girl there too." He promptly told me, "Ah, she got a good thing goin' on, but she ain't all dat." I remembered that he had volunteered the same assessment of Melisa to me on one of the times she came to the last period art class to see me. Now, once he had made the assessment of Serena, he immediately got back to telling me about Leeanne's "nice light skin," and her "pretty long hair." It was also important for him to let me know that he had not done or said any of those nice things to her to make her think he thought she was "all that." He had his "real man's" image to protect. I had my mature adult image to protect also, so I wouldn't let him know that Melisa had shown me the letter and card he gave her with all those superlatively nice things he felt for and saw about her.

Neither Melisa nor Serena had hair growing down below their shoulders. They were both dark-brown And as stated previously, they were both quite attractive. And even though not wanting to seem like a teacher viewing his students lecherously, lasciviously, it would be hypocritical to pretend that my eyes somehow could not see that they were both physically well endowed. But I understood that Medford was a victim of a Caucasian cultural value system that attached a high level of importance to complexion and hair in ascertaining human beauty, judging according to how fair and how long the hair.

All the talk about "Black is beautiful" during the mid-1960's to the late 1970's obviously had not made the kind of impact to result in significant change, no more so with the psyche of people of African ancestry than with the racial attitude of Whites toward Black people.

I had overheard countless conversations among so many Black students based on "boy-girl" relationship, an obsessive preoccupation of American kids, in which I heard mentioned so often, "the pretty light-skinned girl," "he got light skin," "long, pretty hair," "real good hair," "real nice complexion" (meaning light). All said in a tone of adulation, of course. I also overheard these comments so often flying around among Black students to cause me to wonder who raised and told them about themselves: "You too black, nigga;" black ol' ugly nigga; " "monkey-ass nigga."

I was witness to a case that epitomized this so well back at HSGCA. A White female teacher had come to the classroom to see the teacher, a Black male, who was absent. A Black female student of the absent teacher loudly announced, with much indignation, "She be always up in his face. I wonder what she be seeing in him. Imagine, she's so beautiful, wit' such pretty long hair but like such a black, ugly nigga." The teacher seemed so very embarrassed. She smiled and quickly made her escape from the classroom.

I must say that regardless of the examples of Black-against-Black negativity given here, the males were the ones who engaged in it most. I must also add that while many of the males were seen in the company of the light and light-brown Hispanic girls, the same was not true of Black girls and Hispanic males. When Black girls spoke of the "light-skinned boy," they did so in reference to light-skinned Blacks. I theorized that the negative attitude against self was stronger among Black males because the White society, in the effort to demonize and dehumanize Blacks, targeted the male with extra vengeance; hence, the reason why they more often kicked themselves in their own ass.

As a Black man who considered himself quite enlightened and with a mind opened to differing ideas, and not willing to admit to being totally free of all elements of male chauvinism, it certainly gives me no pleasure in "downing" on Black males. However, I must confess that even in the area of responsibility, I thought I saw that in the case of comparable age between males and females, the latter generally gave a more mature accounting of themselves.

For instance, though I frowned on the deplorable trend of teenagers becoming parents, even viewed it as detrimental to family life and to society, especially as the trend picked up pace in a fashion statement-like manner, that the teen fathers exacerbated the problem by denying they were the fathers. Like at HSGCA, I met several girls at Jeff, in a much shorter period, who were also mothers. In fact, Melisa was one. That hurtful and disappointing complaint that the teen fathers were fine once it was all about having sex but absconded out of their lives once it turned into pregnancy. Taking this and other male teenagers' idiosyncrasies into consideration left me with little doubt that, generally speaking, teenage girls were emotionally at least four or five years ahead of teenage boys of comparable chronological age.

Another situation in which I observed a clear disparity in attitudes of Black male students and Black female students was the way they treated Black male teachers. It is imperative, though, that I first state for those who know but conveniently push it down into the cellars of their minds, this horrendous fact: The absentee rate of fathers in Black American households is phenomenally higher than it is in all other ethnic groups.

Quite often, Black female students perceiving of positive characteristics in a Black male teacher tended to gravitate toward him as if being so happy to have such a father figure around to be close to. With Black male students, on the other hand, there seemed to be this eagerness to let the same teacher know that "you ain't nobody." I wondered if I did hit on a plausible idea in thinking: since the mothers were the ones almost always present in households, could this have given the girls a greater feeling of security than the boys, whose fathers – the image of themselves – were the ones almost always absent from households?

Hopefully it will be noted that I don't make statements that implicate everybody. For instance, I have not stated that all Black male students were this way and all Black female students that way. For indeed, there were some male students in my graphic arts classes in particular who treated me in the manner of "I got your back, Mista Brathwaite." "Man, Brathwaite he's one cool teacher." "That Brathwaite is one proud Black brother." When students harbored such attitudes for the teacher it helped him to control his class more than he might ever realize; in fact, more so than if he was assigned a teacher's helper in many cases.

Having touched on the issue of my graphic arts classes, I should mention that I had in these classes students with mixed attitudes. There were a few, who though not having a don't-give-a-damn attitude, aspired to be rappers and at times wanted to ignore the class work to demonstrate their rapping skills. They had to be stopped. Fortunately, they never defied me to the point of the situation turning into a major problem.

A problem I consistently had to deal with was that male mindset of those who had taken a liking to operating the printing machines and insisting on not letting those girls who wanted to do the same to do so because it was something for males. They felt the girls should stay on the light tables and design their books, pads, postcards and other stationery and the boys would do the printing of all these projects. And some of the projects were being done with meticulous care. They also initiated making their own "business cards" with their fancy street names and crazy notes. The classroom eventually became quite a popular place because so many students in the school thought they were so important that they should have their stationery with their names printed on, a novelty to them then, not the simple thing as today because of the popularity of computers. But this was a time when computers were not so popular; there were very precious few to an entire school compared to a few years later, mostly in main offices and classes such as mine.

There was a group of about five Black and Hispanic girls who occupied two light tables in a corner. Initially, whenever I tried to do something, I was sure to hear from that corner, "Mista Brathwaite, get over here...Mista Brathwaite...Mista Brathwaite...Mista Brathwaite, come over here a minute." Sometimes I wouldn't respond. They would become "aggie," as they say about being agitated. They would demand to know, "What kinda teacher is you anyway dat won't help your students when they be callin' for help?" I would respond in a tone mixed with seriousness and humor: "Mister Brathwaite is a great teacher, but he would like to hear the word "please" once in a while at least. They would, even at their young age, go into a take-off of the 1960's James Brown soul hit "Please! please! please! baby, pleeeease...!" thinking they were ever so funny.

In time, after becoming more familiar with using the T-square and understanding measurement the way they never did before coming to the class, for instance, they would call on me less. In fact, I couldn't help but observe Mirriam, a white Hispanic girl, and Tanya, a Black girl from the U.S. Virgin Islands, how involved they always were with their projects, using the T-squares, rulers and pica gauges. One morning I went over to them and made a joke with them that elicited more laughter from them – and other students – than I aimed for or anticipated: "You know something about you two young ladies?" I said, "you really got the American way down pat."

"What's that?" they wanted to know.

"Even if you don't know what you're doing, you act so much like you really know that you convince me you do."

It must be said here that not knowing about measurements was a common shortcoming with students. They didn't know things like 12 inches made a foot, 3 feet – or 36 inches – made a yard. In fact, so many students were unfamiliar with the times tables. I had to tell them that these things, along with liquid measures and weights, I had to know by heart during my school days, long before I had even reached their age.

I recall going over a blackboard lesson on "how to read the inch" when Mrs Lorde made an impromptu visit to my classroom. I didn't think she had come to stay, but after a while she pulled up a chair and observed how I discussed the 16 component parts, one-sixteenth each, that made up an inch and how these sixteen basic fractions could be easily broken down. I told them that if they ever became employed in the graphic arts/printing field, it was imperative that they learned this. And even if they would never be so employed, by learning this they would discover that it would be of much help to them when doing fractions a bit more complex. Each component had the denominator 16 but their numerators started from one to 16. 1 over 16 read as one-sixteenth because it couldn't be reduced. With 2 over 16 both numerator and denominator could be divided evenly by 2 to be 1 over 8, read as one-eighth. 3 over 16 could not be reduced so it remained as is to be read as three-sixteenth. With 4 over 16 both numerator and denominator could be evenly divided by 4 to the lowest form of 1 over 4 to be read as a quarter. And the process continued to 8 over 16 which could be reduced to 1 over 2 and read as half. To the last 16 over 16, both could be divided evenly by 16 and would end up as 1 to be read as one inch. For the youngsters, it wasn't as simple, though, as I thought it to be or as it might seem here. I anticipated how much more difficult it would be when the time came for me to demonstrate the transformation of picas (the official graphic arts-printing method of measurement) into inches.

Mrs. Lorde was seeing such a lesson being taught for the very first time. She was very impressed and told me so.

One couldn't be adequately teaching this subject without also dealing with the issue of spelling. These youngsters, to use one of their sayings, "had it real bad." Another problem they had "real bad" was that of using words (homonyms) in the wrong context. There were many but I will give only a few examples of the constant misuse: its, it's; they, their, there; to, too, two; no, know; accept, except; your, you're; advice, advise; stationery, stationary; whose, who's; effect affect.

A question I frequently asked myself was, why is it that these students somehow consistently select the wrong word?

They also "had it real bad" in their use of language, of which I will again give only a few examples: More better; more prettier, more stronger; most beautifulest; most ugliest; most strongest of the two; I don't have none; don't have nothing.

Perhaps what was most disappointing was that after pointing out these errors over and over, explaining why they were wrong, telling what was correct, most of the students continued with their way as if they felt it didn't make sense to bother about something they didn't see "the big deal" that made it worth bothering so much about.

As the teacher – and a foreigner, and one brought up on a British-type education at that – I understood that I could be faced with my own problem of knowing that some of these errors made by the students were slowly becoming acceptable as far as American English was concerned. In the many years that elapsed since America had put such a dent in the behind of the British Empire to reach the point of actually setting up itself as the new Empire, it had also instituted so many changes as far as the English language is concerned, spelling and grammar. For instance, there are those "our" ending words of England that became "or" ending words in America. Then there are the same-sounding, different-meaning words of England that are spelled differently, a few examples being: tyre, tire; check, cheque; center, centre; irrespective of different meaning, they were eventually given the same spelling in America: one "check," one "center," one "tyre," as it is with the many other similar cases not mentioned here.

I would tell my students about such conflict in language, grammar and spelling and jokingly express how happy I was that they were in the United States and not the United Kingdom, for if they could have so many problems with, say, a single spelling for all same-sounding words, they would be certain to go crazy in schools in Britain. Maybe they should move to Canada, with its cultural connection to England and geographic connection to America; hence, the elimination of the conflict because of the general acceptance of both ways.

I stated earlier my intention to bring improvement to the graphic arts program at Jeff. Well, by now all the school's old stationery had been redesigned and reproduced. All the old stationery, to use the youngsters' vernacular, "was history." The professional-looking difference was Immediately observed. Written and oral commendations came from different sources. The same was true about little publications the egotistical mostly, in different departments of the school, had to have produced in the graphic arts classes. I use the term "egotistical" because I thought some not at all necessary outside of making some individuals look more important than they really were. Some even came with their private projects, some I might have refused to accommodate but for the importance of keeping the students busy. And beyond an iota of doubt, many of them were "stuck on" hands-on activities, a hell of a lot more than hearing about measurements, fractions and correct spelling.

I had to keep my eyes on their every move as far as production was concerned. Errors they considered to be "nothing to make a big deal over," I saw otherwise. I kept telling them that "Mister Brathwaite is a professional; he believes in doin' things to the very best of his ability and so should you all."

Whenever a product was finished, they assumed the responsibility of delivery and took the credit for it production.

I had no objections. They could convince their peers of this, but I had no doubt the principal and other rational adults knew differently.

By the ending of November the graphic arts classroom had become a very popular place. Even students who were not programmed there saw it as a place to congregate. As much precaution as was taken to keep out those not assigned, I must admit it wasn't successful. Some just found ways to weasel their way in, to do little projects, get a friend to do little projects for them, or just to observe what was going on. My administrative and free periods were hardly ever utilized as they were intended to be, for students were always knocking on the door. On those occasions when I wasn't willing to tolerate their presence, I would seclude myself in a corner and let my out-of-sight silence convey the falsehood that I was absent. It wasn't unusual that they wouldn't fall for this deception. They would keep up their obstinate knocking, calling out my name, and making loud false threats: "Mista Brathwaite, I know you be in there hidin'." "Yo, Brathwaite, man, open up the door or we gonna kick it down." "Please, man, it's only three of us. We just wanna do this procject. We ain't gonna bother you. Swear on my mother's grave." And there were many other deceptions. Sometimes I would hear that I was "in there locked up wit' dat girl," in reference to Melisa or Serena, who took turns in being around me so often that it made me a bit uncomfortable as I anticipated what obviously didn't bother either: the gossip. Each would even question me about my relationship with the other.

At the beginning of November I thought it time to get serious about the production of The Thomas Jefferson Star. I was a bit disappointed that I was expected to work with an English teacher, a Jewish woman, because she had previously worked with the other graphic arts teacher. Her role was to help in getting articles from the students. Mr. Hookes knew of my ability to do it on my own. He didn't want it this way, however, not wanting to offend the English teacher.

In any case, I let her know that unlike the teacher she previously worked with on this project, I had a writing-journalism background and as she would be selecting students she would work with in writing articles, so would I. She knew that I could produce the paper in it entirety without her while she couldn't do so without me.

My first problem with her working out of my classroom was her chain smoking. When we sat together to discuss articles or photos, the smoke from her cigarettes, mouth and nostrils was annoying. I always had a low tolerance for cigarette smoke. There were times when she would put her end of cigarette down and not remember where she had laid it down. Next, I learned that the students were ill at ease with her, seeing her as "a nervous wreck, too quick to go off" (shout too much), didn't like the way she "talked down" to them. That she wanted no mention (or photos) of some of her colleagues to appear in the paper lessened my desire to work with her.

In addition to preparing the newspaper to be handed out two or three days before the day we would leave for Christmas break, I was working with the students on preparing the four best Christmas card designs to be printed in large quantities so they could be handed out to many – if not all – students in the school. These were finished ahead of the newspaper. When the students witnessed the beautiful multi-colored cards coming off the press, after the confusion they saw in the pre-press stages that they couldn't perceive of as leading up to this stage, they were full of excitement. The excitement grew more after the folding and trimming for the finished product.

Bear in mind that I am writing about something happening in 1986. There would hardly be any excitement among students over the production of a multi-colored card today. Using computers now can make it so very simple. And students now have easy access to computers in school, at home and through other sources. This was far from the case in 1986. A multi-colored job had to be printed the graphic arts way: design and layout; the shooting and developing of a negative for each color; the correct stripping of the negatives for proper registration during the printing (press) stage; the developing of a (printing) plate for each color; the registered printing of each plate.

It is imperative that all this is mentioned so when I mention how well received, how highly spoken of these cards were around the school, it would be understood why. Surprisingly, though, the excitement soon took on a sour twist. The messages the card conveyed were in English and Spanish and some Jewish staff members made it known to the administration their feelings that it was discriminatory that such salutations as "Merry Christmas, Happy New Year," "Feliz Navidad y Anos Nuevo" and "Happy Kwanzaa" were used but nothing about "Chanukah, " meaning there was no acknowledgement of their presence in the school. I assured Mrs. Lorde and Mr. Hookes that no discrimination was intended, and I wouldn't say sorry in the issue of the school paper soon to follow, not even if it meant the paper not getting published. And I wanted so badly to have it published. I knew it was going to be very well received. I had already taken steps to elevate it from the skimpy 8-pager to a 16-pager, with nicely printed photos and color printing on the front, back and center pages. I must admit, too, even at the expense of seeming on a self-serving mission in this case, the publishing of the paper wouldn't be all about making the students happy. Copies of it would be sent to Principal D'Amato at HSGCA, let him feel the shame of his school, with so much state-of-the-art equipment, producing a skimpy-looking newspaper, while I, at such a great disadvantage in TJH one graphic arts classroom, could yet produce a paper so much better. So if Mrs. Lorde or Mr. Hookes wanted to make that apology, I would gladly insert it. And I doubted if they would refuse to do so.

Some teachers had taken more cards than the students got. But when I set out to produce the cards, I did so with the student population in mind, not staff members. And I saw in the student population almost all Black and Hispanic; among the few of other ethnic groups *not one* was Jewish. Judging by the trend, this was as likely as seeing a Martian walking down Pennsylvania Avenue.

I had no reason to believe that Mrs. Lorde or Mr. Hookes was trying to give me a hard time. Rather, as administrators they knew of the importance of appeasement, especially if the source wherein lurked the feeling of having been offended was thought to be strong enough to exact retributions – even when totally unnecessary.

I think one of the reasons why the paper was so skimpy was because of the policy of selecting student writers only from among the English classes and those students with the reputation of being "smart." But there were students who were neither in these classes nor had the reputation of being smart who had interesting ideas. I would search for them even if the stories, poems and jokes they wrote and stuffed into their bags and kept hidden in their exercise books, never to be seen by anyone but themselves and a few friends, needed some polishing up.

It was extra work with no financial reward. But it wasn't unusual for me to do this. If I was working on a project and lunchtime came when it could be finished in another 15 minutes, I would be crazy enough to lose 15 minutes off my lunch break. If at the end of the day I was faced with a similar situation and I had to stay at school for an extra hour to finish up, not wanting to have to continue working on the same thing next day, I would do so.

I used the term "crazy" because later I would learn that this time was considered per session and I could have been paid for it. Previously, I thought such extra time was only considered per session if the teacher was asked to do it, as in the case of my teaching adult evening classes at HSGCA. Mr. Hookes knew I was doing this but never told me I could fill out a form and at the end of the month add up all the bits and pieces of extra work and get paid for the total hours. He did it for himself.

Of course, I had my shortcomings, the foremost of which must have been dealing with those made-out-to-be-of-ultimate-importance things known as lesson plans, which supposedly would faultlessly guide a teacher through every period. Following these plans accomplished this as well as one jumping from the Empire State Building and flapping arms in an effort to fly safely and not crash down to the pavement. Lesson plans no doubt worked 40 years earlier. But with today's students it was wise to use them for what they really were: statements on pieces of paper to pretend to be following when an administrator turned up – cover your ass.

< 8 >

The holiday season came and passed and I was back at Jeff on January 3, 1987. I was in good spirits. So were my students, many of whom – girls overwhelmingly – had, before the holidays, given me Christmas cards, and those who had not then were doing so now.

I knew that my classes were still popular with the students. With the staffers it was the graphic arts class only. They always had things they wanted reproduced or done from scratch. As for the students, they immediately started off from where they had left off prior to the holiday break. Ever so often one would come to me wanting to have some business cards printed for a mother, a sister, an aunt who had or was opening a hair styling salon, offering cleaning and other business services; or a father, brother or an uncle offering their services as handymen, barbers, movers, DJ's and others. I allowed these things because it not only kept students practicing and learning but it helped people who were trying to help themselves. I had to be always vigilant because there were those who were bent on producing and reproducing things that were sex and drugs related. They knew I disapproved of this so they would get into collaborative efforts to outwit me. Of course, when they couldn't outwit me they resorted to pleading with and pestering me to "lemme do it and I promise you I won't let nobody see it." It wasn't at all easy to get them to give up. But there were certain cases for which my tough-love philosophy reigned supreme. When they insisted on trying to break down my will was such a case. I just wouldn't engage in that soft hearted refusal tone of "if I could I really would but I'm not allowed to do that." "The principal wouldn't like it." Doing it this way left too much room for continued pestering. The answer was an emphatic no, or you can't do that here. And I was nice enough to repeat this three or four times. If the pestering persisted, my absolute silence took over.

    TJH was, as earlier stated, located in a rough-looking neighborhood. With many of the students coming from the immediate and surrounding areas, it wasn't surprising that some of the students acted so tough. But credit must be given where it is due. It was obvious that there was a concentrated effort in the school to uphold some behavioral standards. Though the structural state of parts of the building begged the question, "Is this really New York City?" there was obviously a good degree of success in keeping the school clean. And that very disruptive factor of boombox radios being brought into the school by students – joined by the growing new fad of the miniature Talkman TV – was pretty near under control, unlike being out of control at HSGCA. Students caught bringing these things to school at Jeff had them confiscated. To have them returned guardians of the offending students had to visit the school and claim them.

The two situations here showed me a minor side to that accusation heard about "politics in the schools." TJH had that dubious label of "worst school in New York City" attached to it. HSGCA was not even slightly berated, but I honestly thought it was a worse school than TJH. I had seen happenings in the hallways and on the stairways of HSGCA that were definitely more disgusting and frightening than I had seen at TJH.

I noticed that at TJH, though within close proximity of most of the students it served, Black parents attended Open School Night, in the interest of their children, in the same low numbers as they did at HSGCA which wasn't within close proximity to most of its Black students. Hispanic parents, on the contrary, attended in higher numbers. Even in cases where some didn't speak English well or not at all, they came and brought an interpreter.

During the early part of February 1987 I heard two sets of news circulating that were not at all pleasing to me: budget cuts, teachers excess. I heard also that the teacher I had replaced no longer thought he was so ill to continue entertaining the thought of retirement. His friends at Jeff were looking out for his interest, believing the administration had a preference for me because of dissatisfaction both over how he did what he did and how he didn't do what he was expected to.

One morning in my overcrowded home-room class of noisy students, two of the girls came to me wanting to know, "Why're they gonna fire you, Mista Brathwaite?"

"Firing me?" I responded. "I didn't know that."

"Dat's what the man in the program room told us when we went there to register for your class," one of the girls said. "You know, the dirty-lookin' little man who be givin' out the class programs," she insisted on getting in her unflattering description.

Students describing teachers in unflattering ways, even

when they knew their names, wasn't unusual. I must say, though, that the girl's description quite accurately revealed the identity of the person of whom she spoke, a frail little White guy about 40. He was one of those teachers/staffers who came to school dressed in a manner quite similar to drunks seen hanging around on their selected spots of the pavement, not at all like what people would normally expect of teachers. And while there is no intention here to demean drunks or drug addicts, I had also seen a look on his face that stereotypically represented that of one "spaced out" on drugs. Overall, his physical appearance, particularly the unkempt beard and shoulder-length hair conjured up in my mind thoughts of the infamous mass murderer Charles Mansion.

As I walked to my classroom when the home-room period ended, I saw Leeanne on her way to class. I asked her to go to the program office and seek out this man and tell him of her desire to register for one of my graphic arts classes and let me know of his response. She was soon in my early period art class telling me in a low voice, "Mista Brathwaite, dat crazy man told me that no new students were being programmed to your classes 'cause you ain't gonna be here...that you're gettin' let go."

With a concerned look on her face, Leeanne asked, "Mista Brathwaite, you ain't getting' fired, are ya? You such a good teacher. Kids like you."

"I don't know," I told her. "I guess so."

"What you mean you don't know. If you be gettin' fired, you should know. They ain't got no right doing shit like dat to a good teacher like you."

I told Leeanne not to worry about it, that I would be alright, not wanting to let her go away thinking I was depressed.

That very morning Mrs. Lorde came to my classroom. She found me at the blackboard on which was drawn a pH scale that I was using to explain the mixing of chemicals the right way and not by guess. This meant that they had to know about the acid end of the scale, the alkaline end, the neutral position, extreme acid, weak acid, extreme alkaline, weak alkaline, and how to test for these things. My intent was to show them how guess work in mixing chemicals often got things going wrong from the start: problems in developing negatives, plates and fountain solutions.

I thought it was a very interesting lesson to be covering while the principal was visiting the classroom unannounced and sat there looking on. It was especially interesting in that the students were mostly listening, taking notes and asking relevant questions in a more studious manner than they generally did for lessons such as this.

I had asked Mrs. Lorde when she entered the room if she wanted to speak with me. She indicated that she did but I shouldn't put the teaching of the lesson on hold. When she was ready to leave, she told me how interesting the lesson was. Then she told me, "I'll speak with you later."

She didn't speak with me later that day as I anticipated; Mr. Hookes did, though. After lavishing me with praise for the "really great job" I had done, and expressing his surprise that "it didn't even take long for the students to get to like you," he reluctantly and diplomatically told me how Mrs. Lorde had asked him to inform me that because of circumstance beyond her control she had to excess me and that I should come to her office the next day so she could discuss the situation with me. He went on to tell me that it wasn't easy for him to break such news to me, considering that I had done so much in a few months. Then observing my calm demeanor, he commented, "After you worked so hard and did so well, I expected your reaction to be different, but it seems you're taking it better than I did."

"It's not a matter of taking it better," I told him. "It's more a case of me always trying to be practical. Will getting myself all uptight change anything? I don't think so. Plus you must understand that this isn't new news to me. I already knew that you all were getting rid of me."

My saying this shocked him. "You knew?" he asked surprisingly. "How was that?"

"Well, you see that Charles Mansion-looking freak in the

program room, who I think also plays the role of counselor, and is perhaps very much into that thing the Board of Education calls 'professionalism?' Once he heard from you all that I was about to be let go, he had to open up his big mouth to my students about it. So my students knew about me what I didn't know about myself. Ain't that a damn shame?"

"It is. The sonufabitch."

"Mister Brathwaite, I heard you gettin' fired," a male student loudly announced on entering the classroom later that day. "Is it true?"

The statement caused a stir among the others because the rumor (now fact) had not yet reached their ears. They insisted on knowing if it was true. When it became obvious that the issue would not be laid to rest, I decided to respond. "Well, I might as well tell you that I'm not going to be with you all much longer. The school doesn't have enough money – or something like that – to keep my classes running. Or the teacher before me is coming back for his job. I will miss you guys."

They responded with words of disappointment and anger, mostly aimed at "dat bitch Miss Lorde." It wasn't easy stopping them, but I eventually succeeded. Again, Leeanne surprised me. "We should stop dat bitch from firin' Mista Brathwaite just like dat. We should get the students to sign a petition." There was unanimous agreement. Next, she wanted to use the typewriter. She plugged it in and asked for some paper. Across the top she typed: To Mrs. Lorde, Principal of Thomas Jefferson High School, From the Students. Please Please Do Not Fire Mr. Brathwaite, He is A Real Good Teacher.

She got started by getting the students present to sign their names. Then she was ready to take the petition around the school for other signatures. A student reminded her that there were "thousands of students at Jeff" and she alone couldn't carry out the mission. Leeanne promptly went back to the typewriter to type the message against firing me on a few more sheets of paper. It wasn't long before they were ready to get started. I was still trying to dissuade them, mainly because I got the feeling that it would not be believed that this idea came from students but from me, standing in the background and rallying support to keep my job. Since they were intent on doing it, I reminded them that it was their idea and that I had nothing whatsoever to do with it.

I didn't get to see Mrs. Lorde the next day but two days later. She expressed the same sentiments as Mr. Hookes. She also expressed her regrets that students knew of my impending excess from the school at all. She seemed a bit embarrassed knowing that while she was in my class observing me as though everything was going as per the norm, I was already privy to the plans for – or against, I might say – me.

Mrs. Lorde picked up a folder from her desk containing some sheets of paper, looked them over briefly, then said, "For the few months you've been here, Mister Brathwaite, you have certainly had a positive impact on so many of the kids." She informed me that the sheets of paper in the folder contained the signatures of "so many of the kids" in support of my retention at the school. These were copies. I had already seen the originals and was very surprised at how swiftly so many signatures had been signed. I assured Mrs. Lorde that I truly appreciated the students' effort on my behalf, that it was totally their idea, with no input from me whatsoever.

Mrs. Lorde said she wished it was in her hands to reverse the decision against me but that it was not. What she could do, however, was to have me at the head of the day-to-day substitute teachers list and contact me first when a teacher was out, which was often. Day-to-day substitute pay wasn't bad for those who were comfortable with such an arrangement. And indeed, if I couldn't find a regular position, I would do it too. But at this stage I had already been receiving some differential pay; hence, my salary had improved over what it was when I started teaching. Secondly, day-to-day substituting wasn't like per diem ATR that would guarantee that I got paid as a regular – including summer vacation pay – as was the case at HSGCA.

Mrs. Lorde also promised that she would make sure I was rehired on a regular basis come the beginning of the new school year in September. But I was getting to know the Board of Education for what it really was. More – or *less*, I might say – than a human being, a teacher was a number or a unit, susceptible to being ignored and forgotten, especially if at the per diem status level. So the answer for me was in the popular category: cover your own ass.

I was especially inclined toward this because I had learned from the teacher who had appraised me of the problems I initially encountered in my early period art class that Mrs. Lorde's continued position as principal of TJH was quite tenuous. After the white system had destroyed the school, she was given the position to perform "the miracle" of getting it back on the right track in that "save-your-people" manner and she couldn't get it done. Knowing that she was operating from a weak foundation, that she was "too soft and nice," many of the White teachers who smiled in her face worked against her behind her back. I couldn't doubt it because I had heard a similar assessment – only with more subtlety – from Mr. Hookes during my early days at the school.

By the time I next went to my home-room class, the news of my fate at TJH had made its way all around. The students who were always so happily noisy sat so quietly I couldn't believe the change. Not one shouted out, as had become a regular thing, "here comes Mista Muscles" or "tough guy."

Obviously, they assumed that my being "fired" meant my inevitable slide into the ranks of the homeless. They couldn't take it. They showered me with comments of sympathy. They made sure they let me know that they had signed the petition to stop me from getting fired. They wanted me to know how much they were going to miss me if I did get fired.

After a few minutes of the melancholy mood, I felt obligated to give them a little lecture.

"I really thank you all for looking out for me. Even if I'm

Brooklyn Before Jailhouse Jeopardy   129

let go, I still thank you. I'm going to miss you all too. But I really don't want you all to worry about Brathwaite too much. He's a guy who was living a man's life ever since he was fourteen years old. He's a guy who doesn't know what it means to give up. The harder things get, the stronger he gets. Deep in his heart he's a true survivor."

My fate at TJH helped to strengthen my belief that the Board of Education had some extremely stupid policies, some of which were responsible for creating much of the problems plaguing the schools.

At any rate, my continued relationship with Thomas Jefferson High School was no longer to be. And so, this is what led to my ending up at a school in volatile Rikers Island Jail.

This student was a dedicated graffiti artist while free in East New York and he didn't give it up when he ended up in Rikers Island Jail.

< 9 >

Journey Through Jailhouse Jeopardy

For the new school year, starting September 1987, there were some staff changes at Island Academy, some who got their excess from Mrs. Gee, others who voluntarily did themselves the favor and moved on elsewhere. This sort of thing would become the norm.

I would eventually get to learn that many staffers felt they were as much inmates to Mrs. Gee as the incarcerated felt they were inmates to the Department of Correction. In fact, some inmates were so defiant that they sometimes acted in such a manner as if they thought they had a right to stand up to correction officers. The same couldn't be said in the case of teachers versus Mrs. Gee.

One of the teachers not returning was the art teacher in the little classroom adjoining mine. She was so bent on not returning that she had finalized plans to move to Ontario, Canada where her sister had taken up residence after marrying a Canadian citizen. She had told me at the ending of the previous semester that her sister, also a teacher, was able to get a teaching job in the city of Toronto and had sent her back information that teaching there was so much less stressful than teaching in New York City.

I concurred fully with her own assessment of the bad relationship she was having with her students: "They drive me up the damn wall," she told me. "If I don't get away from them soon, they'll drive me gawddamn crazy."

It was because of the thin partition wall supposedly separating our classes that I was always privy to the on-going commotion in her classroom and often heard that "crazy-ass lady" taunt hurled at her by some of her students, along with their supposedly harmless threat of "we should rape you in here." They also often attacked her habits of constantly smoking and drinking coffee. At times, she did reciprocate by hurling back at them her own threats and accusations, using language no less unsavory than that used to her.

A major change of staff came to the school as a result of the sudden decision to close down the Rikers Island annex facility located around the downtown Brooklyn area, known as the Brigg. There was a little school located within that facility. Since it came under Mrs. Gee's guidance, the staff there was transferred to Island Academy. There were those among the staff coming from the Brigg who also believed that Mrs. Gee was a mean woman. But among them she also had a few staunch supporters. Mrs. Sitro was the head among them. I wasn't so sure if she was already an assistant principal, but she did serve at the Brigg in a supervisory capacity and filled in for Mrs. Gee when she had to be at Island Academy or elsewhere. She was now serving in the same capacity at Island Academy.

Mrs. Sitro was a Black Hispanic whose preference would soon clearly manifest itself to me to be the same as that of so many Black Hispanics to be categorized as Hispanic, Spanish, Latino or dark-skinned rather than Black, and whose allegiance was to the first three categories with a devotion so strong as to totally exclude any ties to being Black. Following along these lines, Mrs. Sitro was able to get about four Hispanic staff members to follow her lead.

It couldn't be determined if Mrs. Sitro's support of Mrs. Gee was genuine or was primarily about her obvious aspiration to climb the ladder of success and, hence, saw Mrs. Gee as a pivotal source of success. Whatever the case, as far as the eyes could see, theirs was "a relationship made in heaven." This new alliance would in time lead to ugly staff factionalism and divisiveness, so much so to lead me to think of them as "the gang of six."

With the changed staff situation, the issue of seniority raised its head. An unwelcome change came in the form of teacher's helper in my classroom. I found myself now having Mr. Martin assigned to me for a single period. One Miss Darcel was assigned for one period and one Mr. Melendez for the rest of the day. As much as I showed my dissatisfaction with the major change, I had no say in the matter, which was unusual, considering that Mrs. Gee was still very much in my corner. How else could I see it when she was able to obtain for me a D.O.C. gate-one pass guaranteeing me the convenience of driving right into the little parking lot at the front of the school building? It was a privilege the D.O.C. was exercising mean-spirited control over the parking lot, denying parking rights to ordinary teachers. They preferred to see the space almost empty.

And it was indeed punishment. Having less than a gate-one pass meant that you could drive across the bridge but not allowed beyond the control building; hence, had to park in one of the two huge parking lots to the left or the right. There were other parking lots on Rikers Island, smaller, that you dared not park in. I must also state here that prior to working in Rikers Island Jail I had often read of how much money it took to keep a person in jail and never believed it could be so much. But now seeing how many vehicles were always parked in these lots – for day shift employees only, not those on night shift – I couldn't believe so many people worked in a jail, but I believed now that it was true the amount of money it was said was spent to keep one prisoner locked up. There were so many cars in those lots that many times it was difficult to get a parking space in the two that were so big. So you had to wait on an available spot, then wait on D.O.C. transportation to take you to the school.

The wait on D.O.C. transportation to get to the school was often annoyingly long. Consequently, there was a lot of lateness.

It was said that I had a special place in Mrs. Gee's heart. So when I did get that gate-one pass – "the gold card," as teachers called it – it came as no surprise to anyone. It was, instead, attributed to that supposedly special place in Mrs. Gee's heart for me. In time, though, I would think that I saw another side to the situation:

The publishing program conducted in my classroom was doing wonders for Mrs. Gee's reputation with her superiors and colleagues. And it was a fact, not an ego thing, that finding a teacher with my versatility, abilities and dedication to run the program wouldn't be the same simple task as, say, finding a social studies teacher who could "succeed" in teaching social studies without proving the same high level of competency that was absolutely necessary for running a program such as I was running. So was Mrs. Gee making every effort not to lose me and be faced with the strong possibility of hiring others no more competent than Mr. Crown turned out to be?.

I still couldn't stand in the way of Miss Darcel and Mr. Melendez. Mr. Martin was quite unhappy with the change. I gathered, though, that he was very disappointed that I couldn't influence Mrs. Gee to let him continue from where he had left off as my helper from the previous semester. It didn't help the situation that he had somehow convinced himself that that she would have bent over backward to please me. This being the case – his mindset – I had no doubt that he felt I wasn't trying as hard as I could have.

He tried to change the situation himself, not through Mrs. Gee but through consultations with Mr. Melendez and Miss Darcel. He could get neither to budge from exercising their seniority rights.

As it is in the schools, news of my two new paras was

soon being volunteered to me by personnel from the Brigg, none positive:

Miss Darcel was portrayed as one "meaning well, but with so many loose screws upstairs, teachers preferred not to have her help." The news about Mr. Melendez was no less unflattering. He was "one of those born-again Christian freaks that kids quickly figured was an easy target to walk all over."

Regardless of what was going through Mr. Martin's mind to the contrary, I would have much preferred it had he been allowed to continue as my main para, for as afore stated, he had proven to me that he could deal with the students in that effective manner many paras just couldn't. Like me, he knew how to interact with the students amiably but wasn't afraid to take a stand in the face of their unacceptable behavior. He obviously didn't think his role as a para was to always disengage me from what I was doing to solve every student problem that developed; he showed, instead, that he was quite capable of solving some of these problems on his own. He also willingly helped out, unlike some paras who thought their duty was to show up in the classroom and keep the teacher's company or "do their own thing," nothing.

I had not served in the U.S. military like Mr. Martin, but having served in the British Army from as a teenager – as was the case with him in the U.S. Army – I was able to identify and appreciate some of that military-like discipline he utilized in the classroom.

At any rate, since I couldn't budge the seniority system, and being endowed with the belief that "it ain't necessarily so" how others observe situations, hence, I should observe for myself, I elected to adopt this attitude toward my two new paras. In time, they would do nothing to cause me to dispute the characterization of them as given to me. They were both the exact opposite of Mr. Martin.

She could be as adolescent-like as the students. For every sickening story they told to elicit laughter and get attention, she, too, had one similar to tell. She was a physically well endowed woman about 28 to 30 years old.

Whenever students would discuss her physical endowment, she showed that she was obviously pleased. One very bad habit she had surfaced just about every time a student threw one of those attention-seeking tantrums. Invariably, she would soon be cradling the student's head in the palm of her hands until his face was eventually rubbing into the breasts area. This would be followed by her words of compassion. The students loved it, of course.

Undoubtedly, Mr. Melendez thought he heard God's calling to save adolescents in jail. That he was hired by the B.O.E. as a teacher's aid, obviously meant little to him. He assigned himself the mission of constantly trying to corner students and point out passages in the Bible to them. When he had no one cornered, he sat at the teacher's desk all during class time and read the Bible.

What Mr. Melendez excelled at was getting into heated confrontations with the same students he was trying to save, assuring them of their impending journey down to hell, constantly disrupting me from teaching to solve everything he perceived as unacceptable behavior, not ever taking the initiative to solve the most simple of these problems. Other than taking the attendance, he rendered no other help in the classroom no matter how I tried to get him to.

It became a habit of students to give Mr. Melendez a hard time. And so I also got saddled with having to solve his stream of complaints about what students were doing to him. I told him that I was fully aware that some students derived a great deal of happiness out of upsetting teachers and that it was only natural for teachers to sometimes defend themselves in that manner the system claims to be unprofessional. In spite of my awareness, though, I thought I saw how Mr. Melendez was helping to cause the students' bad attitudes toward him. True, he was a native of Panama and was nearing age 50, and in third world countries there wasn't that right given to children, as in the United States, to "do as you damn please;" not even in the 1980's, much less during his younger years. But he had been living in the United States long enough to be able to better negotiate himself around this deplorable situation. I, from a third world country also, and not many years younger than Mr. Melendez, often had to negotiate in this kind of situation – as did other teachers – in spite of the fact that my tolerance for it was perhaps no greater than his.

And so I told Mr. Melendez on a few occasions that it was necessary for him to not always let the words and actions of the students precipitate in him a confrontational mood. Many of these teenagers grew up having confrontations with, and disrespecting and disobeying their own parents several years before attaining the age of 13. Many of their parents didn't know how to deal with them, gave in to them less they solicited the sympathies of the law, psychologists and sociologist – who themselves couldn't control their own children – to side with them against the parents. It wasn't unusual that gung-ho cops who were so mean to members of the public, military personnel who would shoot and bomb nations almost into oblivion were not able to go home and control their own children. All of them, though, expected teachers, viewed by the youngsters as the most vulnerable, and perhaps the most disrespected across the board, to be able to educate and control these very youngsters.

It turned out that Mr. Melendez carried within him an entrenched belligerent characteristic which didn't belie that scowl almost always present on his face. He tended to stick to his ways. He wasn't going to render any help which he thought he shouldn't.

I understood and spoke a fair amount of Spanish but could get lost in the language when those of Spanish-speaking backgrounds spoke the language at their usual rapid speed and utilizing colloquial terms as they did also, so I asked Mr. Melendez to stop his deliberate act of speaking "Spanish only" whenever he was communicating with Spanish-speaking students. Spanish was his language and no one was going to stop him from speaking it under any circumstances; he felt he had a right to. He would exercise this right even when such students continued to communicate with him in English.

Clearly – beyond a doubt – Mr. Melendez was of Black African ancestry, but he resented being called black, an attitude I had not previously observed coming from Black Panamanians.

I was totally dissatisfied with Miss Darcel and Mr. Melendez as my paras. And as time went by the situation didn't improve as both continued with their ways. Miss Darcel added to hers by supposedly secretly observing my teaching methods and writing little negative reports to Mr. Brines complaining about the same.

On learning of her malicious actions, I insisted of Mr. Brines that I should be shown what she had written. He played the issue down primarily by assuring me that "nobody takes that girl seriously, Mister Brathwaite. I don't. Misses Gee doesn't. She took one look at that nonsense that girl wrote and that was that." He admitted that the "nonsense" was more than likely still in his desk drawer. I insisted on seeing the "nonsense."

True, I had already concurred with the "loose-screws-upstairs" description I often heard attributed to her. In fact, I had concluded otherwise: that where there were supposed to be those screws, rather than being there loose, they were actually missing.

However, I wasn't about to simply ignore what she had done. I took her to task in a harsh manner that entertained no room for subtlety. I also told her that in future she should make verbal not written complaints because there were so many misspelled words in her writing.

She obviously did not take kindly to some of the things I said to her and took her displeasure to Mrs. Gee.

Mrs. Gee was of the opinion that some of the things I said were "unprofessional" and too harsh. However, she wanted to know how I knew that Miss Darcel had written reports about me. I could have easily satisfied her curiosity there and then with simple truth: Miss Darcel had used that run-off-at-the-mouth habit of hers to divulge her surreptitious activities to her friend, and her friend, who was not yet my friend, informed me of what "that nut" told her. I kept it to myself.

It took some time, more than it should have, if the common sense approach was given priority over seniority, but eventually Mr. Martin was back as my helper for most of the day.

Island Academy being a school made up primarily of new teachers who were neither appointed nor tenured, as time went by I saw that teachers were being let go when they least expected, in an inhuman manner. It was conspicuously evident that most of them feared Mrs. Gee.

Principal or not, it baffled me as to why adults showed so much fear for another human being, how they tolerated her talking down to them. The excess experience was nothing new to me but I didn't see it as being so bad to drill the thought of kissing any administrator's ass into my head for the sake of not losing my position. I would follow rules and regulations, put tremendous effort into doing my job, even continue to extend myself to extra efforts when I thought it necessary, but I won't be subservient.

"Was around for a while, then was suddenly gone," is an appropriate way to describe the presence of Assistant Principals Mr. Roker, Mrs. Shore and Mr. Brines. Then there were Mrs. Elders and Mrs. Sitro. Then there was only Mrs. Sitro.

Eventually, into the scheme of administrative changes came Mrs. Lorde. Yes, the same Mrs. Lorde I left at Thomas Jefferson High School, still principal. So it was true what I was told about her situation there, that the B.O.E. was about to replace her. Though, the first morning I saw her at Island Academy this wasn't on my mind. I thought that, like so many others, she was on one of these curiosity visitors to this school in infamous Rikers Island Jail. When finally I learned that she was actually joining the school's administration until such time as the B.O.E. could find another position to stick her into, I knew how wise I was that February day in 1987 when she promised she would rehire me on a regular basis when the next school year started and I paid no attention to the promise but went out and sought another position.

Keeping with the trend of constant changes, it wasn't long before Mrs. Lorde, too, was gone from Island Academy. She remained in Rikers Island Jail, though, having been made principal of the school for adolescent female inmates.

Of course, there could be no such thing as co-education in Rikers Island Jail. Learning later that the girls' obsession with this American dream, sex – getting "my meat" permeated almost all their conversations – was no less than I already knew existed among their male counterparts, I was sure that even with the correction force tripled, co-education here would lead to a pregnancy revolution. And if the reputation circulated about C.O.'s, that many of them were morally and ethically only one step above the inmates, then the tripling of their force certainly would be of not much help. And what of their dangerous habit of sometimes turning their backs and allowing inmates to settle their own differences?

Co-education would perhaps help in cutting down on the chronic students' sleeping problem in the classroom. How much it would cut down on the sneaky habit of masturbation can't be fully determined, for even if there was enough sex to go around, it would still have to be taken into consideration that "this is jail," as inmates constantly say whenever the issue of what's fair and equal are concerned. The weaker males wouldn't be allowed to share equally in the goodies without paying the usual high price to the stronger.

Being locked down In jail didn't lock the Valentine's Day feeling out of the heart, according to the student artist.

< 10 >

At the beginning of another semester, the trend of changes saw more new staff coming to Island Academy to replace those who had been let go at the end of the last semester.

One of those let go was the school secretary Miss Perry, an African-American, perhaps in her late 20's. She had been with the school for only one semester. In that short time, however, teachers in general developed a liking for her, and not simply because she was attractive. She was one of the few in her position who readily addressed teachers' problems. One problem in particular was not being able to get supplies for their classes. It was obvious that solving this problem improved significantly once she came to the school. Once it was learned how abruptly Mrs. Gee let her go, most teachers became very annoyed.

It was customary to give out excess letters well ahead of the end of the semester. Apparently, Mrs. Gee waited until Miss Perry had gotten everything in order both to end the semester right and to get the new semester started smoothly when she returned.

It was generally accepted by staffers that they would be returning if that excess letter wasn't issued at least a week before the semester ended. In the case of Miss Perry, Mrs. Gee waited until the very last minute of the last day when Miss Perry was about to go on her vacation to stick an excess letter in her hand and wish her "luck elsewhere."

I would eventually learn from Miss Perry that it wasn't the act of Mrs. Gee letting her go that bothered her – for she was able to go back to her old school and get away from the inconveniences of working in the penal setting – but the way she did it, including the sarcasm in her tone. She was also certain that it had a lot to do with Mrs. Sitro and her Hispanic supporters ganging up on her.

I would eventually hear also from Mrs. Gee about Miss Perry's sudden excess. Her way of handling teachers' supplies, she said, threw the school's budget into a state of disarrays. There were, however, two other reasons already circulated around the school: Mrs. Gee thought Miss Perry thought she was too cute and didn't appreciate her flaunting her body by the sexy way she dressed around so many sex-starved adolescent males. Mrs. Sitro harbored a strong resentment for Miss Perry that was petty but quite mean-spirited. She had the support of her Hispanic clan – and Mrs. Gee's, of course.

It was always strange to me that Mrs. Gee backed Mrs. Sitro more so than she did African-American assistant principals. In fact, it was generally believed that she had no time for Mrs. Elders, an attitude that clearly hurt Mrs. Elders. True, Mrs. Sitro, a Puerto Rican, was also Black. But most Blacks felt strongly that she epitomized the kind of Black Hispanic known for expressing a desire not to be identified with the rest of the Black population. Justifiably so, I thought, because I thought I saw how she displayed a strong preference for Hispanic students over Black students, often using insulting remarks to the latter.

The letting go of another African-American teacher at the same time came not as a result of meanness, but it was an example of the stupidity many teachers knew could often emanate from the offices of administrators. This young woman, perhaps in her mid-20's, started at Island Academy about the same time as Miss Perry, which was also the time Mrs. Gee came up with her wise idea to always have a teacher walking the hallway to help the C.O.'s in quelling the disruptive activities of students who habitually roamed out there. It was also supposed to help in stopping C.O.'s from being too rough with the students.

The assignment period of this young woman and students' pandemonium went hand in hand. Their numbers in the hallway increased. They would also be bunched up at the doorways, all eye-raping this "so fly sister" and making non-stop sexual comments. She obviously wasn't one of those who reveled in this attention and at the end of the period would seek refuse in the teachers' room and complain of headaches. At this stage, giving her this assignment in the first place was nothing but stupidity. Even if it could have been said to be a bad mistake to give her such an assignment, especially knowing that she was new to this kind of environment, and the rough attitudes of many of the students, what better way could there have been to stop the circus-like pandemonium it caused than to simply withdraw her from the assignment? But this wasn't to be done. Every day it was the same thing. Undoubtedly, administration had concluded that she was a teacher and should be able to find a way to solve the problem. But she solving this problem wasn't the same simple task as the sex-starved students solving their problem of having a sexual fixation on her; they just went somewhere and played with their penises. Was she supposed to find a way to let them all have sex with her?

A new teacher joining the staff at this time was Miss Cicera, hired as a Spanish and an ESL teacher. She did not possess all those physical curves like Miss Perry, but this 30-year-old lady, on the slim side, possessed physical attributes many men regard as epitomizing beauty: facial beauty, for one; and jet-black hair that cascaded down her back to her behind. There was also this strong male fixation – t eachers, correction officers and students–on Miss Cicera.

As I, like other staffers would often go to the teachers' room during lunch period to prepare lunch, I noticed that rather than being involved in the conversations going on, Miss Cicera would be quietly having her lunch and reading the newspaper, or otherwise personally engaged. One day I went into the teachers' room and almost all there were looking through the latest issue of the Academy News. A teacher said, "Well, here comes the publisher and editor in chief." Miss Cicera was also there and looked up to see the person who was described in such lofty terms, the person responsible for producing the paper she was now reading. As soon as I walked out the room with my heated lunch, heading for my classroom as usual to eat in solitude – for I preferred not to be stuck in the midst of too much noise, Miss Cicera came out too. Our eyes met and I said the usual "hi."

She stopped me and told me how very impressed she was with the paper, that she had never seen a high school paper so nicely put together, that she found the articles and poetry by the student very interesting. I told her there were some back issues still available from my classroom and she was welcome to have any copies she wanted. She followed me to my classroom. I showed her the equipment from which the paper and other publications were produced. I told her of my wish that more staffers would be more helpful with the paper rather than checking out the finished product looking for any typographical errors, and severely criticizing choice of articles published. I was especially looking for at least one Hispanic staff member to help with the translating and correcting of some articles written in Spanish by students who had a problem reading and writing English.

When Miss Cicera left my classroom at the ending of the lunch period, I had no doubt that, unlike many staffers who made promises of help but never did, she was going to live up to her promise. But I couldn't know or even guess that there would develop between us a relationship so close to generate a lot of bad feelings in some circles – racially motivated, I was sure.

As time went by, Miss Cicera proved herself a dedicated helper, bent on learning all she could about producing a publication. Her help with the word processing/typesetting was especially appreciated. For one, she was much faster at it than me. For another, she was also much faster than the students who helped out in this area. Then, too, the student helpers, unable to pay attention to what they were doing because of their desire to hear, see and get involved with the activities being played out among their peers at the same time, made a lot of mistakes.

Admittedly, when I was through correcting articles some of my red pen corrections were not easy to decipher, sometimes not even by me. I was now being surprised that Miss Cicera was able to decipher so many of these corrections. I was no longer assuming that I had to withhold articles from her because I felt too many of my red-pen corrections were too jumbled to be understood by anyone but me.

Busy with publishing projects or not, Miss Cicera, who I now called by the first name Madeline, according to her wishes – though I habitually addressed all staffers as Mister or Miss and would continue to refer to Madeline as Miss in the presence of students and she reciprocated with me – became a fixture in my classroom.

We had lunch together. If she had a free period when I didn't, she came and spent that period in my classroom, sat at my desk and busied herself with things she had to do. If there was a time when neither of us had a class and I had to be in the darkroom developing negatives/photos, she would join me in there. When neither of us brought lunch to school, we drove out of the jail together to get lunch. At this time when the D.O.C. was still being mean-spirited about issuing passes to B.O.E. personnel to drive up to the school and not too many had passes, those males who had passes were always so eager to give Madeline a ride out, but she would wait on me to drive her out. If she was late for school and was stuck on the other side of the bridge, she got on the phone and called for me to come and get her.

Our togetherness so aroused the curiosity of the students that many of then, instead of addressing Madeline as Miss Cicera opted to address her as "Misses Brathwaite." And of course, they certainly didn't neglect to tell – in their manner to generate maximum shock effect, what they knew we were doing with each other in privacy.

Staffers didn't speak in this graphic sexual language but it was obvious that their curiosity was no less aroused. The attitude of some of them, particularly Hispanic and White males, shocked me more than that of the students.

Some of these guys who hardly ever entered my classroom were now doing so to engage Madeline in conversations. It was a common thing for them to pretend to be joking while questioning her about her relationship with me. I don't know how many times I heard their "jokes," "What he got that we don't?" "Mister Brathwaite must have some hidden power to have such a beautiful girl like you falling all over him." Even when Madeline did smile – not responding verbally – it would clearly be a smile saying, "I wish you would stop that bullshit." And indeed, after their reluctant departure, the way she would suck her teeth and roll her eyes in disgust justified my making this statement.

Madeline was an ordinary teacher, not an administrator/supervisor, yet often when she came to my classroom a Hispanic or White teacher would soon come rushing in to solicit her help for one reason or another. Hispanics, whenever they came in, would give me the exclusionary treatment by speaking to her in Spanish, quite rapidly. What was also very obvious was that they became pissed off with her for ignoring their wish to exclude me by responding to their conversations in English only.

Two of the Hispanic staffers primarily responsible for this behavior – one of whom it was well known had "the hots" for Madeline – were Mrs. Sitro's supporters; hence, were always in Mrs. Gee's office. In their efforts to recruit Madeline to be a part of their inner circle, I got to know a lot about the inside goings-on that I otherwise wouldn't have, for I had opted from the very beginning not accept that "opportunity" to be a part of the principal's inner circle. They told me little; they told Madeline a lot; whatever they told her she told me.

I knew that they told her how much better off she would be in the school if she would only join them. I learned, too, that Mrs. Sitro's attitude regarding her closeness with me was no more tolerant than those attitudes I perceived to be racist.

These two guys engaged themselves in some of the most ridiculous tactics to keep Madeline away from me. The most ridiculous one must have been that one afternoon after summer classes had ended. Anticipating that she would be leaving school with me as usual, they set themselves up like undercover sleuths in an effort to see that this didn't happen. One stood by her classroom door and when she came out told her of "the little get together" the inner circle had arranged for that afternoon and they wanted her to come. She politely refused, telling him she already had other plans. The other one had positioned himself by the door of the main office so in case she refused his friend he would have a chance to get to her before she reached my classroom door to enter. He, too, told her of the little get together and how much her company would be appreciated. Her response to him was the same. "What, we're not good enough for you?" he asked in an angry tone. Madeline did not respond, rather, she made her way to where I was waiting by my classroom door and asked me if I was ready.

For a while, as we drove along, no words were exchanged. I knew she was angry. I finally broke the silence. "Some men can be such jackasses," I said to her. "I wouldn't be caught dead making such an ass of myself, like those two clowns do. And it wouldn't matter what the woman looked like. If she showed me that she didn't appreciate my friendship, I would leave that woman alone and not disrespect myself."

"Those two are real assholes," she responded. "They keep bugging me all the damn time. And that Mrs. Sitro, she ain't all that innocent here herself. See, they full of that shit that because I'm Hispanic I should be in some kinda clique with them. But one day they'll see the real bad side of me... this woman who was born and raised in one of the roughest parts of New York City ... East Harlem ... raised by tough

Puerto Rican parents. They have some nerves trying to control me...a former army officer."

I told Madeline that I didn't want to see her ostracized from her "Hispanic people" and if she didn't want this, either, it wouldn't bother me if she didn't spend so much time "hanging out with me." She assured me that she was quite comfortable with my companionship and saw no reason to change it unless I was no longer comfortable with hers.

That day the depth of our conversation got deeper. I told Madeline that she had to understand that even though it was habitual of White Americans to categorize Italians and Greeks, for example, as White while excluding from this category Hispanics who looked the same, and even though she – bearing this resemblance – did not categorize herself as White, there were occasions when White Americans were not so unwilling to categorize Hispanics bearing her physical image as White. White Americans might be unwilling to see her as such, might even disparage her as "a spick," but when she got too close and friendly with a Black male they would have no problem seeing her as a White woman and should not be engaging in this act so very intolerable to their cultural upbringing. Certainly, she must have noticed how whites looked at us. Even when they were driving past and suddenly saw the sight, they would automatically forget about road safety to give that mixed stare of curiosity and resentment.

Madeline was also socio-politically conscious. Yet I had my doubts that she understood this issue as well as I did. And so I told her furthermore that while White society had a problem with interracial relationships between Whites and non-Whites, the most intolerable of these was Black and White, particularly that of Black male and White female. She being with me would not have caused so many stares had I been, say, Japanese, Chinese or light-skinned Arab. And this wasn't just being said by me; studies on the issue substantiated this. She had observed the things I had. What's more, she "didn't give a shit" about those people who had this problem. She suggested that I shouldn't let what

White people thought bother me. I told her it wasn't just a "white thing;" I wasn't singling out the White race, for among Japanese, Chinese, light-skinned Arabs and other non-European peoples could also be found widespread abhorrence for the act of Black males infiltrating their ranks. In fact, sometimes their abhorrence ran deeper than that of Whites. But that historically the dominance of Whites has impacted most internationally, makes them the most visible.

As time went by the closeness between Madeline and I remained intact. I must also admit that I was developing a healthy trust in her such as I had for very, very few in the school.

With all their higher education – degrees in various areas – colleagues yet exhibited a lot of unhealthy pettiness. There was a lot of hypocrisy, ignorance and other "weirdo" characteristics among them. Initially when I came to the Board of Education, I used to question myself as to how it was that this institution, representative of intelligence, attracted these types. Now, however, I was wondering if their working with the B.O.E. didn't play a significant part in molding some of the "weirdo" attitudes they displayed.

For one, it wasn't unusual for administrators to drive teachers crazy by demanding the impossible of them, making demands of them to handle situations that they themselves couldn't resolve as teachers, but after becoming administrators could see no reason why what was impossible for them then wasn't possible for teachers now. It was expected of principals that they produced success and when they failed to do so they escaped from their failures by making scapegoats of innocent teachers. So they, too, were believers in that philosophy of cover your own ass.

Indeed, it is not unusual, in spite of all that is known of the daily bad behavior of students, that many teachers become convinced about most of their stress and unhappiness coming from the principal. Sadly, though, they still end up engaging in the displaced psychology practice of making their colleagues the victims of their pent up feelings. So for the time I was teaching, I became convinced that it was better to keep that safe distance away from potential problems.

So why was I developing this trust in Madeline that other than Mr. Martin also, I didn't feel safe extending to others?

There were also Black female staffers at Island Academy, some I knew before I knew Madeline, others after. We got along to a certain degree, not that kind of close. A few now claimed that I had a preference for Madeline because she wasn't Black. I had done nothing to encourage Madeline to be around me, nor was I consciously doing anything to stop her from distancing herself. I resented that this was said. It was a damn lie.

They should have faced the truth. They were all like so many Black women you seem to meet wherever you turn: Christian zealots totally, always armed with their Bibles, thinking that they had to call on Jesus of Nazareth regarding every little thing regarding their existence, always trying to "save" you, unwilling to discuss anything but their religion, and treated everyone who wasn't a Christian zealot with suspicion, fear, contempt, resentment and avoidance.

It was clear to anyone that while I was quite versed on biblical teachings, I wasn't much of a religious person much less a religious zealot. Madeline wasn't a religious zealot and didn't use the bad attitudes against me that these women habitually did, considering me deserving of such because in their minds I was "an atheist." Incidentally, an atheist whose help they often solicited – and got – for a number of things. Madeline and I, on the other hand, discussed just about everything. And disagree, as we did at times, there was no constant condemnation. She was happy to have learned a lot from me: how to use the computer, how to put a publication together, and get my help in correcting her grammatical errors.

Then there came that day of the school's get together. Any staffers thought to have done good things for the school would be singled out during the luncheon and credited for these good things. They would also be given a little gift of appreciation and a letter stating their accomplishments to be placed in their files.

No one could believe it when it turned out that I was left out, such was their awareness of my contributions and their certainty that I would be acknowledged for the same. Nor would I lie and say that my expectations were any less. In fact, I was hurt, even though it wasn't characteristic of me to do things driven in any way by the thought of rewards. A genuine "thank you" usually was reward enough. In this case, a letter of appreciation for my file would have done it. But being totally excluded was stretching it just too far. And in an obvious attempt to add insult to injury, Mr. Martin and Madeline were given gifts and letters of appreciation. For Madeline in particular, the letter showered her with praise, part of which actually credited her with having come to the school and "straightened out the graphic arts class."

It wasn't long before both Mr. Martin and Madeline came to me and expressed their regrets about what had happened. They were both convinced, as I was, that they were being used to perpetuate a villainous act. Neither was sure that I would perceive it this way. I assured them that I did. Madeline especially displayed much anger, and expressed concern that the villainy wouldn't come between us. I told her over and over, quite honestly, that there was no need for her to worry. I understood why Mrs. Sitro and her Hispanic followers initiated such a situation – and with no objections from Mrs. Gee.

Lately Madeline had been making her belief known to me that while Mrs. Gee tried not to show it, she wasn't successful in hiding her contempt for the closeness between us. She wished I could see it also.

In any event, even though I tried to get her not to do so, Madeline yet discarded her pen-set gift into the garbage along with the letter of commendation. It was a little strange because there was no doubt about that initial liking Mrs. Gee had for her. It wasn't strange that Mr. Martin did the same, considering that he never did appreciate the way Mrs. Gee talked down to staffers. I guess, too, he never did forgive her for getting rid of him – as he saw it – from the graphic arts class.

This day was definitely the day that if there was some covert "bad blood" developing between Mrs. Gee and I, it made its overt move. I personally handed her ten dollars, told her I was sure I had not eaten or drunk that much worth at the luncheon, but I wanted to make sure that I had reimbursed whoever was concerned for what I had partaken of.

In time, there was no doubt that he who was one of Mrs. Sitro's followers and known to have the strongest sexual fixation on Madeline, was primarily responsible for using his connection to the principal's office to push the idea of that luncheon, and push it in such a way to impress the object of his fixation, backed by including a strong element of divisiveness. Mrs. Gee wasn't to be excused, either, not even if it could be said that she was unaware of the actual intent.

The villainous act just drew Madeline closer to me. She was more intent than I knew on proving to the gang that they couldn't tell her who she should be friendly with. And so one morning when the one with the strongest fixation on her came into my classroom and proceeded to speak with her in Spanish, it seemed the kind of conversation she was longing for, the kind that would set her off to put this man in his place. She turned red in the face as she interrupted drinking her coffee and jumped up to address him in English, using some street expletives not included here:

"Look, you don't know me. You don't know a gawddamn thing about me. So don't you come tellin' me who I can be with and who I shouldn't be with. Because you and I speak Spanish don't say shit about we gotta be friends."

He beat a hasty retreat out the door, embarrassed, no doubt, because by addressing him in English she had exposed the fact that he was taking her to task for being with me. She was so angry that she was about to follow him out the door to finish what she had on her mind. I didn't think it a good idea, especially because students were beginning to come through the double doors from downstairs. I stood with my back against the door.

Those who wondered why Madeline kept so close to me were not privy to some of her major characteristics as I was and therefore couldn't decode what was part of the reason for this mystery, as they saw it. While she wasn't an unsociable person, she wasn't that kind of sociable to want to be stuck in the middle of a number of people as, say, in the teachers' room, and the inevitable noise found in such a situation. Though not necessarily desirous of total solitude, she preferred a subdued setting. It didn't take me long, either, to know for certain that she wasn't one who would get into a situation such as formulating too close ties with the principal's office no matter what perks doing so had to offer. Although she possessed most of those physical attributes that generally make a woman Miss Popular with men, she didn't want to be such a woman. Obviously, as I saw in her major characteristics that pleased me, that were conducive with my way of thinking, she likewise observed the same in me.

The rumor – or the joke, whatever it was – that Mrs. Gee had this special liking for me still persisted. Mr. Martin and two other African-American staffers liked to have fun about what the principal was going to do to me because of Madeline.

After several semesters of commending me, Mrs. Gee suddenly started to criticize me. And I knew that I had not eased up on my standards. I still wanted to do things so no one could better them. Students had not eased up on accusing me of "always wanting things to be perfect," of setting myself up to "catch a heart attack."

I finally got my first "unsatisfactory" classroom performance report from Mrs. Gee, part of it reprimanding me for "allowing students to sleep rather than instructing." The sleepers in my class still remained relatively few in numbers.

The report was meant for my file; hence, required my signature. I signed it but exercised my right to do so under protest, primarily because Mrs. Gee made it seem that several students were sleeping, as was the norm in other classes.

I made it a point to have a little talk with the class in question, telling them that they were not to sleep in the class because they were "getting me into the principal's bad book" by engaging in this practice which they were told every day by D.O.C. and B.O.E. personnel was unacceptable. Of course, they voiced their objections, telling me what I should tell "the bitch." They also told me about the "muthafuckas" from the D.O.C. and the B.O.E. "not carin' 'bout us...just usin' us to make money...don't be knowin' what it's like in the dorms at nights not being able to close our eyes." And that "besides this ain't no real school; it's a jail."

More criticism came soon from Mrs. Gee. It had to do with two students, Shays and Charles. Neither was bad in the manner of exhibiting deliberate disrespect or orchestrating confrontation with the teacher. But I must admit that I often wished they wouldn't turn up for class.They did nothing as far as school work was concerned. Fortunately, they would occasionally do me the favor and sit apart from each other, put their heads down on their desk and fall off to sleep. Unfortunately, though, they more often than not preferred to continue the argument they brought with them to the classroom. They argued mostly about sex, guns, fast cars, drugs and rap music. These arguments were fighting-mood loud. Then there were those among their peers who had to join in. At times, too, a delinquent-acting correction officer would also join in the argument , making it even more difficult to put an end to because of his "I-am-the-law" ego and can't be reprimanded.

In any event, Mrs. Gee came into the classroom this day when my tolerance for the arguing had been stretched to the limit and I had called a C.O. to remove Shays and Charles from the classroom and they were now waging an argument about their rights to stay. I told Mrs. Gee exactly what the commotion was about. I also explained that arguments between these two led to too much class time being wasted. I wasn't a teacher who was too quick to ask for the removal of disruptive students from my classroom, not wanting to appear as if I couldn't control my classes. I felt the problem could be solved without stopping them from attending the class, but by not letting them have the same periods.

I not only thought this to be logical, but knowing that these two had this disruptive reputation throughout the school, Mrs. Gee was sure to see my reasoning. Instead, she chose to loudly ridicule my suggestion and my decision as "very unprofessional." She told of how she would have handled the situation had she been the teacher – the way she used to when she was a teacher. She also said that no behavioral problem from students should be bad enough to cause the teacher to put students out of the classroom.

Teachers were known to listen to this diatribe and ignore it. I could do the same. But there was one thing teachers customarily did also that I wouldn't: They allowed Mrs. Gee to raise her voice at them, ridicule them in the presence of their students.

I arranged a meeting with her and went to her office the next day for this purpose. I told her that I knew she was the principal and had the right to evaluate my performance but that I was an adult and resented being "talked down" to by her – or anyone else, for that matter. If my performance of the job she hired me to do wasn't up to par, then she should fire me. But I had never disrespected her and she wasn't to disrespect me either.

Within a few days of being castigated by Mrs. Gee for the way I handled the Shays-Charles disruption, she was attempting to demonstrate to a young teacher how to handle her first period class. Shays was in this class engaging in his early morning snooze. Mrs. Gee insisted on interrupting his snooze and it led to Shays "going off" on her, using his special brand of profanity. She promptly summoned a correction officer to have him immediately "thrown out" of the classroom. Incidentally, it was the same C.O. who had done the same favor for me. The news of her doing this made its way around the school, giving teachers something to talk and laugh about. I felt compelled to write her a little note and place it in her mail box: Mrs. Gee, the problem you encountered with my student Shays was brought to my attention. I was not at all surprised that he "went off" on you. I was surprised, however, to hear that you had him "thrown out" of his class.

Let me interject here briefly to note that I wasn't surprised about two years later to see Shays on the TV news under arrest for the murder of his wife – as the youngsters referred to their girlfriends – and the attempted murder of another young female.

It seemed a case of when a stone started rolling, especially from the top, stopping it – and the others stones below in its path from rolling also – was difficult, and that this was now the situation as far as my relationship with Mrs. Gee was concerned. She started to engage in petty complaints, using Mrs. Sitro, I believed, to help her. I noticed, too, that one of her ardent supporters, a veteran C.O. known as Rev because of his obsession with reading the Bible, and with whom I once had a good relationship, was getting increasingly less friendly with me. Other than his strong Christian zealotry, I thought I always saw this subservient Negro attitude in his actions. At this stage, he would often ridicule me as "one of them black militants who believe in dat Malcolm X," and "that atheist."

I had heard it said by teachers almost as soon as I came to the school that Mrs. Gee was in the habit of using him against teachers she no longer wanted around. For as long also, I had heard from his fellow C.O.'s that he wasn't to be trusted, that he habitually bad-mouthed them to their superiors.

Having now attained the status of tenured teacher, getting rid of me wouldn't be an easy thing for Mrs. Gee to do, though not impossible. It would take more than the senseless petty complaints that so easily got rid of per diem teachers.

She had run Island Academy as she pleased until recently when the teaching staff was still comprised mostly of per diems, but now less as a few more appointed and tenured teachers were included and didn't feel the need to be so fearful of her as the per diems were. But there were still a lot of complaints.

There was a time when the tension and unhappiness among teachers seemed more conspicuous than that between the incarcerated students. As a matter of fact, on a few occasions Mrs. Gee had to initiate the coming to the school of a professional to address this situation at staff meetings. There were other factors, of course, but I believed the situation developed primarily because of Mrs. Gee's inflexible leadership, which she perhaps wasn't aware was as rigid as it was.

I had even come up with a "serious" joke about this situation which I told only to Madeline and Mr. Martin: Mrs. Gee attitudes reminded me of the role Charles Laughton played as captain in the movie *Mutiny on the Bounty*. His crew was petrified of him. The horrifying mutiny that finally took place could have been avoided if only Captain Bligh knew that a true leader should be able to get the cooperation of subordinates by utilizing some methods other than instilling fear and showing little or no care.

I recall one winter day when a snowstorm started about two hours after school got started. As the time passed, the falling snow got progressively worse. All the news services were announcing that it would get a lot worse before it got better. It was also being announced over and over that schools in the city were closing early. The teachers were so sure that Mrs. Gee would follow the other schools' lead and let us go earlier than usual so we could manage to avoid the dangerous driving conditions. Certainly, we deserved this consideration much more so than perhaps all the other schools because of the bad transportation problems most teachers faced getting in and out of the penal surroundings, as aforementioned. Mrs. Gee held us back until the last minute. Teachers were shocked and angry.

It must be said for Mrs. Gee that whenever she did something mean to her staff she seemed to get a brief remorseful feeling from somewhere and would turn up next day with a few boxes of doughnuts and other pastries for them to eat away the memories of their bad feelings. This time was no exception. Personally, I always resented these insulting doughnuts-pastries buy off and, unlike many of my colleagues, never fed into insulting myself.

Mrs. Sitro was widely regarded as a woman who was quite loud. Teachers resented this about her. It must be said, though, that on those days when Mrs. Gee was away from school, for whatever reasons principals are often out, and Mrs. Sitro was filling in for her, teachers were a lot happier.

No efforts were being made to mend the damaged relationship that had developed between Mrs. Gee and I. Whether true or false, I had recently heard that she had a few unflattering things to say about me at the district superintendent's office. Though I wasn't sure if it was true, I wasn't willing to doubt it. I wasn't willing to doubt, either, that seeing me out of the school occupied her thoughts, especially now that my being on the union committee made it seem to her that I was a friend of the union representative, Miss Graemes. It was common knowledge that there existed between these two a relationship that could be likened to that of mixing gasoline and fire.

Miss Graemes, a social worker, knew there were goings-on in the school that principals were obligated to address with the union rep and felt that Mrs. Gee, thus far never having had a union rep with the guts to exercise any union rep's rights with her, felt this was the way it should continue. But Miss Graemes was bent on implementing the change.

Mrs. Gee saw in Miss Graemes a woman, who other than the union rep, exhibited some abrasive mannerisms. Beyond a doubt, theirs was a fight of wills. Each felt the other had an agenda to "get" her. And indeed, it was difficult to doubt the validity of their suspicions.

At this stage, Mrs. Gee had no justification for assuming

that I could join Miss Graemes in "getting" her. First, if I had the desire to do so, I had no power base from which to do it. Other than a teacher, I was just a union committee member. I had elected to be on the committee because of my conviction that the union, as it existed in the school, wasn't doing what it could (and should) for UFT members from whose checks union dues were regularly deducted. Island Academy, located in Rikers Island Jail, seemed somewhat "lost behind God's back," so to speak, and not truly a part of the United Federation of Teachers. In the scheme of things, its staffers felt weak and helpless. I knew Miss Graemes saw in me one with the strength that would strengthen her position. I made it clear to her, though, that in spite of the fact that I was becoming increasingly "pissed off" with Mrs. Gee, I "wasn't trying to get her." I had also told Mrs. Gee at the time she started to display her bad attitudes against me that it wasn't my intention to get into a bad-blood situation with her. And I must admit that during my earlier days at Island Academy, hearing that some of the "mean" accusations aimed at her were racially motivated, and taking into consideration that I had seen racial attitudes often played out in New York City, I didn't ignore the possibility that some racist feelings partly precipitated the negative charges. Hence, she had some sympathy coming from me.

At this stage, though, I was of the opinion that Miss Graemes, also an African-American, had made a stronger case about Mrs. Gee's intention to "get" her. She had proven that that fellow Rev was involving himself in activities that left little doubt that he was in Mrs. Gee's corner. And of course, I had not that long caught him engaging in activities that not only convinced me that his attitudes had changed from what I thought were good to what I now saw as almost nasty toward me, at the same time of Mrs. Gee going through a similar transformation.

The fact of this made itself manifest through a confrontation with a Hispanic student one afternoon. I was into the third day of covering this sixth period class because the teacher was absent. From the very first day the student demonstrated his intent to prove to his peers that this was his class and he was in charge, not this covering teacher. Not at all surprising, his disruptive behavior was getting him a lot of laughter and attention. From experience, I didn't anticipate that he would give up being the center of attention.

On this day I adopted a more no-nonsense tone in warning the student to cease and desist his on-going act of rushing up to the blackboard and erasing whatever I wrote on it. This went along with his favorite, "Ain't nobody wanna read dat bullshit. The situation got worse and I asked the student to step outside the classroom so I could have a brief discussion with him. Surprisingly, he complied. It wasn't for long, for he soon rushed back inside angrily complaining to his fellow students, "that nigga, he slapped me. He ain't got no right doin no shit like dat. If I wasn't locked down in this jail I woulda fucked him up." He rushed back outside cursing and threatening. The period was nearing its end so he didn't return. I was unaware that he had gone on a mission to make a complaint against me.

I would learn much later that the first person of authority he met was Rev. And he being what he was, and knowing that Mrs. Gee was looking for something to "hang" me with, made sure the issue was taken to her.

By the end of that day when the accusation was made, Mrs. Gee had me in her office and was ready to confront me with the accusation that I had physically assaulted a student. I was presented with a neatly typed page dictated by Mrs. Gee, requesting that I read and sign it so it could be placed in my file. It concluded with a warning to me, "It is against the law for teachers in the public school system to hit students. You are not to strike students for any reason whatever."

I objected to the letter being placed in my file as I disagreed with its assertion. I was told it was a warning.

I most definitely didn't believe this was meant to be the end of the issue. But suppose it was indeed the end of the issue as far as Mrs. Gee was concerned, then what if sometime in the future my file had to be checked to make a determination about my character? The statement "You are not to strike students for any reason whatever" would be there giving the message, though not said in the statement, that I was found guilty of having committed such an assault. How else would anyone interpret it?

Well, Mrs. Gee maintained her inflexible stand; she still insisted it was just a warning.

That being the case, I wanted to know from her if she had such a warning in the file of every teacher? No, she did not, I was told. So I concluded that it was unfair to put the warning in my file unless it was proven that I was indeed guilty of having committed the act, as the letter strongly insinuated that I had. I wished I didn't have to resort to doing so, but I felt I had no choice but to file my first grievance.

As to the very critical observation of my classroom performance, I used the opportunity to remind Mrs. Gee that I regarded it as a personal vendetta. I also told her that since she had written all negative things about my performance that period, it was obviously meant to be an unsatisfactory rating but that she had neglected to do the usual and state in her report what the rating was. She said she would look it over and if, as I said, there was no rating applied, the error would be corrected.

I received the report the next day. The rating was unsatisfactory. It was applied below where I had previously applied my signature. I might have ignored it, but Mrs. Gee had seized the opportunity to add more negative comments, which I felt sure was an act meant to be mean spirited. Then she placed it in my mail with a sarcastic note saying: "You asked for your rating. Here it is."

This little statement caused me to see red. Yet up to this point I had not yet developed that desire to be on bad terms with Mrs. Gee. True, I had already concluded that she had a mean streak in Her. I felt that she did do some mean things to some people. I was beginning to believe, too, that some of the meanness could be traced to that career woman thing of reaching the top where ultimate happiness was supposed to be but in reality wasn't found. Whatever the case, it wasn't easy for me finding myself getting closer and closer to being openly at odds with this woman, who in the past wasn't bad to me. I must say, too, that I didn't want to find myself in a situation where I would be likened to those Black folk who it is thought and said of couldn't work under the supervision of others of their own race.

And so, faced with these and similar issues, I went to Mrs. Gee's office to make my dissatisfaction known, even masking my anger.

I told Mrs. Gee again that I really didn't want for it to be perceived that I was pulling against her but that it seemed this was inevitable if she insisted on putting in my file statements I was convinced were written out of spite, for whatever reasons.

We discussed the issue for some time. I even reminded her of having taken her side against another teacher, a friend and fellow Barbadian, when she castigated him for sexually suggestive remarks he had made to a female Jewish teacher, telling him to his face that it was a rather stupid thing he had done.

I thought she understood that I was really trying to avoid any kind of tug of war against her. However, she gave me that final trademark under-eyes stare of hers, I-am-the-boss-here and declared: "You know, Mister Brathwaite, I see no point in continuing this conversation. I have made my decision."

The look and the attitude with which these words were delivered made me so angry. "Well, Misses Gee, I am really sorry that it had to come down to this, but you have convinced me that you are looking to have a war with me. That's the way you want it; that's the way it will be. And may the right person win."

By now grievances filed against Mrs. Gee could no longer be said of to be a thing unheard of or done "once in a blue moon" as was the case in the past when there existed such fear of doing so. I filed my grievances against her.

With the step one level of grievances decided within the school, it wasn't surprising that she won those. It wasn't surprising, either, that she won at the step two level held at the district superintendent's office, well known for siding with principals in such cases. Once losing at this level teachers generally gave up, not willing to go to the step three level, which would go all the way to the chancellor's office and be subject to much serious scrutiny. Failing at the step two level, I took my grievances to the step three level.

As this process lingered on, as usual, my relationship with Mrs. Gee certainly wasn't changing in any way to be thought of as improving. As a matter of fact, another bad situation developed between us one morning when she came to my classroom displaying the kind of behavior normally associated with a spur-of-the-moment observation. But very soon she was accusing me of having "the wrong students" in my class.

All teachers were constantly told not to allow students into their classrooms who were not officially programmed there. Of course, it never worked. All teachers did allow some of their favorite (good) students to "hang out" in their classrooms at times. I can't honestly say I was an exception. Obviously, she was hoping it would be this way on this morning. It wasn't. Every student there officially belonged there. Yet Mrs. Gee kept up her accusation that I had students there who didn't belong there. I got my register and called out the names listed therein for that period. It proved that each student there was represented by a name listed and called. Mrs. Gee still insisted that some of the students there did not belong there. Again, I told her that as far as I was concerned they were all officially programmed there. They were given their programs in the Orientation room, where all students got their programs. In her bossy manner, she demanded to see the program of each student. As usual, very few had a clue where theirs were to be found. By now, their disrespectful mood started to take over and they started directing profanity at her for, as they saw it, "comin' in here and dissin' us 'n' shit first thing in the morning."

Mrs. Gee, rushed out the door, upset, heading for the

Orientation room.

She was soon back, causing the profanity from the students to get stared all over again, something I knew I was better at putting an end to than other teachers, but wouldn't attempt to do so now; let them curse at her. Let her suffer the embarrassment of being "Miss Tough-Ass" principal who had little control over her students, students who could be her grandchildren.

The class list from Orientation proved that every student present was assigned there. However, Mrs. Gee still had some criticism to throw around. As the teacher, she said, it was my responsibility to make sure students were always in possession of their program cards. When she was a teacher, she boasted, she had control of her classes. I wasn't at all prepared to let her escape her embarrassment by making a damn fool of me.

"Misses Gee," I said, "my students are not little kids. They are teenagers. Some have more kids than I do. They should be responsible for their program cards. They make sure they have their D.O.C. ID cards because without them they are subject to many penalties and disadvantages, like not being allowed to go to commissary and having two dollars taken out of their commissary money to pay for a new ID. My responsibility is to make sure they have a program card when they first come to my class. In this way I can compare program cards with ID's, considering that so many of them think it's so slick to get away with lying about their identity, then I know that I am registering the right students. As for your claim of having such control of your students during your years as a teacher, I wonder what went wrong. After all, you're now a principal with much more power. I can only assume that you are either overstating your performance, or that you can't be bothered to take into consideration that today's youngsters have been given so much rights to do as they please that they can't be controlled by even their own parents."

Obviously intent on leaving on a victorious note, Mrs. Gee decided she had to get the last knock in on me. "Mister

Brathwaite, there certainly should be no reason why you shouldn't know that a few of these Hispanic students in here speak very little English and should not be here but in an ESL class. Unless you are proficient in Spanish, how can you expect to instruct them properly? Who are the ones who don't speak English well?"

I pointed them out: two Mexicans, a Colombian, a Puerto Rican and a Peruvian. One Mexican spoke no English, the others a little and a little more, though, as was usual in this kind of situation, they somehow frequently used all the popular American curse words – and in proper perspective.

In any case, I told Mrs. Gee that I saw no need to complain about having such students in my graphic arts class. Why now? This has been going on a regular basis from the time I first came to Island Academy. I had always accommodated the situation by resorting to what Spanish I knew and regular translation from Spanish-speaking students who were also proficient in speaking English.

Why could she not have left the issue there and gone on her business instead of allowing me time to figure out that she was sent on a mission by Mrs. Sitro and her Hispanic supporters? And to make matters worse, she took a red marker and proceeded to carelessly cross out name from my register book while addressing me in that "talk-down-to" manner of hers. Then she was through and dropped the register book back on the table, saying, "There's your register, you need to make the changes I've made for you." I looked at those red marks and I suddenly became a bull, raging, when taunted by the matador waving that red cape in its face.

I picked up the register, along with a ream of paper it was sitting on and vehemently threw them across the room. They hit the wall so hard that the ream of paper opened up. "There goes your register, Mrs. Gee. You can have it. I don't want it anymore. And what's more, if you're no longer satisfied with the way I do this job, you can have that back too. I am an adult man. You'll never catch me disrespecting people because I don't like to be disrespected by anyone."

Other than a brief scamper by the students to find my glasses which flew off my face onto the floor somewhere, such silence took over the classroom to warrant the mentioning of that saying, "you could hear a pin fall." I almost immediately sought to bring normalcy back to the class by asking for undivided attention. Just then Madeline walked in to borrow some pencils from me. I asked her if she had a minute to translate what I had to say into Spanish. Even Mrs. Gee halted her intended exit from the room.

I told the students that what they had just witnessed was a display of anger taking control. Quite often things would happen to make them angry. But it would be best if they would stop and think for a little while before acting. This would help them to control their temper.

I wasn't at all surprised that they were vociferous in their unanimous defense of what I had done. The principal, they said, was "always dissin' the teachers" and it was time that she was "dissed right back". Logical or not, I told them that I stood by what I said, they were to think for a little when they got angry before they acted.

Of course, I later explained to Madeline what had happened. She had also heard about what precipitated it from some of the very students who also had a class with her. It wasn't until about two or three day later that she brought up the issue and took the students' side. Mrs. Gee was "a mean, disrespectful bitch," she said. And from what the students told her about the incident, she didn't deserve any kind of apology. I reminded her that I had not apologized to Mrs. Gee. What I did was to acknowledge to my students that I felt badly for having done something I so often was critical of them for doing: lost my cool.

Later on the very day I had lost my equilibrium, Mr. Martin couldn't contain his laughter. Why would he laugh at such a serious matter, I wondered. When he did explain, I found that I couldn't contain my laughter, either. In fact, for a long time after, when this part of the incident would come up, as it often did, the laughter was still there. It was because on that morning when my glasses went flying off my face to be temporarily lost behind a locker, I gave what seemed to be a military order to the students, "You guys, find my glasses," and seemingly the tension between teacher and principal was so high that they exhibited none of the usual slowness to cooperate when asked to do such a task, rather, they all immediately dropped down to the floor and started a desperate search. Among the first to do so were the Mexican students whose understanding of English was so limited they couldn't, under normal circumstances, possibly have understood what I had asked to be done. Actually, it was one of them who found the glasses and ran to me with them, frantically saying, "Profesor! professor! aqui! aqui! aqui."

.Even Madeline, who wasn't there when this happened, would tell me, laughing, how she broke down with laughter when Mr. Martin first told her of the role of the Mexican students.

Another incident soon followed. It happened at the Friday Staff Development meeting. The topic being dealt with once again was the conspicuous unhappiness displayed by staff members and what could be done to change this. Mrs. Gee was present. It therefore came as no surprise that in spite of all the complaining heard from staff members about the unprofessional treatment they were often subjected to, very few of them – least of all, those who complained most – were willing to voice a complaint now, undoubtedly waiting for a safer time and place to do so. Then Mrs. Gee could walk away from the meeting convincing herself that every-

According to the student caricaturist and comic, his drawing, right (significantly reduced), represents "Mr. Brathwaite's helper, Martin, always jumping to act beeeesey when he sees the principal coming."

thing was going smoothly in the school.

I had a new issue of the Academy News almost ready for distribution. It carried a long editorial, which among other criticisms of bad policies of the administration, addressed the issue at hand this day. I didn't want to address any of these criticisms now, thereby lessening the impact when they appeared in printed form. But then I thought, suppose someone should now focus on one or two of these issues, when they appeared in print it would seem that my written ideas had come from elsewhere.

And so I suggested there and then that I believed a major problem in the school was that there was "an ever-present shadow of intimidation that teachers feared and resented, felt helpless against, and their feelings therefore trickled down to their colleagues." I also focused on the phenomenal rate at which staffers came to and departed from the school, a relatively small school, meaning there wasn't much time to settle down and accomplish meaningful things. Finally, I asked for an explanation as to why the school was designated an "alternative" high school – understandable because it was so different – but teachers were forced to utilize traditional teaching methods which didn't work, and for which, after being judged according to traditional school standards, were severely criticized.

Getting answers to these issues proved to be an exercise in futility. It was obvious that it was thought the best way to deal with them was to ignore them. Posing these issues wasn't supposed to upset anyone. However, it did upset Mrs. Gee, even though she feigned otherwise.

The new issue of the Academy News soon followed. As anticipated, it fueled the consternation. Mrs. Gee summoned me to her office and instructed me that this issue was to be the last one published under my autonomous editorship. In future, it was to be seen and authorized by her or Mrs. Sitro before it was distributed. She obviously though that "shadow of intimidation" remark was aimed at her – as did staffers – though I had taken every precaution to make sure that nothing was said in such a manner to directly implicate her.

One White veteran teacher, known to be a favorite of Mrs. Gee – both having been teachers together from some years back – because of the special privileges accorded her, approached me in her defense. "You should not have made those accusations about the principal," she admonished me. "Mrs. Gee ain't that kind of person." Then she gave me a short article stating the same, along with others statements written in defense of Mrs. Gee, which she said was a rebuttal to be published in the next issue of the Academy News – if I was an editorial advisor objective enough to publish something that disagreed with me.

As I had frequently done, I made it clear that I didn't believe in stifling opposing views, especially because I strongly believed they brought some special interest to any publication. But I did inform her that nowhere in my editorial was there a single mention of Mrs. Gee's name, position or school. How then was she so sure that the editorial was about Mrs. Gee that she would come up with the defense, "she ain't like that?" Realizing that her defense had come very, very close to saying that she clearly saw an association between those unflattering statements the editorial attributed to "those principals...," "principals who...," the defending teacher suddenly decided she didn't want her article published; wanted it back.

She wasn't the only one who came to the defense of Mrs. Gee as though the editorial was directly aimed at her. There were about three or four others. But there was a difference: they didn't stick their feet in their mouths with the written word.

I must confess that even Madeline, as she was typesetting the editorial on the computer, was sure Mrs. Gee would see it as something aimed at her, the fact that she wasn't directly mentioned not withstanding.

We had debated whether or not the editorial should be published. She wasn't as forthright as usual. She didn't want it to appear that she was somehow taking a stand to exacerbate the Mrs. Gee-Brathwaite problems. Nor did she want me to think that she was telling me to be afraid to say what I felt should be said. She wouldn't be critical of me if I decided to publish the editorial. In fact, if I wanted her to add her name to it to create that joint responsibility appearance, she would. It wasn't necessary, I assured her. It was my idea and I would assume the responsibility for it.

Other than the few who defended Mrs. Gee, all others, believing, too, that it was aimed at her, were elated about the editorial. I must admit here, though, as I did to Madeline and Mr. Martin, if I could have seen how publishing this editorial would cause so many staffers to constantly thank me, I would not have published it. I felt quite badly that it was perceived that I had taken a knock at Mrs. Gee for them. Not so at all. I thought she had allowed a few opportunistic flunkies to set her up against me. I resented that about her perhaps more than anything else

I didn't even know some of my colleagues that well. We hardly communicated much beyond the casual "hi," "morning," "thank you," and "you're welcome" when they would thank me for all the little favors they customarily had done in my graphic arts classes. Sometimes I wasn't so sure they didn't deserve the talking down to they got from Mrs. Gee. They were adults and shouldn't have been so cowardly. When they came to shake my hand for what they perceived as my taking a stand against Mrs. Gee for them, I assured them this was unnecessary because while my stand might have improved their lot in the school, I didn't take the stand for them at all.

Why should I waste time standing up for a wimp like Mr. Jewison, middle aged, White, apparently always ready to tremble whenever Mrs. Gee approached him. He never uttered a word in defense of himself in her presence, but had a litany of complaints against her in her absence. And Mr. Perkins, whenever she confronted him the way a drill sergeant would a new recruit, he would resort to thanking her for the last boxes of doughnuts she brought in for the staff. Then the moment she was gone, his tongue would automatically go into motion belittling her with the words "that's a real crazy woman." And there was Mr. Starks, the merriment in his laughter increased dramatically whenever he saw Mrs. Gee. His constant agreement with her obviously embarrassed even her, the way she would give him that under-eyed look. She undoubtedly saw in him, as I did, the super-Negro hypocrite he was. If he was with Jesus Christ he would tell him how he found out that Satan was even more wicked and evil than he was said to be. And if as he walked around the corner he met Satan, he would tell him that he really wasn't such a bad guy, and how he found out that Jesus Christ wasn't so righteous after all. And there were those two African-American ladies, both middle-aged, one who loved herself immensely, the other who loved nobody. The first one had tremendous professional ambition and thought that if she could be a part of Mrs. Gee's inner circle it would help her in achieving her goal. But disdainfully rejected, resorted to proving to Mrs. Gee that those she wasn't fond of, neither was she. And as she blamed them for her failures, she also concocted reasons to bad-mouth them to her. As to the other one, once a pal and confidant of Mrs. Gee, but now bearing for her a silent and deep resentment for what she perceived as Mrs. Gee having allowed her new inner circle to slowly but surely push her out, there was no certainty that if accepted back by Mrs. Gee she wouldn't grasp the opportunity and again go back to exhibiting those attitudes that were no less unpleasant than Mrs. Gee's.

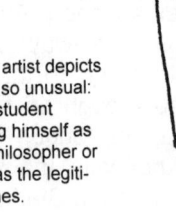
Student artist depicts The not so unusual: inmate/student believing himself as much philosopher or lawyer as the legitimate ones.

In pensive mood from the eyes of the student artist.

< 11 >

It was a tough school year. It felt like an exceptionally long one. Teaching summer school didn't help the situation, for summer school started very soon after the end of the normal school year, creating the feeling that the normal school year and summer school session were one and the same. And the break before the start of the new school year was quite short.

During the short summer break rumors were circulating via the phone that for the new school year there would be more changes at Island Academy than previously. I had already been giving serious thought to leaving. I really wasn't comfortable there and being at odds with Mrs. Gee. The situation wasn't helped, either, when I learned that a number of other staffers had filed grievances against her. I wasn't surprised that Madeline and Miss Graemes had done so, but was surprised that three or four others, who I considered too gutless to do so, actually had.

My resolve to leave Island Academy was strengthened when I received some correspondence from the union a few days before the new school year was to start. The Office of the Chancellor had investigated my grievances against Mrs. Gee and I was totally exonerated. On the contrary, the letter from the Office of the Chancellor showed that Mrs. Gee was severely reprimanded. In no uncertain terms, she was instructed to "immediately remove" from my file that letter instructing me not to strike students. This letter and all copies of it were to be "immediately destroyed," for there was no evidence presented to show that the teacher had committed the act, therefore the teacher was right in deeming that a letter with such a warning indicated that he was found guilty. Mrs. Gee was also instructed to "immediately remove" from my file the observation report and all copies of it and "immediately destroy" them. For one, it was wrong to have someone sign a document and after the signature add more information to the same document. For another, the observation in its original form wasn't given a rating and this, according to the rules and regulations, is regarded as satisfactory, something every principal should know. She didn't know it and neither did I.

Clearly, decisions as profound as these coming from the very top couldn't possibly help our working relationship. I would definitely make a serious effort to leave Island Academy, let Mrs. Gee run her school how it pleased her to.

The first day back at school revealed changes that shocked us all. Mrs. Gee was no longer the principal. She had opted to accept a retirement package deal. Mrs. Sitro, who as Mrs. Gee's special protégé had the mistaken belief that she had the power to pass on her position to her, discovered it was a stupid assumption. Not only was she not even considered for the position, but after allowing the disappointment to cause her to unleash her tongue against the superintendent, she was "thrown out" of the school all together.

The new principal was now the person the inner circle was so united against: Mrs. Lorde. In fact, the B.O.E. had also made the decision that Rosewood Alternative High School – the school for adolescent female inmates – of which Mrs. Lorde had been appointed principal, was to come under the banner of Island Academy, also always known as Austin H. MacCormick Alternative High School, though very seldom ever referred to as such. Included in these and other changes were two new assistant principals, one African-American male, one Jewish female. These changes would lead to problems never anticipated.

Since Mrs. Gee's and Mrs. Sitro's departure came at the last minute – so to speak – of the preceding school year, the decisions made by them for the new school year couldn't be suddenly reversed. Those staffers who were put through the excess mill would be ground up.

Later, on the first day of school – students not yet attending – Mrs Lorde summoned me to her office and I learned that one of the changes Mrs. Gee and Mrs. Sitro had decided on, under the pretext of a shortage of funds, was to close out my program for at least one semester. As a tenured teacher, the superintendent had instructed that I should come to school as usual until his office instructed me as to my new assignment. I would do this. Of course, had I not now had tenured protection, I would have ignored that "closed out for one semester" pacifier and forthwith set out to find another position.

Mrs. Lorde expressed her sorrow that the position had been closed out. I knew that she knew that having the program was a big plus for the school. It was widely accepted as the most popular program in the school. It already had been beneficial to Mrs. Lorde's reputation, for it was through my graphic arts classes that the Rosewood News was produced and she liked it so much. She informed me that she had nothing to do with making any of the changes. She urged me not to seek a position elsewhere but to wait for words from the superintendent's office.

I didn't think that her memory was bad. She had to have remembered that she was principal of Thomas Jefferson High when I was suddenly put through the excess mill. I told her there was absolutely no need for her to feel sorry. I truly felt that I had been at this school in Rikers Island Jail for long enough and it was time for me to move on; return to the traditional school setting. Among other reasons, I was growing increasingly disappointed that an overwhelming percentage of the youngsters in the school was too dedicated to the ways of prison life, convinced that they were prisoners and that the B.O.E. idea of calling them students was pure bullshit. I had the audacity to psychoanalyze them and was convinced that my analysis was correct.

These guys were in a very rough environment. Too many of them thought they were tough guys and were dedicated to that very negative philosophy advocated by the rap singer known as Tu-Pac Shakur, "thug life." They even nicknamed themselves after gangsters, cons and other Whites of dubious reputation, and had no intention of letting the Board of Education trap them into falling for education and thereby reducing them to chumps. Working with this entrenched mentality meant falling very short of the degree of achievement. I anticipated, not making a significant positive change. It disappointed me to the point where I was now asking myself if what was being achieved in the school wasn't far too little to justify all the tax payers' money that was spent to keep it functioning.

Eventually, with mixed feelings, I learned from Mrs. Lorde that the decision from the superintendent's office was that my program was to be immediately reinstated.

Maybe I should not have said it, seeing that the revelation was made at the teachers' meeting. But I announced quite frankly that as far as I was concerned it didn't have to be reinstated because I had made up my mind to move on as soon as I was assigned to another school. Certainly not one in another penal setting, and perhaps not another alternative one, either. Mrs. Lorde still announced how very important the program was to the school. The teachers, so surprised when the discontinuation of the program was announced, generally agreed with her.

I then announced that in spite of my readiness to move on, if I did stay on at Island Academy, "Mrs. Lorde, you know me from at Thomas Jefferson High as a teacher who always endeavored to do the best I can; it is a characteristic that is an integral part of me."

Mrs. Lorde seemed a happy woman. Little did she know that there were some trying times ahead waiting for her.

She was neither liked by Mrs. Gee nor Mrs. Sitro. For the most part, teachers were euphoric that Mrs. Gee was gone. But both she and Mrs. Sitro had their supporters that Mrs. Lorde inherited. First, there was this stupid rule that the school being on D.O.C. "turf," the D.O.C. had to have a certain amount of say in selecting the principal. The deputy warden in charge of the C.I.F.M. area in which the school was located, a Hispanic, wanted Mrs. Sitro to be the new principal. It didn't work out the way he wanted. The two senior C.O.'s assigned to the school, one Hispanic, the other Rev, handsome and with the very dark complexion of Mrs. Lorde, were known to be close to Mrs. Gee and Mrs. Sitro. And as afore-mentioned, Rev was generally regarded by B.O.E. personnel as Mrs. Gee's henchman, the one she would set on those not in her favor. Bear in mind, too, as afore mentioned, his propensity for "sucking up" to his superiors. So taking into consideration that Mrs. Sitro and especially Mrs. Gee had left him to carry out a mission of vengeance against Mrs. Lorde for them, and that he felt obligated to defend the stand of his boss, the deputy warden, then there should be some understanding as to the depth of his mission against Mrs. Lorde.

He started this mission immediately, aided by those who supported Mrs. Gee and Mrs. Sitro.

Part of his undermining of Mrs. Lorde was in the form of acting like he was the new principal. It wasn't long before Mrs. Lorde found herself being regularly summoned to the downton Brooklyn Office of Investigations to answer to accusations made against her.

In time, some B.O.E. personnel started to act in such a manner as if this man Rev was above the principal; this man who was widely regarded as the C.O. least capable of getting inmates to obey orders. Then, too, it became the thing to do, for other B.O.E. personnel to join those already against Mrs. Lorde. Especially pathetic about this was that a few of these were the very gutless cowards who used to have tears in their eyes when Mrs. Gee talked down to them.

Mrs. Lorde was a very soft spoken Christian woman from South Carolina who would never talk down to anyone. I had no doubt that this was the major reason for people taking advantage of her. They interpreted her politeness as softness. Now, even the gutless saw what they believed to be the kind of vulnerability that allowed them their chance to put on a show about having some guts.

I saw it written all over Mrs. Lorde's face that she was being stressed out, pushed to the limit. It set me to thinking about those concepts "happy medium" and "middle ground." Were they not mostly idealistic shit? And realistically, there was one extreme or the other: tough and no-nonsense like Mrs. Gee or pleasant and tolerant like Mrs. Lorde. Who knows if Mrs. Gee had not had reasons to examine the kind of ways of Mrs. Lorde and felt justified in concluding that such ways were too frequently taken advantage of.

I observed over a period of time that Mrs. Lorde spent a lot of time going out of her way in trying to get those known to be most against her to like her. It wasn't working.

It was a microcosmic example of folly and failure that would soon reveal itself in the City of New York on a macrocosmic level: That of David Dinkins becoming the first African-American to become mayor of the city though resented by certain groups. But would be defeated in his quest for reelection by Rudolph Guiliani because he (Dinkins) while proving himself to be a good human being proved himself a bad politician, by his spending of too much time trying to be liked by those who didn't vote for him because they didn't like him, and didn't want his kind to be mayor. Guiliani, on the other hand, proved himself a bad human being but a good politician. While he talked a good game of being "mayor of all the people," unlike Dinkins, he specifically looked out for the interest of those groups he knew were against Dinkins and displayed callous disregard for the group he knew liked Dinkins most. It was because of this Dinkins' strategy that he wouldn't be elected to a second term and Guiliani would go on to be showered with national adulations for which those of the group who most supported Dinkins would never see the justification.

At any rate, there prevailed at Island Academy the general belief that while others found it convenient to jump on the bandwagon of hate against Mrs. Lorde, those driving the wagon, along with Rev, were two White females, one a teacher, the other not a teacher, not even a UFT member, but known to have been always in Mrs. Gee's corner.

Though not yet at the disgusting stage it would reach, the idea that B.O.E. personnel were to acknowledge their place behind D.O.C. personnel was obvious, and that if the former should find themselves on the wrong side of the latter, they (the latter) could find ways to make them suffer. So it was understandable why some elected to join the bandwagon. It was hard, though, to accept that a number of these were actually Black. They were expressing their disappointment that the position of principal wasn't filled by Mrs. Sitro.

It was obvious that Rev was enjoying the new "promotion" he had given himself – or that those who were in the background trying to create an unworkable situation were using him to help in the creation of. He was now in the habit of going into classrooms and acting in the manner of principals and assistant principals, observing what was going on and making known his dislikes. And there were those teachers, aware of little things C.O.'s could do in the penal setting to inconvenience them, who muffled their resentment.

He had come into my classroom a few times and looked around. At no time did he voice the criticism I had heard from other teachers that he had when entering their classrooms. I realized that this being a school in a jail and the students being inmates, often engaging in forbidden activities, a C.O. not only had the right to, but should check on them, though not in the manner of being the teacher's boss. This being the case, I had no objections to Rev coming into my classroom. I must say, though, I anticipated a change in the situation. The only reason it had not yet come, I felt sure, was because Rev knew that any attempts by him to act as if he could exercise control over me wouldn't be accommodated as in the case of other teachers, but would be problematic.

As anticipated, so it eventually turned out to be. Rev came into my classroom one morning and ordered me to supply him with an inventory of "all that equipment in here." I told him that I would do no such thing unless I was asked to by my supervisor, the principal. If it was an issue regarding safety I would readily recognize the need to cooperate because of the environment I was in. But this wasn't the case. He simply was on a mission to set himself up to be seen as the one in charge at the school.

He flew into a rage, a fighting kind, and started hurling at me those accusations he had hurled at me in the past: Black militant, atheist, don't like to listen. Then he went to Mrs. Lorde. She eventually came to me and in her soft-spoken manner requested that I should do the inventory. I agreed, realizing how badly she wanted to get this man off her back and believed that every move she made to appease him would help. Even though at this stage I was not yet as aware of the great depth of his propensity to be a hypocrite and a cut-throat as I would later on, I yet knew him well enough to doubt that he would ease up on his mission against Mrs. Lorde no matter what she did or didn't do. As a matter of fact, I had already suggested to her that she should do herself a favor and cease having any discussions with him without someone on her side present. She obviously saw the sense in it because now whenever this situation arose the assistant principal Mr. Welles was there.

Rev kept pressuring me for the inventory. I would let him know that as a teacher I had classes to teach and the inventory would be done when I could find the time to do it. When it was done and he asked about it, I told him it was done but that since Mrs. Lorde was my supervisor I felt it was appropriate for me to give it to her and he could get it from her. He didn't like this decision at all. I knew it was because that as simple a decision as it appeared when looked at superficially, it represented a major slight to him that I didn't treat him like the boss he thought he was.

Mrs. Lorde came to my classroom during the sixth period one day when I had no students. She praised the recently published school newspaper, to which I had just given a major new look. She thought it was the most interesting issue she had seen, and that it made her so proud when she gave out copies and nobody could believe it was produced entirely in a high school classroom – and in jail at that.

Since the two schools were now combined, I made the decision to insert extra pages into the Academy News to serve as Rosewood News. The girls didn't like the idea of having their news hidden inside another publication and I wasn't keen about publishing two separate publications when the two schools, though still physically separated, of course, were yet combined. And I certainly wasn't going to stick pages inside another publication to serve as the Academy News. Hence, came the final idea of adding those extra pages for a single publication that served as two. There was no back page. If you picked up the publication and saw the front page reading Academy News, you read it through to the center page where Academy News ended, with this page serving as its back page. To read Rosewood News you simply flipped the publication over and instead of seeing a back page you would see another front page reading Rosewood News, to be read through to the other middle page where this publication ended. In actuality, the two center pages served as a back page each for both publications. And so, all concerned were satisfied. I suppose the novelty of it not only helped in the area of appeasement, but in the general agreement with Mrs. Lorde that it was the best issue.

I told Mrs. Lorde that I, too, had an extra feeling about this issue. I worked with the female adolescents more than previously. They often seemed as obstinate as their male counterparts as far as topics were concerned. They, too, wanted to write articles about criminal activities, sex, and wanted to use a lot of profanity. Of course, in spite of their initial persistence to do it their way because "the paper is for us not you," I prevailed with my insistence that these topics they found so appealing would not dominate the pages of the publication. When working with the females, though, it did make for a welcome change.

On this day that Mrs. Lorde came in she said she had only come to have a brief chat about the new issue because she was once again summoned to the investigation office to answer to more charges made against her. And that worried look took over her face.

"Mister Brathwaite, you know, I just wonder what I did to these people," Mrs. Lorde said. "maybe I'm too black for them."

"Misses Lorde, I don't think that's it," I said. "You're a very nice person. And it's nice to be nice. But sometimes being too nice works against you. You see, there are people who see niceness as softness. And they walk all over you and actually enjoy the feeling of strength and importance it brings them. They only stop if you take a mean and nasty turn on them."

I certainly didn't think that Mrs. Lorde would accept this advice. She didn't. The mean-spirited actions against her persisted. I knew that she felt quite comfortable having the occasional conversation with me about issues not necessarily on the professional level. I think her role as my principal at Thomas Jefferson High created in her a feeling

According to the student caricaturist and comic, his drawing, right (significantly reduced), represents "Mr. Brathwaite, trying to fool students that he's Mr. Tuff Guy."

of trust in me.

In our most recent such conversation, she had expressed to me her dual feelings about the student at TJH who had not long ago shot to death two of his fellow students inside that troubled school. She felt so hurt that "such a horrible thing" happened at "my school." But she also expressed how very happy she was that she was "so fortunate" to have been "let go from there in time so as not to have the deaths of those two youngsters – and the problems of the shooter – on my mind for the rest of my life."

I told her how badly I felt when I heard the news. And she shouldn't think that I was being mean, but I agreed one hundred percent with a girl at the school who told a TV news person that the principal who took over from her should have been arrested for having metal detectors available to the school but refusing to use them, thinking that doing so would be a question mark against her ability to control the school.

Not much longer, Mrs. Lorde would be faced with what had to be her worst trauma. Her only son, Willie, just turned 22, was fatally gunned down out in Long Island.

I had first met Willie when Mrs. Lorde came to Island Academy, though he would assure me that he had seen me while I was at TJH, and would laugh hysterically when telling me that the first time he saw me he thought to himself, because of my huge Afro and Chinese-like beard, "Damn! Dat's one funny-looking Black man."

But He ended up working with me three periods a day as my para and had so much respect for me that he consistently asked for my advice and opinion on many issues. He wasn't such an effective helper, certainly not like Mr. Martin. But I understood that it was primarily because of his boyish looks that the students thought he looked too much like them to be telling them what to do, so they did what they thought was appropriate: showered him with the same disrespect and disregard they showered on one another.

At any rate, like so many others, I found Willie to be a respectful and very likeable fellow. He looked forward to lunch period so he could munch on his cheeseburgers and French fries.

The White youngster who worked at the garage saw it differently. So when Willie took his car back to the garage, dissatisfied with the way it was fixed, and became engaged in words of disagreement, the White youngster, he thought it necessary to put a shotgun blast into Willie's chest from close range because "he looked like Mike Tyson" and that's why he "was so afraid of him."

No matter how ridiculous the alibi, the White judge thought it a justifiable reason and let the murderer go free.

I sat with Mrs. Lorde in her office before the trial, tears running down her cheeks, and suggested that she should solicit the help of the activist Reverend Herbert Daughtry. I felt sure she wouldn't be comfortable with the activist Reverend Al Sharpton because of his more controversial reputation. Though not as controversial, Daughtry would be as effective at drawing attention to the case. The help of neither was solicited. The case never got a line of coverage in the mainstream media. To me, it was a testament to Mrs. Lorde's desire not to create waves. Leave it in the hands of Jesus and everything would be taken care of in the hereafter.

True, Willie was her son. She truly loved him. He truly loved her. His death was painful. Now, I felt the same pains in my conviction that not enough was done to make his murderer responsible for his wicked deed.

Knowing of her great loss didn't deter Mrs. Lorde's detractors from pursuing their acts of villainy against her. It certainly didn't matter to Rev. This man who was so often seen reading the Bible, discussing its teachings, and trying to "save" the youngsters with it refused to even sign a sympathy card from the staff to Mrs. Lorde. It was said when he was approached with the card his reaction was: "Serves her right; God doesn't like her, either."

Eventually the time came to have the union election to elect the school's new UFT chapter leader (union rep). Three people were running for the position. Miss Graemes announced that she was no longer interested in filling the position a second time because it was a thankless job, pleasing the teachers was almost impossible. I thought there was a more significant reason. She felt that she wouldn't be reelected. There was too strong a general opinion that her attitude was often too abrasive. Personally, I was a bit disappointed that this abrasiveness would surface in her dealings with Mrs. Lorde, without justification, I thought.

My name ended up among those vying for the position, though I was the only one who didn't initiate my own candidacy, not having any interest in being union rep, even if I was overly concerned that the others running were a bunch of wimps who would take the union back to that scared-stiff-of-the-D.O.C. state in which it existed before Miss Graemes took over. I felt they only wanted the position because it allowed them one less teaching period a day to deal with union issues. And even after my name was entered by Miss Graemes, I made no attempts, as did the other candidates, to get votes.

I was elected. The other candidates got very few votes. It was surprising because I wasn't regarded as Mr. Popular, not being the extroverted type.

When it was announced at the teachers' meeting that I was the new union rep the news was well received. I had no doubt it was because they felt I, though not the friendliest fellow, had the strength to handle the position. Whatever the case, I thanked them for placing their trust in me and seeing in me the characteristics they thought best to represent their interest. "I didn't set out to be union rep," I told them. "Matter of fact, I was pushed into it. And now that it has happened, I accept. Be assured that if I ever find that I can't defend you if the need arises, that I can't represent your interest when I should, such as was the case with other union reps, I will not hold on like they did; I will voluntarily give up."

As the school year progressed, nothing really changed. Mrs. Lorde was still having her problems with her detractors, notably Rev. My relationship with him had definitely deteriorated significantly. If there was that remotest of chance of it improving, then my becoming union rep destroyed that.

"Union rep? Union rep?" he often grunted when he saw me. "Dat union rep stuff don't mean nothin' around here. This is D.O.C. turf. We can handcuff you and take you back 'cross the bridge." It became his motto.

There was a new deputy warden (dep), African American, who had started to make his presence at the school felt. It was becoming a habit of his to use the teachers' meeting to speak on the issue of security, as he claimed. It seemed, though, to have more to do with inflating his ego. There was no doubt that his attitudes encouraged Rev to continue his.

The Dep liked to express himself in this tough-guy manner: "And you teachers had better understand that I can have you arrested." The teachers would sit there and never ask for an explanation.

One Friday afternoon when he made this statement, I suggested to him that having heard it so many times, I was beginning to detect in it a tone of disrespect, as if when he spoke to the teachers, adult professionals, it was the same as if he was speaking to the adolescent inmates. The statement always sounded as if he was saying that he had the power to arrest teachers "just like that," without them having broken any law, and if he did so the teacher couldn't file a lawsuit against him. I guess I could have ignored him, as I felt sure he was trying to impress some of the female teachers.

It was not up to the UFT to look out for Mrs. Lorde. She was a principal and had her own union. However, after a while I concluded that she was being persecuted too much and it wasn't good for the school on a whole. I approached those staffers who I felt believed as I did and suggested that we should go to the B.O.E. Office to which she was frequently summoned and stage a demonstration to let it be known that we believed that she was being unjustly set upon, and that we had observed that, for some strange reason, those staffers who were summoned to the investigation office to be questioned about her were those generally regarded as her foes.

Some staffers were ready to take this stand. Some expressed the wish that they could but didn't want to upset anyone from the D.O.C. by openly doing so. But why be disappointed with the latter? We were taking a stand for Mrs. Lorde and she seemed the one most timid of the idea. We perhaps understood better than Mrs. Lorde what this persecution and the recent loss of her son were doing to her.

The demonstration didn't take place. Two of the big shots at the office suggested that rather than the demonstration they would sit with six of us and hear what we had to say.

It made a difference. After we had our say Mrs. Lorde was not summoned back to that investigation office again. Her detractors still disliked her, but it was obvious that they thought it best to find a different way to attack her.

For having the audacity to initiate the taking of a stand in defense of Mrs. Lorde. Rev and the Dep for whom it was widely believed he was doing this dirty work, set out to teach me a lesson about how not to oppose them on their turf. Rev spoke often and openly about me being "a black militant who don't listen," vowing "I'm gonna get him, make sure he's taken outta here in handcuffs, show him that dat union rep thing don't mean nothin' around here."

By the end of that semester Rev had proven that he was quite serious about his plans to get rid of me not only from Island Academy but from Rikers Island. He fed a stream of complaints against me to the assistant principal, principal, his fellow C.O.'s, captains and deps. Thankfully, after hearing these complaints from him so often, some of his own captains started to disregard them And, of course, many of his fellow C.O.'s already distrusted him as the major cut throat among them.

Teaching graphic arts/printing in my classroom meant

that in addition to using blades, scissors and T-squares – all made of metal and could yield potent pieces of contraband for inflicting serious wounds, as was the case with so many production equipment – provided Rev with ample sources from which to build security complaints. Youngsters inflicting cuts across the faces of each other was an activity the D.O.C. guarded against most, much more so than against, say, their pounding on one another, or the raping of the weaker by the stronger. The evidence of the latter two wasn't as lasting or conspicuous as that of a gash across (down) the face. The more conspicuous the evidence of violent acts, the louder the message it sent out that the D.O.C. wasn't quite succeeding at doing its job. And there was no doubt that the youngsters regarded it as the ultimate show of victory to inflict that facial scar. Hence, they were constantly on the lookout for contraband to do the job. Increasing their need for contraband was that D.O.C. policy of rewarding them –less jail time notably – for handing in such contraband they supposedly "found." So Rev had no problems in soliciting their help in this area and giving to my classroom that dubious reputation of being a danger spot that should be eliminated.

And to buy these youngsters off didn't require the giving of major rewards such as mentioned here; something so insignificant on the "outside world" as the giving of a few cigarettes or bringing them ham on a roll with cheese, lettuce and tomato motivated them to do things for you.

With all the things that went on, this school year seemed so very long. Opting to teach summer school didn't help; it made the one school year seem like two.

Once the summer session was over, September and the new school year came so fast it didn't seem to me that I had went off to London to "get away from it all" by reacquainting myself with the city where I had lived part of my teenage years and had not visited for a number of years. So eager was I to get away from it all, I even squeezed in Paris and Amsterdam.

Retuning to New York City and realizing that my final

summer school check was there, I thought, why did I not remember this so I could have given myself another week getting away from it all?

Well, it was not to be. I was back at Island Academy the first week of September. Surprisingly, Island Academy and Rosewood were no longer one, no longer under the same principal. The B.O.E. had made the sudden decision to return the schools to their individual state and send Mrs. Lorde back to Rosewood and assigned to Island Academy an interim principal, Mr. Hines, a White guy. Also gone was Mrs. Lorde's trusted assistant principal Mr. Welles. The lone remaining A.P. was Mrs. Straus, a Jewish woman, who had proven from the previous semester that she was not at all capable of dealing with the students. In fact, she had exhibited an attitude of downright fear and disregard for them. They, in return, treated her with the utmost disrespect. She obviously didn't have a good relationship with Black teachers, either.

I guess Rev, knowing this, and being the type he was, saw it as the great opportunity to prove himself Mr. Nice Negro, for he was always up in Mrs. Straus' face grinning and whispering.

It turned out that Mr. Hines was not at all keen about being principal of a school in jail. His appointment was an emergency one. He couldn't wait for the emergency to end.

Armed with their street and jail "smarts," the students soon saw the instability of the prevailing situation and gladly geared their behavior accordingly.

A second A.P., Mr. Dudley, White, came later, adding some strength to the administration.

Most teachers saw in Mr. Hines a laid-back style of leadership, a style helpful to them. However, though they were often critical of his style, critical of Mrs. Straus' inability to make a helpful impact, none of the criticism ever took the mean-spirited, destructive turn as in the case of Mrs. Lorde, or even on a lesser scale, as in Mrs. Gee's case. It might have had something to do with the fact that of late the number of White staff members had increased significantly, to the point now where even the administration was all-white, heading in the direction of the public schools in general. So excusing away shortcomings was the normal and easy thing to do.

Rev seemed quite satisfied. He no doubt recognized that there would be no objection coming from the administration to the "promotion" he gave himself.

This would be put to the test when he tried to set up the computer teacher, Miss Helen. One day she left her box cutter blade – a tool she needed for using in her class – sticking out of her bag, which was sitting on her desk. It certainly would have been a dangerous and negligent thing if students were around. But not only was it during the lunch break when no students were around, her classroom door was locked. On returning to the room she realized that her bag had been tampered with, that the box cutter was missing.

Panicking, as any teacher, especially a per diem such as she was, would do, Miss Helen came to me and related what had happened. She was of the opinion that while she was in the washroom Rev, as was his habit, unlocked the door to look around. Seeing the box cutter, he thought it a grand opportunity to take it and show his supervisors how this incompetent teacher was contributing to danger in the school and how much he was "on the ball" to have prevented it. To make matters worse for Miss Helen, their relationship was definitely in the "no-love-lost" category.

I wanted to be sure that Miss Helen was sure that the box cutter was in her possession after all the students had left, that one of them had not taken this kind of contraband with the potential of it resulting in three or four slashed faces before all the pieces it was broken into and distributed among his homeboys were recovered. If she wasn't sure she had the blade in her possession after the departure of the students, she should report it missing so the D.O.C. could have a "search down" of the students, something they dreaded. In fact, most teachers preferred not seeing them put through this. But the violence they perpetrated against each other made it necessary.

True, teachers from whose classroom contraband was missing were reluctant to report it, mainly so because C.O.'s would show no mercy in ridiculing them for being incompetent, though it was common knowledge that C.O.'s themselves were regularly outsmarted "big-time" by inmates, adolescents and adults alike. But they could excuse themselves. Island Academy students not only beat the safety system and managed to take contraband from the school floor back to the dorms; they beat the wider safety system by somehow taking contraband back to the dorm which was slipped to them by family members and friends on visitations. As for drugs, they might not have gotten all they wanted, but they certainly got quite a bit.

In any case, if missing contraband that could inflict wounds was missing and not reported, as insisted on by the D.O.C., but then turned up during a fight or a search down and was traced back to a classroom, the D.O.C. could have that teacher removed from the school for neglecting to report the contraband missing.

By the time Miss Helen went to Mr. Hines to discuss the issue of the missing box cutter, Rev had beaten her to it. The way he explained it made it appear as though he had retrieved it from a student who had taken it from her bag. He even had a report written. She came back and related the story to me. She also told me that Mr. Hines had informed her that Rev's report would be typed up and she would have to sign it so it could be placed in her file. And of course, she still had to answer to the D.O.C.

Miss Helen stuck to her version of what had happened, as I suggested she should. Let Rev prove his version. As to the issue of whether she should sign the report which she disagreed with, I told her I would have to read it first.

When I did go to see Mr. Hines, with whom I was getting along with quite well thus far, he had the report typed up and ready for Miss Helen's signature. As the union rep, and with Miss Helen having a problem with the report, I explained to him that she wanted me to read it before she would sign it. To him, it was like a simple issue. Then I realized that more than this there was that fear B.O.E. personnel had about displeasing D.O.C. personnel, even those at the lowest level. Mr. Hines was definitely no exception to this rule. Of course, I didn't see it his way. Having read the report, I thought it not only made the teacher look incompetent but like she had brought the box cutter into the school as a contraband gift.

The still panicking Miss Helen was eager to know from me what she should do. I told her I couldn't tell her what to do. But if she asked me what I would do if I were in her shoes, I would tell her quite honestly that "I would not sign that report." The contents had to be changed.

I sat down with Mr. Hines and showed him the things that should be changed. He grudgingly agreed and commended me for the way I defended the teacher. I wasn't so kind to him, though. I told him that I was disappointed that as principal he seemed to have wanted his teacher to throw up her hands and plead guilty. Rev, on the other hand, was very angry with me. He again vowed to prove to me that "union rep don't mean nothin' around here. This is D.O.C. turf." He was particularly upset that Miss Helen had come to me for advice, as if she dared to think that I, a teacher, had some kind of power to question his authority. Yet there seemed a little more that was slapping around his ego. I heard it in this sarcastic remark he made to a fellow C.O. for me to hear:

"I guess these Hispanic women hangin' around him done gone to his head." I knew he was alluding to the fact that Madeline had been so very close to me and since her recent leaving from Island Academy for another school, Miss Helen, also of Spanish roots, raised in France, coming to the school after Madeline, was often in my classroom to do some of the things Madeline used to do.

As far as I was concerned about this matter, I saw it in accordance with a popular saying: Miss Helen "was no Madeline." As much as I appreciated her help on the computers and in translating, and that we had a very good relationship, and the fact that she never allowed the sexual innuendoes thrown at this relationship to bother her, I quite often tried all I could to get rid of her because she spent so much time helping herself, even on those times when I arranged it so she got per session pay for help she rendered after normal school hours. I even had disputes with both these women based on race. I doubt a fellow like Rev would have done this under the circumstances, fearing it would damage that "nice-Negro" image he was obsessed with portraying to Whites especially. A major dispute was about my strong belief that I had observed a trend among Hispanic teachers to relate to Hispanic students much better than to Black students. I must say in defense of Madeline, though, that while she argued against my observation as a case of being overly sensitive, she never doubted that there was a lot of racism all around and that Black people suffered from it most.

    I next had a confrontation with Rev based on a student not leaving the classroom when he was told. All students were ordered out into the hallway immediately by the D.O.C. for "the count." I kept telling this student to stop what he was doing and get out into the hallway with the others before he got himself into trouble. All it took for Rev to turn this mole hill situation into one of mountainous proportions was the sudden appearance of a captain on the scene. Immediately he was screaming and accusing me of telling the student not to do as he had ordered him to. I immediately thought of how he might have already pointed me out to the captain as this uncooperative teacher and this was an opportunity to wrap it in validity, as he had done to others before, as he would tell Whites I was a black power militant, tell religious zealots I was an atheist.

    No, I couldn't be sure that he had mischaracterized me in this case, but the quickness with which the captain got nasty with me left little doubt in my mind that he had

    "Sir," I said to the captain, "I have been teaching at this school for quite a while now. Do you really think that after all this time I've been seeing how things are in jail that I, a teacher with no power, would be so crazy to encourage an inmate to disobey D.O.C. orders, knowing the consequences he would have to face? And this is a student I actually like because he helps me out a lot. When he didn't move with the other students, what I actually did was to tell him to get out of the room before he got himself into trouble. Sir, I don't bother this man. I keep as far away from him as I can. I don't know why he can't stop bothering me. You're his boss and I wish you would do me the favor and tell him to leave me alone, stop trying so damn hard to set me up."

Rev still tried to stick to his fabricated position. It was obvious to me, though – and to him – that the truth and logic in my statement was believed by the captain.

In time, when I was approached by a Black Muslim C.O. asking me to write a letter recommending him as C.O. in charge of the school floor because there was dissatisfaction with the way Rev was handling the job, I was happy to do him the favor. Big Ak, as he was popularly known, had a reputation as a no-nonsense C.O. Students were not at all eager to be on his wrong side, making it easier for teachers. During my early days at Island Academy he had worked on the school floor briefly before being removed to another assignment. For whatever reasons, I don't know. But if it was that he hoped to control, he obviously knew that he could not have succeeded in doing so under Mrs. Gee. Whatever things there were to be said against her, one certainly could not have been that she would allow even the top D.O.C. guys to control her and what she referred to adamantly as "my" school, much less low-level guys like Rev and Big Ak. But if being in control of something was now on Big Ak's mind, with his domineering trait and the wimpy stand adopted by the school administrations ever since the departure of Mrs. Gee, then he would have no problem at all controlling Island Academy now.

Big Ak was reassigned to the school floor. It wasn't long before it became obvious that Rev was backing away from the promotion he had given himself. He quickly faded away into Big Ak's shadow. Bear in mind that he never did do much as far as what he was actually assigned to the school floor to do was concerned. He was always in the habit of avoiding getting involved with the behavioral problems of the students, leaving such to his fellow C.O.'s, unless of course, one of his supervisors suddenly appeared on the scene and he suddenly jumped into his act of portraying himself as the busiest C.O. on Rikers Island.

Big Ak was clearly a fellow who thought he was tough enough to handle any situation all by himself. I guess I didn't see the real Big Ak the first time around. He had me fooled then with all that Afro-centric posturing he did.

Needless to say, most of the students liked Rev but were not at all fond of Big Ak. Their feelings about him were constantly expressed thus: "The nigga be thinkin' he so big an bad;" "he be always beating up on niggas;" "one day some inmate gonna meet him in New York and give him what he deserves;" "dat nigga better learn to keep his hands to hisself;" "he beats the shit outta us just 'cause he know we be inmates and can't fuck him back up;" "somebody gonna kill dat nigga's ass one day."

It must be said that it wasn't unusual for female staffers to side with the students against Big Ak, not to his face, of course. Seeing a student getting roughed up, they would say, "It could've been my son;" "bet he wouldn't like it if his son ends up in jail and somebody treats him like that."

As tough as Ak was known to be, some youngsters still ignored the consequences and jumped into his face. That the female staffers – more so than the male staffers – often sided with the students against Big Ak could be understood. It's only fair, though, to say that at times the youngsters got so out of hand that it wasn't easy to sympathize with them.

By the end of the school year it was known that Mr. Hines wouldn't be back as principal. He was a nice, quiet guy, never made his teachers miserable. What he would leave to work against them was a C.O., Big Ak, acting as leader of Island Academy. By then, I had completely different views about Big Ak: control freak, big ox, and most definitely not the Afro-centric Black man he pretended to be.

< 12 >

So the beginning of another school year was upon us. Again, there was a new principal, Mr. Timothy. It was said that he was one of those fellows who "went by the book all the way." Certainly not a practical thing for a school like Island Academy.

As the union rep, I thought it very important to know of the new principal's plans and to make a few suggestions. I discussed this with Miss Graemes and the two other staffers who formed the union committee. We would meet with the new principal and "pick his brain."

There was one issue in particular that I wanted to put before Mr. Timothy, which I hoped the committee viewed as seriously as I did. Island Academy was indeed on "correction's turf," but would he have the guts to say no to the assertion of Big Ak and Rev that they were the ones "in charge around here?" Would he stand up and be what a principal should be, or would he succumb to the egotistical stand of these two?

Mr. Timothy gave his assurance that he would be the one in control of the school in the manner expected of a principal. Big Ak and Rev would take care of their responsibilities.

The school year could not have been more than a month old when I saw a plaque – not a letter – displayed over the window of the bubble, as the tiny office of Big Ak and Rev was known, commending these two, none of the other C.O.'s on the school floor, for the great contribution they were making toward the successful running of the school. I knew that Big Ak would continue to think of himself as leader of the school without any administrative objections. Great for his ego. Very helpful to the principal's future and career. Extras problems for the teachers as a result of an added display of ego-tripping behavior from these two.

In spite of my disagreement over Mr. Timothy's too-quick move to praise these guys and therefore making himself appear to be a weakling pleading for mercy, in time I had to admit that there were some very good traits about him. Especially admirable about him was his willingness – and courage – to regularly teach a class, a task not required of principals. Those who found an escape out of the classroom never wanted to return there. They usually engineered this escape because of more money, but that desire to get away from being "trapped" in a classroom every day was a major part of the reason. Of course, they would try to play this down by constantly making statements to make it seem that they missed teaching so much.

Most teachers thought Mr. Timothy was a bit "crazy" to voluntarily take on this stressful responsibility that other principals were not known to do. Instead, they constantly criticized the performance of teachers. Then "once in a blue moon" when the situation in a classroom seemed just right for it, go in and demonstrate teaching skills.

Mr. Timothy's inclination to go by the book was evident but not as strong as it was made out to be. He did emphasize the need for high standards. It was obvious, though, that his regular connection with the classroom helped him in separating idealism from reality. He knew that even he, the principal, could be confronted by disruptive, undesirable students' behavior for which there were no immediate solutions such as those magical ones that constantly circulated in the minds of those whose positions never had them dealing with more than one student at a time, much less several.

Mr. Timothy's style truly was one of leading by example. It did a lot of good. I wouldn't advocate that all principals should do the same amount of time in the classroom, but it would be very helpful to the schools if the Board of Education would make it mandatory that not only principals, but assistant principals and clinicians spend at least three periods a week in the classroom so they wouldn't be able to disconnect themselves from the reality of the major problems afflicting the schools.

As the time went by, it was obvious that Rev wasn't pleased that Big Ak, with less seniority, was not only able to take over from him but was able to force B.O.E. staffers to treat him as their boss, even if some did so grudgingly. In truth, Rev would have never accomplished this. His way of doing things just couldn't endear anyone to him as a leader. Consider the extra show of defiance he got from students, for one. But all in all, he just didn't exude any qualities that made a leader.

Little by little the Brathwaite-Big Ak relationship deteriorated. It was primarily about control. Knowing that he was no match for Big Ak as far as controlling was concerned, Rev no doubt passed on his feelings toward me to Big Ak. Endowed with this "control freak (bully)" syndrome, Big Ak set out to show him that it could be done: You couldn't control Brathwaite but I can and I'll prove it to you.

I was no bully, was no control freak, would never want to be either. To me, these characteristics represented a sick mind. Ironically, too, such characteristics sometimes represented a latent cowardice that was struggling for cover. Whatever the case, I knew of myself as one possessing such deep pride in self that it drove me to take a stand in defense of my rights if they were being violated or infringed upon, no matter what the repercussions exacted against me might be. This kind of person, as far as I was concerned, was by far mentally tougher than some control freak and bully.

Undoubtedly, Big Ak didn't understand this, but he would see the futility of using control freak and bully tactics to defeat innate self pride.

These two Negroes consistently worked toward their goal to see me "done in." They resorted to tactics of harassment, using the contraband situation to set me up, making complaints to B.O.E. administration and their D.O.C. supervisors, creating an atmosphere of hostility, and engaging in acts of inconvenience.

If I was outside trying to get in, or inside wanting to get out, because they so effectively exercised that power-tripping monopoly with the two sets of keys to the steel doors, not even wanting junior C.O.'s to use them, they would delay my entry or exit for as long as they could. i must say that I wasn't the only one they did this to. But I was the union rep who had to be taught a lesson that "that union rep thing don't mean nothin' around here." They were very quick to get to those doors for the females, especially the White ones.

Because of the transportation, parking and locked doors situations, being those few minutes late in getting into the building wasn't unusual. Consequently, when staffers finally made it into the building they were often so concerned with moving their time cards that it wasn't unusual for them to forget to go through the required process of changing ID cards. I sometimes found myself in this situation. Every time these two Negroes would take my ID to the administration as opposed to coming to me about the error as they normally did in the case of most others. I got to know about this double standard when on several occasions I went to those who came into the building late with me and had not exchanged their ID's to find out that their ID's were not taken to the administration. Fortunately, administration personnel understood what was going on. Actually they commended me when I told them I wouldn't make an issue out of it. If I did, Big Ak and Rev would use this as an excuse for creating added inconveniences for all concerned and attribute the need for doing so to my complaining, meaning that however they were now being subject to extra inconvenience was because of me. A great contribution to that atmosphere of hostility they were trying to create.

One very nasty act Big Ak engaged in against me started with two students playing around in my class when I stepped out briefly to go to the washroom, leaving the para to look after the class. The playing around led to one student getting a slight cut with the box cutter blade, which I was sure would not have happened had I not stepped out of the room. So slight was the cut that the students – and the para – saw no need to report the incident. I knew that they couldn't be trusted to not make an issue of it, then it would reach the D.O.C. and they would be only too eager to take the teacher to task for not reporting the incident. So I decided it was best to report it. After the tremendous fuss made, Big Ak held on to that blade in his bubble office and because the handle holding the blade could be changed and they came in different colors, he took advantage of these things to periodically go to the principal with a different-looking box cutter under the pretext that another dangerous weapon was found in my classroom. I never knew of this surreptitious act to make me look like an irresponsible threat to security until a C.O. tipped me off. I felt compelled to go to the principal about the issue only to have it confirmed that in the last few months Big Ak had actually brought to him blades said to have been taken from my classroom. It was a damn vicious lie. I was disappointed, though, that the principal, rather than bringing it to my attention, had taken it upon himself to settle the issue with the security captains.

There was also the problem of the graffiti drawings and writings appearing just about everywhere. Because it was known that my graphic arts classes were the ones that most often used markers and inks, whenever graffiti turned up somewhere, the accusing fingers of Big Ak and Rev were pointed at my classroom. Just as I had initiated an almost fool-proof method regarding the blades and scissors, using only one which only the teacher handled, and two scissors which were locked onto chains and nailed to the wall, I initiated a way of proving if those markers students were caught with did come from my classroom. On several occasions it was proven beyond a doubt that the markers were not from my classroom but were coming from other classrooms, taken there by other teachers for students to use and thereby keep them quiet on those many occasions when they didn't want to be engaged with academics. Whenever this was proven, the fuss that was previously being made when the fingers of guilt were being pointed at my graphic arts class would quickly fade away to no fuss at all.

There was one occasion that especially changed the accusations as to whose markers were responsible for the graffiti appearing on the walls. On this occasion it actually came down to a near certainty that the markers had to have come from the C.O.'s bubble office. Big Ak was adamant that such was not the case. But of course, he was even more adamant against my simple request to look into his desk drawer to see if those markers he kept there were still there.

I was sure that they were not too pleased that I had initiated means of proving them wrong. But by doing so I had backed them into a position where, no matter what others told them to their faces to appease them, they knew of their double standards and their propensity for fabricating things.

There was a time when I felt certain that Big Ak was actually succeeding in getting the principal to believe him. Then one day he was in my classroom, when no students were there, having a discussion with me. Big Ak and Rev were where they habitually stood observing and discussing when they were not in their bubble: right outside the door of my classroom. C.O.'s in general tended to hang out at this spot, never giving thought that I could be inside hearing their discussions. In fact, I usually heard things they were saying which I doubt they consciously would have wanted me to hear. In any case, the principal was now privy to a conversation going on between Big Ak and Rev in which they were severely bad-mouthing a fellow C.O. to their captain.

The fellow C.O. was depicted as very lazy, not ever offering meaningful help on the school floor, couldn't be found when he was wanted, wasn't right to be assigned to the school floor. Both the principal and I knew the C.O. to be the exact opposite of the way he was being characterized. I was sure, too, that other B.O.E. personnel would have disagreed with them. The principal and I looked at each other and shook our heads in disbelief over the villainy.

It might have been new to the principal, not to me. I had heard these two bad-mouthing other fellow C.O.'s. But they seemed to have reserved a special kind of bad-mouthing for the C.O. in question here, a native of Ghana. I had heard Rev, in that pit bull-like anger he was known to display, wish "he would go back to Africa where he came from," also saying, "Somebody should tell him he ain't in Africa no more; this is America."

It was known that the Ghanaian had passed the captain's test and soon would be promoted to that position. He had come all the way from West Africa, as they no doubt thought of it, and bettered them.

i certainly didn't think I was giving wrong advice to anyone, as Big Ak and Rev would accuse me of doing. I couldn't see myself doing this just to be at odds with them. When the business teacher, a Puerto Rican, came to me complaining that Rev was constantly harassing him. I asked him, as I had asked of the barbering teacher and the physical education teacher, both African-Americans, to explain how and why he was being harassed. One of his complaints was that Rev kept bothering him when he saw him smoking. I had previously listened to the complaints of the barbering teacher and the physical education teacher and agreed with them that they were being bothered unnecessarily, that they should cease running to me, stand up like men and open their mouths in defense of themselves. After all, the barbering teacher was a man in his late 50's, the physical education teacher around his mid-30's with an imposing stature: height of a basketball player and size of a football player. However, I didn't give the business teacher similar advice about his smoking. I reminded him that there was a "no smoking" order in the school that applied to all. His insistence on going against the order meant that he wanted to be "wrong and strong," and I couldn't agree with him. I certainly wished that it was a case in which he was right because I knew before this complaint that he had demonstrated that he wasn't afraid of Rev or Big Ak, which strengthened my position.

In the past, the outside set of double steel doors to the school were kept closed but not locked. This meant that teachers could enter but had to wait in the small vestibule for a C.O. to unlock the inside set of double steel doors to get into the school. Understandable because students were not supposed to have access to the outside. Soon after Ak took over the outside double doors were also "locked down." Not having these also locked down, he said, was a security risk. Not a single teacher could see the security risk he was talking about. How could anyone get pass those locked steel doors that prevented access to the actual school from the vestibule? Whenever the need to lock down the outside doors was questioned, Big Ak went into his boast about them never being left unlocked again. And so, in the most inclement weather conditions, we had to stay outside and get rained on, snowed on, sleeted on, and to shiver in the cold until it was convenient for a C.O. to come and unlock the doors. Teachers were all sure that this was Big Ak's way of demonstrating his power. Disgruntled as they were, they dared not disagree with Big Ak – not even the principal. Big Ak was obviously enjoying the begging-like manner they would approach him about putting an end to locking down the outside doors.

Of course, the disgruntled eventually came to me. As angry as I was about Ak's power-tripping act, I was reluctant to address the issue. Let the bastards suffer. For being such cowardly adults, they deserved it. Then, too, their parasite-like way of trying to get their union rep to go forward and solve things that displeased them, then fading away into the background and leaving me alone looking like the sole disgruntled one, was displeasing to me.

Eventually, I called a meeting and told them that their complaining among themselves would change nothing. I also admonished them for not making their dissatisfaction known on those occasions when Big Ak stood before them and, in response to their subdued mentioning of the problems they had to endure because of those doors being kept locked down, repeated that "security risk" bullshit of his in that boastful manner. They were being punished, I told them, not because not locking down the doors was a security risk but because of Big Ak's ego. I wanted to know, how could they allow Big Ak, a low-level C.O., treat them the way farmers treated migrant farm workers back in the 1950's?

I would address the issue in a letter, apply my signature to it, then other B.O.E. personnel should apply their signatures after mine. Once this was done, the letter would be given directly to the new deputy warden. Most agreed to sign the letter, but there were those who were still fearful of upsetting Big Ak and the D.O.C.

There were two sets of keys to these doors. One set in Big Ak's possession, the other set in Rev's . In the past one of the junior C.O.'s could get the keys and open the doors. With the coming of Big Ak this was changed. When he and his "pardner" were occupied, it wasn't often that junior C.O.'s would have access to the keys to unlock the doors. We had to wait until the two big guys were good and ready.

There wasn't an iota of doubt that Big Ak was a womanizer. He liked touching, hugging and smooching on the females. Being there to open the doors was his best chance of engaging in these practices. I can't say if such practices were appreciated by the females, but I can accuse some of them – White ones especially – of being prostitute-like in their conciliatory-like response to avail themselves of that "protection" so many of them seemed to have internalized that they needed while working in jail. There was also the popularity factor, and that of getting special treatment, the latter I believe, from experience, to be something many White females were culturally conditioned to believe they deserved over other women.

The females guilty of these accusations were also pathetic in their pretense of constantly running to Big Ak with their "problems" to be solved and to bad-mouth those among their colleagues with whom they didn't get along, or knowing that the working relationship they had with Big Ak and Rev fell into that category of no-love-lost. Big Ak and Rev were obviously exulting in the pseudo importance showered on them by these devoid enough of principles to see the merit in that B.O.E. philosophy of cover your own ass.

Communication from the deputy warden came sooner than was expected. He could see no logical reason why the outside doors leading to the vestibule couldn't be left unlocked. He had therefore instructed the two C.O.'s in charge of the school floor to return to the old policy of not locking down the doors to the vestibule.

Several days passed and the doors were still kept locked down. I had no doubt that Big Ak and Rev had received the dep's edict, for they both were huffing and puffing and bad-eyeing me more than usual whenever our paths crossed. And of course, those favorite comments of theirs had to be made in that threatening and sarcastic manner: "Union rep, hun? Dat don't mean nothin' around here." "Let's see how bein' union rep gonna help when we handcuff him and take him outta here." At least twice I was witness to a teacher going to Big Ak for help and since I was in hearing distance he quickly responded , "Why don't ya go to the union rep and see if he can do it for ya?"

There were times when I would send a student out the classroom to do me a little favor and I made sure I did it the right way by giving him a pass so if his and Big Ak's paths did cross he wouldn't be subject to his wrath. Once Big Ak saw him the student would quickly show his pass and simultaneously let it be known that "Brathwaite sent me to get a broom to sweep up the class...to get a garbage bag to put the stuff on the floor in...to give this to the principal...to go to the cleaning room to clean this off." The mentioning of my name would immediately arouse Big Ak's ire. He would issue the student with a mean warning about the physical havoc he was about to feel unleashed on him if he didn't get back in the classroom right away. "See if Brathwaite can save ya. He don't be givin' no orders around here."

Actually, I was told that the news about the letter to the dep had reached Big Ak and Rev almost as soon as we ended the meeting that day. Female staffers in particular – also a few males – who agreed with the plans, had signed the letter, and even commended me for having the courage to initiate it, still found it necessary to go to Big Ak and Rev gossiping about what had been discussed and planned. This manifested to the depth of the conviction that to avoid retributive actions against them, they were to always take care to be on the good side of Big Ak and Rev. Some of the signers had obviously gone to such length to protect themselves as making their signatures as illegible as could be. I was quite pleased that Mr. Timothy gave his full support to the idea, placing his signature immediately after mine, quite legibly signed.

One morning I saw the dep on the school floor and approached him and inquired as to why the doors to the vestibule were still kept locked down. He being so busy, I diplomatically suggested, the matter might have slipped his mind. Maybe he could find a little time to deal with it.

It had not slipped his mind. He had issued the order that the two doors were no longer to be kept locked down. Next morning, the doors were not locked down. B.O.E. personnel were elated to be able to walk into the vestibule, even if they were delayed there for some time before the doors to the school were unlocked. I got together with Mr. Timothy and we both wrote and signed a letter to the dep thanking him on behalf of B.O.E. personnel for his understanding.

Big Ak was soon coming up with other ideas that inconvenienced B.O.E. staffers and when they were questioned he came up with absurd reasons to show that they somehow had something to do with the outside doors no longer being locked down. So any new inconveniences they were now experiencing could be traced to Brathwaite getting the dep to keep the outside doors unlocked.

With such a grossly inflated ego, I knew it had to be hurtful to Big Ak to have initiated the locking down of the doors, feeling himself so smart to have discovered this "security risk" that would "never be reversed," only to be proven wrong.

Surprisingly, as time went by there was an obvious lull in that we-gonna-get-you-Brathwaite attitude. Of course, this didn't mean that if I found myself alone outside waiting to get into the school, or inside the school and the only one waiting to get out that they wouldn't still keep me waiting for an inordinately long period. Nor had they quite given up on trying to trace anything found and considered contraband to my classroom. They engaged in this practice even as they would shamelessly solicit my help while using the same classroom to have all kinds of personal projects produced, which, by the way, was an on-going practice of Board of Education and Department of Correction personnel alike.

Around the time when there were four Haitian teachers on the staff, it seemed clearer than ever that Big Ak and Rev had taken this little break from harassing me. Had I been fearful of them at all, I would have to say that with the Haitians around they will have brought me some relief. For whatever reasons, Big Ak and Rev – Rev in particular – habitually harassed the Haitians. I wasn't too sure that Big Ak had set out to do so, no more than that Rev always set out to join Big Ak against those he wanted to harass. What was obvious was that they had this dedication to the philosophy of "I got your back." It was a philosophy that was espoused among the ranks of the D.O.C. in general, but also trickled down in little ways as between Big Ak and Rev. And it was a very necessary show of unity for these two, as I didn't see it earlier. For instance, I knew that among his fellow C.O.'s Rev was very much distrusted as the consumate back stabber. But it took me quite some time to realize that among C.O.'s working on the school floor the resentment for Big Ak's control freak attitudes was as strong as the distrust of Rev. They truly needed each other, even if in their hearts, for each other, there was no love lost.

Two of the Haitians handled the situation well. The older one simply ignored Big Ak's and Rev's criticism or brushed them off with a disdainful wave of the hand and some very nasty looks. The younger one seemed to find so much fun in the way Big Ak and Rev acted that when they were engaged in harassing him, he would be looking them in the face wide-eyed and displaying a big grin on his face. Because he was artistically inclined he was often in my classroom and would often give me hilarious demonstrations of how Big Ak and Rev acted. It was clear that he saw them as two clowns, but mocking how Rev acted and talked was his specialty. He could have gotten a whole lot of laughs had he taken this routine on the stand-up comedy circuit. The other two Haitians were even younger. One had no answer to the harassment. His incessant complaining to me about Rev constantly harassing him told me how upset and dissatisfied it made him. I would advise him to "ignore those guys." But while he was ignoring them, he wasn't to do or say anything that would give them the feeling he was afraid of them. They had not that power to have him removed from the school as they often boasted. As to their admonishment of him for being late for classes, they tried to pull off that I-am-your-boss thing on other teachers. He didn't have to tell them as I did that it was none of their business if he didn't want to, but it really was none of their business because he wasn't employed by the D.O.C. Of course, though, their attitudes not withstanding, he should, as all of us should, consider it an obligation to get to school early.

Eventually he, the serious one and the comedian left Island Academy to teach at the school for adolescent females. But there was one left: Mr. Glades.

Even before the departure of the other three Haitians, it

was evident that Mr. Glades was the one taking the brunt of the pressure from Big Ak and Rev – from Rev especially. Mr. Glades was seldom free of their attacks. They called him a voodoo priest, mocked his Haitian accent, told him he was uncivilized, wanted to know from him "how you got to this country anyway? Are you one of them Boat People?" Told him they wished he would "go back to the bushes where you come from." Rev in particular subjected him to this kind of ridicule especially when White people were present.

Mr. Glades just didn't know how to handle the situation. It was a clear case of downright harassment. Realizing that it wasn't going to stop, I informed Mr. Glades on a few occasions of his rights to make a complaint against them, Rev in particular. His response was as always: a friendly grin on his face and the desire to know, "What did I do to these two guys? I never did them anything wrong at all."

Mr. Glades was a math teacher, acknowledged to be very good at it, and very conscientious. The guy would even go around the school looking for his most disruptive students who were cutting classes and demand that they were to come to class. Very few teachers in New York City did such. But he had this dedication to helping the youngsters to get their GED (General Education Diploma). Unfortunately, he couldn't get things under control. The students consistently gave him a hard time. Beyond an iota of doubt, they had more than enough encouragement from Rev and Big Ak to do so. And rather than criticize them for encouraging such irresponsibility, fellow teachers went along with their criticism of Mr. Glades. If a problem developed in his classroom, he could be sure that no help would be coming from Big Ak or Rev in the time necessary to quell it. The students were fully aware of this. And it wouldn't help even if they did turn up eventually. They simply exacerbated the problem, if consideration is given to what the students derive from seeing their teacher being personally ridiculed rather than being helped.

Mr. Glades was a relatively new teacher, still in his 20's. He really needed some help, not with the task of instructing but understanding the reality of the situation he was faced with, thereby making him more able to deal with the terrible behavioral problems in the school, that there would be no solution if he stuck rigidly to those solutions advocated by the B.O.E.

I reminded Mr. Glades on a few occasions that his students were inmates. Some of them were indeed hard-headed, bad-assed guys who were not at all concerned about his dedication to helping them. It was much more important to them to be seen as tough guys. Controlling him in his classroom was one of the foremost ways of achieving this. He wasn't to allow this to happen or he would never be able to turn it around. Then they would be sure to come to school every day with driving him over that proverbial wall a priority.

Mr. Glades was eventually thrown to the excess mill. Fortunately, he was soon "picked up" by another school on the outside. Big Ak and Rev thought it was ever so funny the way they had mistreated him. Some of the teachers laughed with them. I thought it was a damn shame that two adult Black men, both over six feet tall, could be so childish, and Uncle Tomish, thinking it enhanced their image as men being downright nasty to Mr. Glades. How could Big Ak especially be so shameless? The guy used to be posing as a Black Muslim, pretending to be full of Black pride. Did it have something to do with his reverting to Christianity? Or was it about that obsession he had with impressing that White culinary arts teacher? I felt he couldn't differentiate between somebody liking him or using him. I had no doubt that she running to him regularly with her complaints was all about that "Mandingo, please protect and treat me favorably" shit. Her general attitudes always did give me the impression that she harbored racist tendencies.

As for Rev, I was now judging him mostly because of his nasty attitudes towards Mr. Glades, not so much as they were toward me. For I felt sure that in his attitudes toward me there was a strong inferiority element, so much so, in fact, that there were times when he wanted to be mean to me but was reluctant to make his feelings known, as though he was afraid of not being able to cope with the reaction I might unleash against him. He obviously preferred to be mean to me in an underhanded manner. I had actually concluded that he was a natural born Uncle Tom. And I honestly do not write this for the sake of sensationalism, but in my mind this man was the perfect representation of the slave who saw the abolitionist John Brown and his followers on their way to the plantation to free the slaves and he called the slave master to kill the abolitionist who was on a mission to give him his freedom. I felt certain that Rev had a latent hatred for his blackness. I honestly saw him as a slave helping slave hunters to return runaway slaves to the plantations that owned them. I kept wondering why. He was a handsome fellow with an eye-catching thick mustache and a beautifully grown Afro. So his self-hate, I perceived, was because his skin was quite dark. And it couldn't be denied that in the human value system the blacker meant to be more stigmatized; not just from the white perspective, as is readily pointed out, but from the perspective of others – including even Black people.

Well, Big Ak and Rev got that proverbial "feather in the hat" for getting Mr. Glades sent to the excess mill, though there could be no doubt that they would have felt they had received many more feathers in their hats had I been the one. I mention them along with the act in spite of the fact that it was up to the principal to do this. And I had no doubt whatever that Mr. Timothy, good principal though he was, felt he had to excess Mr. Glades to please Big Ak and Rev, Big Ak especially, even though he wasn't the one who initiated the be-nasty to Mr. Glades onslaught, nor was he the one who pursued it most. Or if he did, he gave the task to Rev, as many suspected he did at times while he faded into the background to appear as if he wasn't such a bad guy after all.

As the union rep, ignoring possible retributions for doing so, I hinted strongly to Mr. Timothy why I thought he let Mr. Glades go.

For a long time after Mr. Glades was let go, Big Ak and Rev kept up their laughter and joking about what had happened to him. Apparently they thought it proved that they had the power they coveted. They would say to me, "See what happen to your Haitian buddy? How come the union rep couldn't help him?" I would tell them, "Bear in mind that I am not Glades. I know my rights and that's why you two can't scare me." I would tell them, furthermore, that it mattered not how well they sometimes played that wolf-in-sheep's-clothing game with me, I knew how badly they wanted to "do in" Brathwaite. I wasn't too sure if they knew that the depth of my distrust for them was such that I would never lower my guard as far as they were concerned.

< 13 >

The Religious and the Sexual In Jailhouse Jeopardy

Mr. Timothy had been principal of Island Academy for over two years when we returned for a new school year to learn that he no longer held that position. It was quite a surprise to all since it seemed that he had settled himself into the position quite well and with much enthusiasm. What was perhaps more surprising to all was the person who was installed as the new principal: Mr. Hines; the same fellow who had occupied the position just before the coming of Mr. Timothy.

This time around, Mr. Hines seemed to have found a new enthusiasm.

Giving the situation a retrospective look now, it certainly didn't seem like it, but in actuality, that day I came to Island Academy was quite a few years in the past. In those years I had seen a lot, much of which caused me to formulate some very strong opinions, and having such a belief in their validity to challenge those considered experts on these issues to prove otherwise.

I have already made mention to the obvious intent and dedication of many female students to blatantly flaunt their sexuality, the skin-tight clothes worn to school by them being indicative of this. Of course, because of their mostly oversized jail-issued clothes, adolescent girls in jail couldn't dress in this manner. Perhaps more disgusting were the attempts made by some female Board of Education staffers to emulate this dress code and come to jail to interact with 16 to 18-year-old males. Some of these females were old enough to be the mothers of the adolescent males.

They wore mini-skirts that constantly slid up their thighs, forcing them to constantly pull them back down, as if they were unaware that keeping what they pretended to struggle to not have exposed could have been easily avoided by wearing skirts not as short or as tight. There was also the struggle to not let too much cleavage show, as if all the dresses and tops in the stores were all low cut around the shoulders and breasts areas. And of course, there were those spandex-type slacks, designed to stick to the backside and front part of the crotch area.

Simultaneous with the struggle to not let these things show – supposedly – there was the deceptive posturing to make a sexual statement without incurring the personal embarrassment it would if seen as being consciously done.

Anyone coming to Island Academy found out quite soon how very important things having to do with sex were to these adolescents. There could have been no doubt that these women were fully aware of how much they were being eye-raped daily as a result of the way they dressed and consciously postured to convey sexual statements.

Undoubtedly, they craved the attention, and harboring no less lechery than that normally attributed to men trying to impress women with their supposedly vibrant masculinity.

Maybe these women were not getting the male attention they needed in their lives. Maybe they wanted to convince themselves that that they still had what it took for males to find them appealing, that they were still sexy. And if their needs were not being satisfied under normal circumstances, then there was another way: appealing to the most vulnerable, those males sexually hot but locked away from the chance of cooling down their heat, making women not only old enough to be their mothers, but who under normal circumstances they wouldn't have found sexually appealing, quite appealing under the prevailing deprived circumstances.

I can't say if it was true or false, but it was rumored about three or four of these staffers that they had actually went all the way with adolescents, meeting them after their release, taking care of and having relationships with them.

I must say that some of these youngsters, once in jail, took to pumping iron daily, and despite all their complaints about the "bad jail food," managed to develop muscular bodies. And it is true that I have heard female staffers speak of how "good" they looked in a tone undoubtedly sexual.

As stated earlier, generally speaking, these youngsters were quite forward. "No shame in my game" was a popular motto of theirs. They went after what they wanted, what they believed they could get, with relentless pursuit.

Of course, I wouldn't know of all the things that sexually endears a female to a male. I do believe, though, that possessing a muscular, healthy-looking body helps significantly, the same as a female with a curvaceous body attracts the attention of males. I must also say that because of my cultural upbringing, my mind wasn't open to the idea of women in their late 20's and over having this kind of infatuation with teenage males. Furthermore, I felt, even if they possessed muscles that belied their age but habitually, and openly, engaged in the immature act of trying to out-fart each other, as was the habit of these youngsters, it would negate this infatuation. It didn't. I believed that if the youngsters here were females and the adults males – a situation which has always been more readily met with societal approval – the infatuation will have dissipated in the face of such immature displays.

I would be remised not to mention that age differences notwithstanding, it was common knowledge that it wasn't unusual for women to develop this infatuation for men in jail. It baffled many people that some of the most beautiful women actually launched searches to get themselves "hooked up" with men in jail. Often times, these men were career criminals, poorly educated, with no skills, no positive aspirations, but with the entrenched belief in their ability to bullshit their way into getting what they wanted.

At this stage, I was no longer baffled by this situation. Obviously, many of these women saw these men as being down-and-out, just the kind they would be able to control once they were out of jail, not knowing that at the root of their problems were two mountainous characteristics that got them where they were and kept them returning there: their unwavering conviction that they knew everything; their total unwillingness to ever listen to anyone.

In fact, I now felt justified in blaming these women partly for contributing to the recidivist mentality of these men. Many of these men had an element of disregard for responsibility, meaning that they were not concerned, for example, that wives and grandmothers were saddled with taking care of their children while they kept themselves constantly "locked down" in jail. Additionally, all the things they wanted – and demanded – to satisfy their demanding jail subculture were supplied to them by their women. The growing acceptance of conjugal visits also contributed to their disregard for outside responsibilities. How then were prisoners with these characteristics, and benefiting from the new relaxed rules and regulations, to feel about that absolute need that "I really gotta get the hell outta here?"

Would these prisoners not be more dedicated to getting

out – and staying out – of jail if their women were not so eager to sometimes jump on buses and drive hundreds of miles to visit and prove their love for their imprisoned men? Would the same not be true if these women would stop sending them the special brand of expensive sneakers they craved for – in jail of all places? And how about having to keep an adequate amount of money in their commissary accounts and accepting financial responsibility for the numerous phone calls they habitually made?

When credible surveys and television documentaries prove that free men seldom do the same for women who are locked down, how can credence for the above be denied?

Another act I observed among female staffers that I saw as out of place was the peddling of Christianity to the youngsters, with no regard for the law of "separation of church and state," disallowing this act in public schools. It can't be said that Black females were the ones primarily responsible for this act, for it seemed they were the only females who engaged in this act. In fact, I can't honestly implicate even a single White female, though maybe one White male and two or three Black males.

From my experience, I concluded that the idea of having religion as an integral part of the public school system had tremendous support. From observing the women in question here and those at other schools who exhibited the same kind of religious zealotry, most labeling themselves "Born Again Christians," my support of such could never be. For I was left with much doubt about their lack of wisdom to see the havoc on the school system it would cause. In the first place, Christianity wouldn't be the only religion to be accommodated. Even if it were the only one, within it there are so many different denominations with so many differing views to ensure never-ending disagreements, such as is the case with the numerous churches located on every street corner and elsewhere. The differences among these can be so many to create doubts about them being the same religion and worshipping the same God. And there can be no questioning the fact that the rigidity pertaining to religious ideas and beliefs is more unshakeable and unyielding that ideas pertaining to most other things.

I saw from the attitude of the women mentioned here that they seemed more concerned with "saving" the adolescents than educating them. Once they were saved everything else in their lives would automatically straighten up and go right.

It's a historical fact that people who are very religious are known to show very little tolerance for those who don't share their religious views. So I need not try to substantiate this by pointing out the nasty attitudes directed at me by the religious zealots I have mentioned here, not because I was a bad human being, but no matter how exemplary my human qualities, I just couldn't be that good a human being I showed myself to be because I didn't share in their religious obsession. I should at least be one of the super-religious hypocrites they knew and therefore be seen by them as not such a bad heathen.

All things considered, with the reversal of separation of church and state, how many good teachers would be hounded out of the school system for not having the Christian views deemed absolutely necessary for the making of a good human being. I was of no doubt that in this case these women would have had me driven from Island Academy.

I had no doubt, either, that I had a much better tolerance for views different from mine than they did. They violated the rules and regulations pertaining to religion in the schools by espousing their religious views in the school in different ways. I could have filed a grievance against them doing so, but I didn't.

I believed that school were meant to educate youngsters, not influence them about religion. Considering my propensity for tolerance, I could even see myself not being in full support of separation of church and state if religious teachings were not available to people in vast numbers. But take the Black communities, for instance, there are churches everywhere. What logical reason could there be for turning schools into churches? Suffice it to say, if youngsters are not exposed to enough Christian teachings in their communities, it would have to be because the very parents who are so high on Christianity are faced with that problem that is increasingly plaguing America: no control over their children; hence, by the time they reach age 13 they can't be made to go to church, as if the Fifth Commandment, "Children, obey your parents," had been changed to "Parents, obey your children." And as going to school at this age is still enforced, let the schools serve as partial churches. The youngsters would then have their away-from-school time free to pursue their obsession with playing basketball, hanging out, looking at sex and violence through videos, television and computer.

I frequently heard the complaint from Black females that "good men are so hard to find." As frequently heard was the lamenting over the phenomenal rise of single parent households, mothers raising children without fathers. I was among those who used to agree with the former and blame the latter on the Black male. In recent years, however, I started to adopt the opinion the "poor Black woman" wasn't that innocent as far as these two issues were concerned. For I was now quite aware that there were so many Black women just like the Christian zealots I was around at Island Academy. A man could have all the other qualities they wished for in a man, but if he wasn't fully committed to being "saved" and seeing Jesus of Nazareth forever in every nook and cranny of their existence, then there would be zero change to that idea of theirs that "good men are hard to find."

Among the zealot Christian Black women in question here – as in the case of those similar that I met at other schools and in college classrooms, not to mention the many outside the education arena – they were all either separated, divorced, single, and had no man at all. I therefore understood that joke-fact heard from some Black men: You look into all those Black churches and what do you see? A male pastor preaching to a congregation about the greatness and perfection of a Jewish man. And the congregation is made up of just a few males and an overwhelming number of females singing, clapping, dancing and jumping for joy.

When these women would angrily castigate me for being "an atheist" and act as though I should be crucified, I would no longer challenge them on the falsehood. However, I would challenge them about the anger and violence more evident in their attitudes than in other peoples' far less religious.

They would leave me with no wonder at all as to why in the late 1970's a large group of Black folk from the United States – mostly female – followed their White Christian mentor, Jim Jones, to Guyana and when exhorted by him to drink cyanide to prove the depth of their religiosity and commitment to their leader, they obeyed and poisoned themselves by the hundreds. Not many years later, we saw, though on a lesser scale, many Blacks committing themselves to suicidal actions at Waco, Texas, under the orders of their White religious leader David Koresh.

I would tell these Black women that I had no doubt that they would engage in the same act under similar circumstances.

Undoubtedly, it will be labeled as Black racism, absurd as it will be, but with the nasty racism America subjects Black people to – only in a more covert manner today – what manner of Black people would follow a White religious leader and commit suicide to prove their dedication to his leadership? Hopefully only those ones who in increasing numbers flock to the more affluent-looking churches with White pastors.

Conventional wisdom answers very negatively. But it is said that in everything bad there can be found something good. What if there were more cases like Jim Jones'? Would they not help in the curtailing of the growth of an obvious weak mentality among Blacks? Wouldn't it be especially harmful to the growth of Blacks to have this mentality instilled in the minds of young Blacks?

< 14 >

Some of the Weird Actors of Jailhouse Jeopardy

I couldn't help it that at times my minds would go roaming back to the 1970's and my watching a poignant movie titled *The Education of Sonny Carson,* specifically that part with the youngsters in the gangs, all heading down Negative Street. Yet they paused for a while to actually speak of a future they envisioned for themselves on Positive Street, so positively detailed but the reality of which seemed highly unlikely. I thought how at the time there wasn't the faintest vision in my mind of my daily involvement with such youngsters starting only a few short years later.

In the case of *Sonny Carson,* the youngsters were limited to Blacks in gangs. Obviously, then, I couldn't possibly have envisioned my close involvement with so many more youngsters of so many different racial groups, of so many different nationalities, with such diverse cultural attitudes, some of whom could hardly speak English, some who couldn't, but most of whom held on to the values from the fast-lane of life.

Journey Through Jailhouse Jeopardy   219

As afore-stated, there was a lot more to working with these youngsters besides dispensing traditional education. This was especially so in the case of a teacher who challenged them in such a way that in spite of their I-know-what's-to-know attitude, they yet felt compelled at times to seek out this teacher to share their thoughts with, to solicit his opinions on issues, sometimes simply to be around, or as in their words, "to chill out with." As a result, such a teacher got to observe and learn so much about them. I was a teacher that fell into this category.

During the summer vacation I was able to reflect on my years at Island Academy, an aspect of this reflection being the idiosyncrasies of individual students, some too "weird" to ever escape my memory.

By "weird" I do not necessarily mean to imply bad as much as out of the ordinary; sometimes so much out of the ordinary to make the teacher want to laugh hysterically, but forcing himself not to, knowing of the likelihood of it encouraging the continuation of the "weird" behavior. And though it will not be easy to transfer into writing these idiosyncrasies with the same emotions with which they were played out, I think it is still worth it to try to capture as much as the original flavor as possible. I will also use the funny names they were given and accepted while in jail, even though I habitually called all students by their surnames. And my giving of only one to three examples of the students chosen is not an indication that these were their only "weird" acts but rather a few of the many so similar, or that they engaged in this act consistently.

Hale House Baby was a 17-year-old African-American from Harlem. He was saddled with this name because his fellow inmates, regarding him as extraordinarily weird, concluded that he was one of those kids born to drug addicted mothers and given up to Harlem's Hale House to be raised there.

He always selected a seat apart from all others. And even as he did his first chore in the class, writing down the safety rules, he started what was to be his humorous habit:

220   Some of the Weird Actors of Jailhouse Jeopardy

conversing with himself; questioning and answering himself; laughing to himself; all of which were accompanied by hands, head and facial gestures. There was no doubt that he liked the hands-on activities of the graphic arts class. He was always busy and always tried to do things to the best of his ability. He was reluctant to solicit the teacher's help. It wasn't unusual for him to start laughing to himself to this conversation: "Serves him right. He was nothin' but a punk thinin' he was a man. I didn't tell him to be foolin' around wit' no gun. The nigga shot his own self; I swear on my mother's grave it wan't me. So why am I locked down just 'cause dat punk shot himself?"

Very often he would grab up his folder and loudly issue the frustrated warning: "I'm tearing all this work up and getting' outta this class 'cause the teacher he don't 'preciate all this work I do in here." He was given a lot of help, even though he insisted on not asking for it. And I knew for sure that he had no intention of leaving the class. He wasn't comfortable anywhere else. As I had observed his ways, so had he mine. In time, he had other students laughing hysterically at how he had learned to mimic me to perfection. The moment he made his rush into the classroom he started issuing the students with my regular orders: "Everybody take a seat." "Your folders will be given to you." "Don't touch any equipment that didn't touch you." "Don't operate any of the equipment without my permission." "No cursing in the classroom." And the others.

The students constantly told me about him, "Mister Brathwaite, dat boy is the weirdest nigga in the dorm. He sets fire to your socks when you fall asleep. He would respond, "Nigga, I didn't tell you to sleep in yo' socks. Besides, you should wash them smelly things sometimes."

There was something else about Hale House that made his fellow students laugh. He would often tell himself, "See, these niggas think I'm like them, that I'm a criminal too. But I'm gonna be a lawyer and a judge." A desire no doubt precipitated by his belief that White judges were in the habit of sending Black people to jail for no good reason. I would tell him that if he was really serious about it, he could actually succeed. At his age his records were sealed.

On a day soon after Hale House came to the class I sat in a chair in which one of the students must have deliberately smeared with ink, a common malicious act they usually engaged in. It was usually done against other students for fun. But this day when it happened to the teacher they thought it was so much funnier. Hale house never let go of that day. He would frequently come close to me and exclaim in a shocking manner, "Hey, teacher, there's ink all over your pants." Somehow he always caught me off guard, sending me jumping to check. That the practical joke had worked once again would send him and the other students into wild laughter. "See what I told y'all," he would announce victoriously, "as tough as he thinks he is, I can still make him jump whenever I want to" He didn't play such a practical joke on Mr. Martin, but he never did let up on his laughter when aiming this comment at him: "Brathwaite is the teacher in here, not him. I don't want him to help me wit' nothin' 'cause he ain't no kinda teacher at all. Always be acting like he knows what he's doing when he don't know no more 'bout what he be tryin' to do from a great big hole in the wall."

One thing we both thought was very unusual about Hale House was that he was in the midst of the constant use of profanity, got into shouting matches with fellow students, but never used curse words. Rather, whenever student started with the profanity, he would immediately mimic me: "Do you have to curse so much? Do you want me to get you a dictionary so you can improve your vocabulary?"

Porky Boy was a 16-year-old New York Puerto Rican (Nuyorican), over six feet tall and over 200 hundred pounds. He had a problem from the moment he came to the writing class. The students were unanimous in their demand that I wasn't to let him register for the class because he was "too childish." He insisted on his right to join the class. Even if I could refuse to register him, he did himself the big favor of telling me, "Man, you gotta let me come to this class. I'm the best writer in this school. I wanna be writing for dat paper you be making in here."

It turned out that he really liked writing, was especially good with short stories. He was also every bit as childish as the students said he was. But he was so dedicated to writing that it would have taken a tremendous display of shortcomings for me to get rid of him from the class. There were not many students who actually liked to read and write. It obviously didn't take him long to find out that I needed him, so the childish attitudes he brought to the class with him he maintained them. And of course, immature acting as some of his fellow students were, they kept insisting that I should "get rid of the nigga," as he insisted on his right to stay " 'cause ya all niggas be not owning this classroom. And ya all had better leave me alone or I'm gonna write some really nasty shit 'bout ya all when I write my best selling book."

Part of Porky Boy's immaturity was evident in his ever-present need for instant gratification. He always had to have me there to discuss something "now." Forget about everybody else. And so it was that day at the end of the two periods when I was worn out and looked forward to having a few minutes rest but he had this "masterpiece" he wanted me to read – "now." He pulled up a chair to my desk with the happy and eager anticipation of me reading and discussing his "masterpiece" all over his face. I told him how worn out I was, that when I was so worn out I couldn't "get into" the story, one hundred percent pure truth. The best thing to do was to leave the story with me so I could take it home, go over it there, correct it and bring it back next day ready to be discussed during the first period when I didn't even have a class. He pleaded with me to "please read it and see how funny it is." No matter how much I told him about being too worn out to do so, he didn't want to hear this. When it seemed to him that he really wasn't going to get his way this time, his pleading turned to demanding. He jumped up angrily and threw the sheets of paper down on the desk, slamming down on the desk with his fists.

"So you said you ain't gonna read it now. Well you lemme tell you something, you so-call teacher, you readin' my shit right now. The tax payers be payin' yo' gawddamn salary to do this shit, and here you are talkin' 'bout you worn out. Betcha you don't be worn out taking dat big fat check to the bank. Okay, then, now that I made my point, let's get to it – now." And he sat back down.

Calling him by his surname, I told him, "I don't ever swear when I'm addressing you and you're not to swear when you're addressing me. Anyway, leave the story there and get out of my face. We will discuss it tomorrow."

He jumped back up. This time he adopted a threatening pugilistic stand. "Yo, man! I told you that you gonna read my story now. So what's it gonna be? You gonna read it or do I have to knock your lazy ass out?"

I leaned back in my chair and took a large can of iced tea from my bag. He immediately rushed to the door. "Goodbye. Have a good day," I told him.

"Mista Brathwaite, what goodbye you talkin' bout, man? I ain't goin' nowhere. I'm locking the door so me and you can eat dat ham sandwich I just saw hiding there in your bag and drink dat Mucho Macho drink without these greedy inmates come rushing in here to blow up my spot – wanting some too." And with that, he already had the door locked and was at the sink washing one of the green plastic inmates' cups they usually left everywhere. He came with the cup. "It's months now I've been in here locked down and dying for a drink of Mucho Macho. My mom's always gave it to us."

"Who told you that you're getting any? Even if I had ham sandwich and Mucho Macho, I wouldn't give you any."

"Aw, come on, Mista Brathwaite, You gots to gimme some o' dat shit. How you gonna tell me dat you get New York food every day and want to eat it and don't share it wit' a nigga who been locked down in jail for almost six months, eating dat nasty jail food?"

"Well, first of all, I'm not supposed to feed the inmates."

"So who's gonna know that you took care of me? This is on the down-low between me and you – unless you gonna be snitchin' 'bout it. I sure won't."

"But aren't you the tough guy who was just about to put a hurtin' on me?"

"Aw, Mista Brathwaite, ain't you been knowin' me long enough to know dat I was just punkin' out? Damn, why you wanna go taking me serious? Ain't nobody else does."

"Well, I still can't give you any because you said you want some Mucho Macho and a piece of ham sandwich." I showed him the can and the sandwich and told him, " See, this drink is Mucho Mango; I've never heard of that drink you said your mother raised you on. And I don't eat ham; I have a turkey sandwich."

"Aw, Mister Brathwaite, I forgot the name, so what? Mucho whatever it's called, I don't care. Just gimme mine's. And ya know what, I don't eat ham, either. You must be one o' them Muslims, right? Me too."

I watched him in the corner where I had sent him to be out of sight as he consumed the iced tea and sandwich with a ravenous delight. I couldn't help but laugh at this overgrown kid – a boy in a man's body – who when he was through eating and drinking, left his story on my desk because he was too obsessed with trying to bribe me into bringing "a ham sandwich with lettuce and cheese" into jail for him.

I think Caveman was also a Nuyorican. He was in the writing class and was good at writing, though not dedicated to doing it. For a youngster not yet 18, he had very heavy facial hair growth. When he didn't shave for a few days the stubs of his beard gave him a grizzly appearance. He also had thick bushy eyebrows. He was in the habit of somehow finding old blankets, sheets and towels and making every attempt to hang them up in a corner of the classroom to get behind them and sleep. I was told that he did the same around his bunk in the dorm to cut himself off from his fellow inmates. And why his face was always adorned with that smile many would call sinister, I couldn't say. However, I thought I knew why that name Caveman was given to him.

Though Caveman was a good writer and also a potentially good artist, he showed little motivation in the class. But it must be said of him that when he was pushed, unlike some other classroom sleepers who would get into nasty moods, he would actually get himself involved. Other than showing facial dissatisfaction, he accepted it whenever I dismantled his makeshift bedroom. Unlike Porky Boy whose writing was generally inclined toward humor, Caveman's was generally inclined toward violence as were his cartoon drawings

He was around when a Christmas (holiday season) issue of the Academy News was being worked on. I kept him busy with art for the issue. But he also had a Christmas story he wanted published. For this issue most students wrote articles, poems and jokes pertaining to the holidays, expressing their New Year's resolutions, especially their big, positive plans for the future. The honor of designing the cover for this issue went to Caveman. As was the case with all others contributing to the publication and were duly credited with their names printed in it, he was so eager to see the finished product so he could send home copies to family, girlfriends and other friends.

I told Caveman that his cover idea – nicely drawn even in the rough – of a man disguised as Santa Claus, hiding behind Christmas trees and shooting at unsuspecting community residents out Christmas shopping with a rifle and packing a pistol under his red suit was not what my idea of what the cover should be. He couldn't understand the reason for my disapproval. "Damn, Brathwaite, why can't you ever learn to lighten up a bit sometimes? Get real, man. Whole lotta people nowadays ain't into dat dumb shit 'bout Santa Claus and reindeers like back in the old days when you was a kid." Not long after, he presented me with his story. It was nothing more than his intended cover drawing now expressed in words: A disgruntled man, easily identified as Caveman, positions himself in hidden spots on a Christmas day and uses a high powered rifle to shoot at people on the block. At the end of the day, not satisfied that he had spread enough terror, he tells himself dejectedly, "It's a long time to wait, but they'll hear from me again next Christmas."

Again, Caveman couldn't understand why I had problems with his story. After we had spent some time going over it, and his adamant refusal to consider changes, while looking at me with that "sinister" smile adorning his face, I said to him in a tone of clear concern," Man, are you sure you're alright?" He assured me that he was. "You know the school has a psychologist, right? Why don't you let me arrange for you to sit down with her and have a little talk?"

"Brathwaite, man," he said angrily, "just what me and dat woman gonna talk about? I know that lady. Keep her away from me. The bitch is crazy. See, man, there be a whole lotta people callin' me crazy when they be the ones who're really crazy. Anyway, you don't have to put me in no school paper. I'm gonna be a big cartoonist wit' my stuff appearin' in the New York News...the Post...and a whole lotta others papers. I don't have to be published in no magazine dat's done in jail...and don't pay nothing at that."

He not only ended up designing a different and beautiful cover, and having his story – with a few little changes – published, but his attitude toward the finished product was so enthusiastic, I joked with him, "When your work starts appearing in the big-time papers they'll need the space shuttle to get you off cloud nine. Just don't forget to let people know who gave you your start. And by the way, you better change your ways if you really want to make it. When you get out of Rikers don't go out there shooting another youngster because he took over your drug-dealing 'spot.' "

There was Bam-Bam, so named because his peers thought he looked and acted so much like the newspaper boy cartoon character. He finally got his program changed to be in my graphic arts class for two periods in the morning. Like so many students, once there for a while, he intended to somehow extend these periods. It might not be so difficult because he never tried to play tough guy with the teacher, showed much liking for the hands-on program, and was willing to help out. I usually gave such students a break.

That happy, unassuming kind of grin he came to the class with remained on his face. There was a side to this grin that everyone found quite funny: that space from where two front teeth were missing.

I didn't consider it a character change when he threw a sudden temper tantrum that day the newspaper – now with a different design and renamed Academy Journal because I, like most others, had long believed it looked a bit too "magazinish" to be called a newspaper – was distributed. As eager as he was to see it with his poems and name in it, the one-letter spelling error in his name upset him. He being Hispanic and having one of those Spanish names where the letter "o" or "a" made the difference of identifying one as either male or female was the problem. Where there should have been an "o" in his name there was an "a" instead

"Oh my gawd! Look what this man done did!" part of his vociferous complaining went. "imagine, my mother born me a boy and all my seventeen years I was a male. And just like dat, he turned me into a girl. I ain't no bitch. Everybody take a look at this," he announced as he pulled his pants down. I warned him against "stripping" in my classroom and the consequences if he didn't pull his pants back up immediately. "Well, I just wanted everybody to see that I still have my tool, dat I ain't went through no sex change operation. Here I am waiting for this magazine to come out so I can mail it home and let people see my poems and now I can't. I don't want people to be thinking that I'm one of these guys who come to jail and turn into a faggot. That's what they'll be thinkin' when they see I now have a girl's name."

Once he had his peers laughing, he wasn't about to stop his complaining. And I must confess that even though I knew he was disappointed over the little typographical error that did the big thing of changing his gender identification, there was much humor in his complaining. To bring the curtains down on his stage, I told him of my willingness to correct and reprint as many of that page on which his poems and name appeared as the number of copies of the publication he wanted to mail out, remove the staples from that number of copies and replace the page of error with the corrected ones.

The problem was solved – for a while. Obviously, Bam-Bam enjoyed the attention he was getting. He soon got into the habit of making his lust over the school's beautiful young African-American psychologist a classroom topic. The topic always included his desire to possess her sexually. His details and displays became more graphic with the increased appreciation that was being shown by his peers. I issued a serious warning to him: he was to end his show in the classroom or I would end his presence in the classroom. He wasn't willing to end his show. My demand that he immediately vacate the classroom was made in such a no-nonsense way that he was soon out in the hallway.

"And don't you show your face in this class again," I told him, "until you come with a letter of apology. And I'll know if it's genuine, so don't try playing any games with me."

For maybe three days, whenever the classroom door was opened, I would see Bam-Bam looking in. I knew how badly he wanted to return. One morning when my students were late in coming to class, there he was at the open door looking in. Once our eyes met he started uttering those defiant and critical statements he had been uttering whenever he saw me since his ouster:

"Write you a letter of apology? You gots to be crazy. Not even my father would have the nerves to come telling me what I have to do and what I can't do. Just look at his class. No students. He threw me outta my class not knowing these inmates be my homies and they would stand up for me. Damn, his own students don't like him. Serves him right. I was the only one who liked him, now he don't have no friend at all."

He looked down the hallway and saw one of his Hispanic homeboys. He called him over as if calling him to an emergency situation. "We got the word on him, right?" he said to his homeboy, pointing the accusing finger at me. His homeboy was at loss as to what he was talking about. "What word?" he wanted to know. "What about?"

"What you mean by 'what word,' man? Don't pretend you don't know dat the word is out on him, dat he be damn prejudice 'genst us Hispanics."

"Oh dat! Yeah right!," his homeboy gave his support. "The word been out on him for a long time 'bout dat. He be a teacher and shouldn't be getting' into shit like dat. We can get him fired."

Obviously, Bam-Bam realized that his South Bronx tactics were not helping in any way to improve his situation. He came to me first period next morning when I had no class and handed me a sealed envelope, displaying that funny grin on his face. I opened the envelope as soon as he was gone. I took one look at the letter and actually laughed out aloud. It started, "Dear Mr. Brathwaite, Dear Sir, Sir, this is my apology for dissing you and your class..." He went on to write that I was the best teacher in the school, that my class was the "onliest" class he liked. After lavishing me with more praise, he ended even more humorously: "Mr. Brathwaite, Sir, my very best friend, I am yours truly (he used his real name), the best friend you ever had."

I had to show the letter to his social worker Miss Graemes. She laughed hysterically.

Bam-Bam returned to the class and went back to acting the way he did initially. He pleaded with me to write a letter to his employers explaining that he was sorry for disappointing them by getting locked up and not being able to come to work, that he hoped they would rehire him when he was released. Not long after I got a letter from his employers telling me what a good worker he was and assuring me that he would be rehired.

One day when the students had left and he remained to clean up the classroom, I was playing a 90-minute tape of 1960's soul music. He told me several times how that "old school music was so good" and wanted to know where he could buy it when he went home. I knew he couldn't buy a tape with all those songs because I had taped them from various sources. Then came the day he would be released overnight and he came to me at the end of the day to say goodbye. I shook his hand, wished him the best, then said to him, "Here, these are yours. The letter from your employers, and a copy of that tape of old school music you like so much."

I saw the water in Bam-Bam's eyes. "Mister Brathwaite, I really hope we run into each other some time. But even if we don't, I will never forget you."

Bandit was a 17-year-old heavyweight, African-American, over six feet tall and over 200 pounds. He certainly looked capable of giving a good account of himself if he had to tangle with Mike Tyson, though rather than boxing ambition his ambition was to be a mean wrestler. Rather than calling him Bandit, they might have called him Quiet Storm, for he said very little. But there was always that you-better-keep-to-hell-away-from-me look on his face. The only thing that went against his quiet demeanor, for which I had to admonish him severely, was that occasionally he had to have one of his peers in a headlock or some other wrestling hold from which none could escape.

I think that he was stuck with the name Bandit because of the way he carried himself. Of course, most inmates looked a bit off because of their ill-fitting prison clothes. But Bandit wore his clothes so carelessly that he looked more inmate than the other inmates. And while their footwear was generally sneakers, Bandit consistently wore big boots without laces, tongues hanging out, and looking old. Without seeing him, you knew when he was up and about because of his boots pounding on the floor.

True, he wasn't one for engaging in conversation with the crowd. But when he found himself alone with me, as he often set the situation up, he enjoyed telling me dramatic stories of his life – mostly problematic. He always had letters from girlfriends he wanted me to read. Since breaking up with him was often an issue discussed in these letters, he would insist on hearing my opinion, in spite of the fact he had already planned physical harm against the girls concerned when he was released. There were also the problems he had at home before he was incarcerated that still were confronting him even now that he was in jail. And there were the neighbors who didn't like him, who always gave him a hard time, with whom he was sure he would still be "pissed off" when he got "back to the 'hood." There was also the big problem of his peers who were "jealous" of him. They would still be waiting to "get even" with him and he "wasn't gonna take no shit from them niggas."

He told me, laughing aloud, as he did his usual strutting around and making numerous hand gestures, how he used to let air out of tires, put holes in them, break off antennae when people got him mad. And there were times when he would pick up trash cans from one side of the street and hurl them over to the other side or dump them in the middle of the street. One night he hurled a trash can right in front of a car that was coming down the street. The driver was "a grouch who couldn't take a joke" so he backed up and "took a shot" at him.

One day Bandit came to me in an unusually happy mood. "Brathwaite, man, you gotta read this letter from one of my homeboys." I read the letter after he pleaded with me to because by now he knew I no longer wanted to commit myself to the chore. In any case, his homeboy was complaining about "how boring" the 'hood had become in the months he was in jail as a result of the easing up on the thuggish deeds he had credited himself with initiating. When I was through reading the letter Bandit had not yet contained his laughter. He had interpreted his homeboy's "boring 'hood" complaint as representing the general sentiment of the neighborhood having missed him so much.

"See, Brathwaite, ya don't miss the water till the well runs dry. When they had me around they didn't want me. Now I ain't there they miss me. Serves 'em right. They didn't know how to appreciate all the fun they used to get from me. The bastards are now bored to death."

Once again, I tried to show Bandit the other side to the story. Once against, he couldn't accept it that I was trying to correct him. And though he would be back again to get my opinion, he had to let it be known again, as he stormed off expressing his disappointment in me: "Oh, Brathwaite, man, you don't ever see it my way 'cause you old niggas don't know how to lighten up a little and try to understand kids."

Billz was a 17-year-old little fellow from Brooklyn. He had a cantankerous streak in him that was well known to teachers. Even his peers would often wonder aloud, "Damn, what's wit' dat nigga?" There was, however, this ironic twist to Billz: he was independent and motivated and if you knew how to bring out these characteristics in him, his cantankerous streak could be subdued.

    He was programmed to my second and third period graphic arts classes. It wasn't long before he was trying to extend his time in the class to the fourth period. Failing this, he wanted to start first period. Failing this also, he would be the very first student at the door for second period. If he didn't get immediate entry, if he wasn't given his folder as soon as he entered, if he didn't get undivided attention, his cantankerous streak would accelerate to a high without any delay. And if through his too-hurried look through his folder he thought that one of his projects was taken by one of his peers, his treats of physical harm to whoever the culprit was were frightening.

    I made it a habit of going to Billz' first period class about 10 minutes before it would end and he would be rushing to second period with me. It wasn't unusual that I would have to ask his teacher to please wake him form his sound sleep so I may have a few words with him. When I first started this he would come to me wearing a look of dissatisfaction and wanting to know, "What now? What did I do wrong? I ain't done nothing."

    "That's right," I would tell him. "You didn't do a thing wrong – not yet. But in a few minutes you will be coming to my class and I want to remind you not to bring your bad attitude with you. I'm in no mood for it today. Just remember that you're not the only student in the class."

    Sometimes he tried to wage an argument in his defense.

Sometimes he simply settled for those facial contortions which conveyed his resentment as much as his verbal anger would have. Then when he came to me for second period, I made sure to give him my own facial expressions to remind him of what I said to him a few minutes earlier. It didn't always work but it was obvious that there was some improvement in his attitude. Sometimes I would notice how hard he struggled to hold back the impulse to "go off." Sometimes I thought I saw anger in his smile.

Billz was also in the barbering class. He had a reputation among his peers as the top student barber, of which he proudly bragged, almost as much as he bragged about all the money he was making in New York. I guess this was how he acquired his name.

I made it my business to ask the barbering instructor how Billz was doing in his class. I wasn't at all surprised that his evaluation was similar to mine: "A hard-working youngster who always tried to do his best but would drive you crazy with his impatience if you let him get away with it." He also confirmed what the students said about his barbering skills.

Because he was convinced that he was as good a writer as he was a barber, Billz pestered me to let him come to one of my afternoon writing periods sometimes. I finally agreed under the condition that when he could do so the teacher with whom he officially had that period would have to give him a permission slip. The plan worked out and when Billz came he worked on writing his poetry. He did very well. Consequently, he was one of those students chosen to have a little chapbook of his best verses printed.

When eventually he saw his little book, so neatly produced, cover printed in colors and even laminated, he was transformed from grouchy to happy. Every day he would be seen reading it with a smile on his face. He was also in the habit of signing copies for his teachers and fellow students. He also signed and mailed out copies. And for all those copies that would be left over, he intended to take them home when he was released. And as it was just a small book, he would sell them for two dollars each.

When he came to me with the idea of doing barbering for a living when he was released, I encouraged him. With the obsession youngster had with always displaying a "fresh" haircut, I assured him, and with a haircut costing eight to ten dollars – and tips generally given – he should do well enough to not end up on the road back to jail like so many. I even helped him to put a professional look to the business card he was struggling to design to advertise his barbering business.

Then when he was released unexpectedly and all those cards remained in the classroom, I took it upon myself to get his address and delivered them to his apartment. He and his grandmother were so surprised that I would do this and thanked me over and over. She showed me the barbering tools she had bought for him and told me she had already arranged for him to get a chair at a barber shop. A few weeks later I phoned to see how he was doing. His grandmother told me elatedly, "That boy is always at the barber shop; he's doing real good." She spoke of wanting to pay for the business cards. I told her to forget about it. Billz was working and that was payment enough for me.

A short time after joining my third and fourth period classes 17-year-old Romero proved that he had those qualities to make him my main student, meaning that he learned fast and was able to help the teacher in ways some teachers' helpers wouldn't. Teachers had a great appreciation for such a student. I trusted him, even though by now my experience had taught me that trusting anyone in jail was a dangerous thing, on-going deception and downright con-artist activities being as characteristic to such an institution as sand is to a desert.

Anything wrong Romero observed going on, he brought it to my attention. When the classroom started to take on a look uglier than previously with graffiti writings and drawings constantly appearing everywhere – walls, desks, chairs, equipment, lockers, light tables, computers, and even T-squares and rulers – I needed extra eyes to help me catch the culprits. Of course, finding them wasn't going to be so easy because as much as inmates distrusted one another, knowing that in jail "snitches get stitches" is a reality, there was that inmates' wall of silence to contend with. This was especially so in a case such as this with me being regarded as an outsider.

It must be known, of course, that graffiti desecration – or decoration, as youngsters see it – of everywhere and everything in New York City is at the top of the list of youth value system. So this wasn't a problem confined to my classroom by any means. But I had this thing against situations that made it seem that I might not be quite as observant in my classroom as I could be. I even had a huge computer-made banner on the walls reading "No Graffiti of Any Kind Anywhere in the Classroom," along with the "No Profanity in the Classroom" sign.

Romero knew how much I hated this sudden increase of graffiti in the classroom, how badly I wanted to find out who the culprits responsible for it were, especially the leading one by far whose signature of "Tragedy" – all looking exactly the same regardless of size or color – popped up everywhere. He set about diligently to help me find this culprit Tragedy. He would point out those he strongly suspected. He would threaten them with physical harm for "comin' to this class and dissin' my man Brathwaite like this." I even had to step in at times and make this little fellow, of Dominican Republic ancestry, release his hold on the collars of those he said were the culprits. He also had endless ideas for me about solving the mystery.

Then one morning Fame, one of Romero's homeboys, came in and approached me angrily. "Brathwaite, I hear you be lookin' for dat nigga Tragedy. Dat's the nigger there," he said, pointing at Romero. "The one you be trustin' so much."

Romero immediately put up a loud argument in defense of his innocence. He wasn't that culprit Tragedy. After all his efforts to help me find out who Tragedy was, and helping me out in general, I knew he wasn't the guilty one. Fame saw the doubt on my face. He rushed out the door and was soon back with King Sunny and Little Mexico – both, like Romero, members of the Hispanic gang the Latin Kings – and tackled Romero. After a good struggle, they ripped his shirt off, forcing him to try to cover up the tattoos on his arms and chest. Then they had him subdued and invited me to take a look. The signature Tragedy was there on his arms and chest looking exactly like all the others everywhere.

Tragedy couldn't say another word toward his innocence. He never admitted to being the culprit, either. But it manifested itself in his silly laughter. He was undone by two who were known to be his homeboys. And why? He had received payment (cigarettes) in advance from Fame to design and make him sweetheart cards – something he did with a professional flair – but having taken on the responsibility of doing similar projects for others, he was too long in delivering to Fame. He also had not repaid (in commissary goods) a debt to Little Mexico.

For a few minutes I could only look at Tragedy with surprise and disbelief as his grinning and laughter showed clearly that they were dominated by his regrets and guilty conscience. Finally, he told me, "Brathwaite, man, something is definitely wrong wit' me and this graffiti shit. I've always gotten myself in trouble 'cause of it. I know it be wrong, but it got a hold on me like crack gets a hold of crackheads."

It was only a few weeks ago that he had so enthusiastically introduced me to his mother, when parents and friends visited the school, as "my man Brathwaite, the best teacher in the place." She was happy to have met me, telling me of all the good things her son had told her about me. Now, she wanted us to communicate with each other since she felt sure I was capable of helping to turn him around. He was such a "problem child," she said, that when he was out and the phone rang the first thing that would come to her mind was that once again somebody somewhere had a gun in his face, as was the case within a few days of his release from Rikers a few months earlier. "It wouldn't have been so," she lamented, "if only this boy had listened to me and went and stayed and work with his uncle in Georgia. But he thinks he can't live without hangin' out in New York City with his so-called friends."

Meeting her personally, it strengthened a belief I had conjured up in my mind after meeting and listening to other mothers like her, so young-looking that the first impression was that they were either the sisters or girlfriends of their sons. And could the fact that they looked as young as their sons resulted in the subconscious lessening in the eyes of the sons regarding their maternal authority. Bear in mind the generality of this situation being that of mothers minus fathers, or fathers seldom meaningfully involved.

Like so many other mothers who visited the classroom and saw the computers and the graphic arts equipment, Tragedy's mother was enthusiastic about her son learning a skill that seemed to have so much potential for a youngster to succeed. I assured her of my wish to teach the skills to the youngsters. I didn't bother to tell her of those absolute needs necessary for learning the skills, which so many youngsters just didn't see as necessary: discipline and following the program.

At any rate, what was I going to do regarding Tragedy's transgression? I finally concluded that his promises to "never do it again" were honestly meant but wouldn't be lived up to. And the fact of having had my wallet and money stolen by a "trusted" student, having been set up to have dangerous contraband taken from the classroom by "trusted" students, and being aware of how many teachers were similarly set up by "trusted" students," also that I had worked long enough in this "trust-nobody" environment, it had to be partly my fault that Tragedy was able to outsmart me like this. So I assured him that I wouldn't try to get him to lose days. I wouldn't even try to get him to lose commissary privileges. But complain as much as he did, I wanted that he be made to clean up all the graffiti in the classroom that could be cleaned up with chemicals. As for that on the walls that couldn't be chemically removed, the walls should be painted. True, as he protested, he wasn't the only culprit. But I reminded him that he was the one who was undone.

Some of the Weird Actors of Jailhouse Jeopardy

Moreover, since he was my main student, looking out for me, who was there in a better position to catch him than he himself?

So I took my case to a no-nonsense correction officer. Tragedy didn't lose any days or any commissary privileges, but he got to clean up and paint the classroom for three days. It certainly made him angry. His angry mood lasted for two or three days after the cleaning up was done, then he took his relationship with me back to the friendly state of "my man Mister Brathwaite."

Mr. Romero," I said to him the day he was about to go home and came to give me high-fives, wish me goodbye, and ask that I keep in touch with his mother, "it was so good knowing you. Listen to your mother and stop trying to make a career out of coming to jail. You apologized for making a fool of me, but I'm glad you did; it helped to strengthen my distrust in a place where it's absolutely necessary. I only hope the way I made a fool back out of you helps you to get out of that nasty graffiti addiction you have. Because out there some victims of graffiti addicts like you don't ask them to clean it up; they hurt them physically."

Others I will always remember, not for their display of an array of strange idiosyncrasies but for never giving up on the same habit every day:

There was Shorty-One-Forty with his helpless attitude. He kept himself busy. Ironically, though, he was always calling out for help: "Teacher, please come here and help me. I can't do this. Help me, please."

After I found out it was mostly a case of a bad habit he had of wanting attention, I would tell him, "Just try a little harder and you'll see it's not as hard as you think." He would turn to my new para, who was a follower of the Islamic faith, not ever addressing him by his name, and plead pitifully, "Muslim, please help me. Please, Muslim, help me." Eventually I instructed Muslim not to keep running to his assistance. So he would turn to his friends, one after the other. "Homeboy, help me. Damn, nobody here won't help me." Eventually I would go to his assistance and he would show no signs whatever of wanting me to show him how to help himself but would pass the responsibility off to me completely. "Here, teacher, do it for me, please. I don't know how to do it."

Little Perez came to periods seven and eight every day for about four months before he was released. True, he would copy all the lessons I wrote on the blackboard, more willingly in fact than many others. I must also credit him with voluntarily cleaning up the room on a regular basis. As to other class-related work, motivating him to get involved was quite a difficult task. He preferred to consistently try to occupy the doorway and specifically observe the correction officers. He would bad-mouth them almost non-stop, not for them to hear, of course, but for the enjoyment of his peers. He was especially severe on Big Ak: "Just look at him...ol' mean-ass himself...be always messin' wit' inmates and treatin' us like a bunch of criminals...the big dufus...walks just like a muthafuckin' gorilla. He always be trying to give Brathwaite a hard time...he wanna be like Brathwaite. But he knows he ain't never gonna make it. He can never be cool and intelligent like Brathwaite. Dat's why he be so jealous."

Chang was another one who obviously came to the class because he was programmed there. Little Perez at least copied the lessons from the blackboard and made feeble attempts at doing the quizzes and tests. Chang made no attempts to do anything. He preferred hiding behind the excuse, "I no speak English so good." In my opinion, it was a pitiful excuse. Except for sometimes resorting to a corner and going through Bruce Lee-like karate moves and grunts, and complaining that his mother was in New York's China Town waiting to get a letter from him from Hong-Kong, where she thought he was, Chang usually fell into a deep sleep within fifteen minutes of entering the classroom.

Maybe it was a legacy of sorts from his initial coming to

the class and when the periods ended I asked him to clean up that had him voluntarily doing the chore each day when the last period ended. I tried (unsuccessfully) to stop him for a very good reason. His cleaning up was a bit too thorough. He would scrape everything left on the light tables onto the floor, sweep everything up and put all into a garbage bag and head with it for where the rest of the garbage was placed to be thrown out. Those students who didn't heed my classroom rule that at the end of the last period they were to put their unfinished work in their folders and either give them to the teacher or para or place them on the teacher's desk, but not to leave anything on the light tables and elsewhere, would find out next day that they were missing.

As Chang cleaned up he would constantly utter these same words with contempt: "Garbage! Garbage! Garbage! Anything left on light table when class finish, garbage." Students who previously didn't heed the rule were soon doing so.

I never did ascertain Chang's nationality. One time he would say he was from Hong-Kong. Another time it would be China, sometimes Taiwan, Malaysia and Indo-China.

He answered to the name of Too Black as if it was the name on his ID card. There was no need to wonder about the name; he was very dark-skinned. Just looking at the same sour look on his faced every day said that he had some problems, perhaps more than having to face the daily teasing of his peers about being "so black." He not only kept his distance from his fellow students, he resisted every attempt by me to communicate with him. Whenever I found a reason to offer him some help, he would refuse it abruptly, saying, "I don't want no help from nobody. I don't even wanna be in this stupid-ass school." Finally, one day at the end of classes he surprisingly wasn't the one to immediately jump up and rush out the class first, as he had done every day since his first day of attendance, with that sour look on his face. Instead, he lingered behind and was last. "Hey, young brother," I said, wanting to get a conversation going with him, " see you're not in a hurry today." That barrier he had placed between us, he tore it down abruptly. But not in the manner I wished he would. "Man, don't you be callin' me no brother. " 'Cause, see you, I can't stand you, nigga. You be just like everybody else…don't like me 'cause I'm too black…no different."

"So that's what you think?" I quickly replied.

"I don't think nothin'; I know what I'm talkin' 'bout."

"Really?" What you just said tells me that you don't know what you're talking about. If you know what you're talking about, prove it to me."

He stood there trying to find something to say to substantiate his charge, to no avail. I told him there was no truth whatsoever in his statement about me. On the contrary, if there was only one person in the city who didn't subscribe to the feelings he expressed, I would have to be that person. I understood, though, what he was trying to "get at." I told him that it was an undisputable fact that we lived in a world where the darker one was the more one's human worth was disregarded. I didn't see it changing, I reluctantly told him. But it was how one viewed one's self that mattered most. Liking yourself while not being liked by others is not necessarily disastrous. But even if you're liked by others and you don't like yourself, that's a certain disaster. I stressed to him how very important it was to not appear to be weak and vulnerable.

He told me about how much he hated his father. He hardly ever knew him because "the nigga" was always in jail.

By the time he left the room, I felt sure that sour look he always carried on his face wasn't now there.

His attitude toward me changed completely. In fact, He would often tell me about seeing in me what a father, a teacher and a Black man should be. He didn't change his attitude toward his father, who he constantly referred to as "not a real man," "a small-time drug-dealing punk." I had to put a stop to his often telling me how he intended to prove to his father he was a punk and he (son) was more man than he ever was. "Imagine," he had said to me initially, "the nigga be thinkin' he's a man and never even made it as a major drug dealer. He ain't never even killed nobody. Well, I've gotta prove to him that I'm a more better man than he ever was by doing all the shit he never had the guts to do."

"Son, if he's a 'punk' and 'not a real man' because of his life style, what would you be if you do more of it than he did?" I asked. "It would make you more of a 'punk' and more of a 'no real man.' If he's such a bad man for having done these things, it can't make you a better man by doing worse than he did; that will make you a worse man."

Several weeks later when he was about to be released, with that barrier he had built in his mind against me having long crumbled, he came to me to say goodbye and tell me how sorry he was for being so mean to me when we first met. I told him he wasn't to bother about it. What I wanted from him was that he become a better man than his father. "But do it the right way; achieve positive things he did not." He gave me his promise that he would.

When Santana first came to the class, the questions he considered of most importance to put to me didn't in any way pertain to the class or education. He wanted to know how he could get muscles like mine. This 16-year-old had six more months to do before his release and he wanted badly to "go home with muscles."

As the days went by, he never let up on his questioning. It reached a point where I had answered the same questions so many times that I often had to remind him of my purpose for coming to Rikers Island: to be a teacher.

When he came to class what was foremost on his mind was going into a corner and doing push ups. I was told that he was always exercising, in the gym, in the dorm and when he went to the recreation yard. I thought it necessary to let him know that while there was merit to that iron pumpers' motto "no pain, no gain," grossly overdoing it wasn't a wise approach.

Apparently, he was a bit too enthusiastic, and having worked so hard expected significant progress in a relatively short period. After a few weeks of pumping away he didn't see the muscular improvement he thought he should have accomplished. What he actually expected was to have my kind of development, which I had achieved over a number of years, in two months. So disillusioned, he gave it up. From then on I heard his disgruntled and accusing voice every day that he came to class: "Yo, man, I worked out real hard. How comes I ain't got like Brathwaite. I know, Brathwaite be on steroids. Yeah, he be on steroids. He gotta be on dat shit. How else can an old man look like dat?"

"Santana," I would sometimes say to him, "you have to keep it up. You don't get to look good like me in two months, not even if you take steroids."

He still kept up his accusation every day. "You know, Santana," I said to him one day, I wouldn't know steroids if somebody came and stuck some in my face. You know that but you're just jealous of old man Brathwaite because he looks better that a young weakling like you." I never heard that accusation from him again. He was soon moved to another wing of the jail for several weeks, in which time I didn't see him. He eventually moved back to his old dorm and to school. His body development was good for the time he had been working out.

"Santana, is that really you?" I asked. "How did you manage to get steroids in jail?"

It ain't steroids," he boasted. "It's what you said to me dat day, that I was jealous of how you look." Man, I don't want no old man be lookin' better than me. I'm gonna make sure that if you see me two years from now I'm gonna be looking better than you."

This youngster from Detroit, Michigan had the distinction of having more than one jail name that stuck with him. The two main ones were Detroit Red and Detroit Debbie. He was given the first name because he was quite fond of coloring his hair red, the second one because he was a homosexual who obviously took great delight in flaunting his femininity.

I must admit that I held it against him how every day he

flaunted his effeminate ways, for so much of it came in the form of his graphic details of his gay activities, which he said started at age 12 with adult men. Apparently, having started so young equipped him with the street smarts to use most of the years from 12 to his present 17 accepting money for sexual favors. Some of the stories about his activities as a gay prostitute were so wild and dangerous – especially his con games – to not only belie the age at which some took place but to leave some doubt as to their credibility. Whatever the case, his fellow students delighted in hearing him tell these stories – every day. So much so that on the occasions when I would admonish him, they made it clear that they wish I would "leave her alone.". I thought he had some respect for my authority as he would always say he was sorry and end his conversation, though he would soon start back from where he left off.

His presence led to classroom disruptions, notably with students wanting to touch him in various ways. Some did so in a manner of teasing and joking. Others, I was sure, did so under the same pretext but with serious intentions. It was during one of these touching sessions that, without even the slightest warning, a fight erupted among Detroit Red and two other students. When the C.O. came most of the students exonerated Detroit Red and blamed the other two for starting the fight because of "jealousy over her." I told the C.O. that from what I saw they were equally guilty. Detroit Red became angry over this assessment and made the accusation "you know I didn't start it but you went against me 'cause you think of me as just a faggot."

I told him I was not a supporter of the gay lifestyle but that I certainly wouldn't go around doing wrong to gays. If I were to do so it would be to those who advocate things like having sex with both genders, with little kids, and championing the legality of two people of the same sex marrying each other. I held him equally guilty "because it's the way you show so much disrespect for your gay self that leads to others disrespecting you more than they normally would have. You don't have to keep disrespecting yourself

Some of the Weird Actors of Jailhouse Jeopardy

because others expect it of you, and it makes them happy"

As much as I didn't like having fights in my classroom, I wasn't too disappointed about this one. It was the best excuse so far to get rid of Detroit Red from the class. I must credit him, though, with coming to see me one day to apologize and tell me, "You know, Mista Brathwaite, I was thinkin' real hard 'bout the stuff you said to me. You was right."

The student artist recalls how he and his homeboys used to "bugout" on their way to school in the Bronx before he ended up incarcerated on Rikers Island..

< 15 >

Tragedies Out of Jailhouse Jeopardy

As was the case with watching the movie *The Education of Sonny Carson,* I recalled also that back in the 1970's I read a book by Orde Coombs titled *Can't You See My Love For You Growing.* Part of the book documented the author's experience of working with teenagers in Brooklyn, New York. Once again, his experience didn't involve dealing with the vast numbers of youngsters as mine did, or the diverse cross section of races, cultures and nationalities. When reading Coombs' account of the youngsters who lost their lives foolishly, I wondered if his account wasn't a bit exaggerated. However, now that I was involved with youngsters every day, I had no doubt about his account, for youngsters losing their lives foolishly started almost as soon as my Rikers Island experience started.

There were two brothers in my class of Cuban background. The younger one, just 16, and extremely childish, was released first. About three weeks after his release the older brother got the news from home that he had been shot to death.

There was the 17-year-old who was known as Crazy Carl by his fellow students, all of whom kept a safe distance from him because of his inability to lead a conversation which didn't end on a nasty note. He had told me that he had nowhere to go when he was released because his mother had disappeared and left him with his father when he was 10 years old. Now his father no longer liked him. Shortly before he was arrested he had "beaten the shit out" of his father. His father went and got his gun and told him, with tears in his eyes, "Son, I used to love you so much, but in the last few years you forced me to really hate you. I'm sorry it had to come to this, but I gotta kill you."

When he saw the tears in his father's eyes, he told me, he knew he was "dead-ass" serious. He jumped out the window and never went back.

Carl would often back me into the proverbial corner, trying to force a character analysis of him out of me. "What you think about me, Mista Brathwaite? Tell me the truth. I ain't such guy, am I?"

When I felt I had no choice but to give an answer, I would chose my response very carefully, not wanting to hurt his feelings, but not wanting to be hypocritical and make him think I approved of his consistently "uptight" bad attitude. To be honest, I felt he was trapped in this three-way dangerous situation: He very likely would kill someone; someone would very likely kill him; he might take his own life. And if my analysis was right, I thought, the third stated action would be best. For considering his constant temper flare-ups, the possibility that he would kill an innocent person was as strong as the possibility of the person who killed him was forced by his actions to do it. If he committed suicide, however, the hurt and the guilt would be on him.

It turned out that a few months after he went home he was fatally gunned down by a police officer.

Why they called him Bugsie, I never knew. He was a loner with a temper problem. It must be said for him that the heated arguments he got into were never initiated by him, though if he was more mature some of these arguments wouldn't have started. He somehow felt that his peers were always trying to pick on him and would jump to defend himself against any of their comments he thought were directed at him in a "put-down" manner. I never did get much details about this 17-year-old potentially good artist who worked with dedication on his art, but it was confirmed that shortly after returning to his East New York neighborhood he was fatally stabbed in the chest.

Gene the Dancing Machine was one of those students who often came to my classroom, either wanting to work on a project or to "hangout" for a while. There was no need for music to be playing to set him off demonstrating his slick break dancing moves and other slick dance steps. He obviously somehow had the music stored in his head. As I would say to the rappers and dancers when they started to rap, sing and dance in the classroom, knowing of the disruption it was sure to soon lead to, "You're in the wrong place; take it to the music class," I used to get rid of Gene the same way. When he tried to make a case for his staying, giving the assurance "I ain't gonna do it no more, Mista Brathwaite, if you lemme stay," I would take my "tough love" stand and let him know that I knew for sure he was going to start again as soon as he thought I had forgotten, so he should "hit the road, Jack, and we'll remain friends."

The last time I saw Gene was in my classroom, dancing with joy to that music he carried around in his head. I didn't even bother to make him leave because I knew he was so happy that after several months in jail he would be going home early the next morning and I wouldn't have to put up with his break dancing after today. Not long after he went home the news came back to us that he had been murdered.

Christmas was just around the corner. Like other inmates

who would be released to be home in time for Christmas, Flintstone was very happy. It would mark his second going home from Rikers in the same year. Before leaving earlier in the year he had written a nice article for the Academy News. Since he wouldn't be there when it came off the press, I promised him I would mail him copies. And so I did. When he was incarcerated again maybe two months or so later, I joked with this friendly, regular classroom sleeper – labeled Fred Flintstone after the popular prehistoric cartoon character by fellow students who said they resembled – about making me waste money to mail copies to "your cave" when I could have kept them for him until he returned to jail. I also reminded him that in that article he had written about not ever getting himself locked up again and how interesting it would be if he would write another article before he left addressing the fact that his boastful promise fell apart, why it happened and what he would do this time to make sure it didn't happen again.

He was happy to write the article, criticizing his bad judgment, but gave the assurance that this time he was going to get a job as soon as he got home and "keep away from those so-called friends" who were responsible for getting him locked up again. These were friends, he said, who if they were not locked up too couldn't spare the time to visit a friend in jail. He gave the assurance that it would "never happen again." It was his New Year's resolution.

Before I left school for the Christmas holidays, I mailed Flinstone his copies. He may or may not have seen them. When I returned to school on the second day of January, I was given the news by the D.O.C. that Flintstone was shot dead in the Bronx while on a night out with friends relieving cars of their radios.

He had a burning desire to be a rap singer. I was of the opinion that he had the potential to make it. If I wasn't a good enough judge of this genre of music, the youngsters who were very much "into it" were high in their praise of his ability. So much so, in fact, that they called him Little-D after the then popular rap star Heavy-D. He also had the same light-brown complexion, but was little in stature compared to the one he was likened to.

While the youngsters might have judged him primarily because of his performing ability, I saw another side to him that helped in my concluding that he had potential; he was constantly writing poetry (rap lyrics). And though there was that generation gap as far as the message he conveyed was concerned, I had to tell him that he wrote very well and should pursue his ambition with the conviction that he could make it. I would also joke with him about the absolute need for him to make a lot of money, for he had just turned 18 and already had two children from one girl, one with the girl he was living with, who also had two before she met him.

Almost as soon as he went home he sent me a signed eight by ten photo taken with his rapping buddy, asking me to keep it so when he made it big I could look at it and say, "I used to be this guy's teacher."

Very soon after I received that photo Little-D was confronted by a youngster who wanted to relieve him of his cell phone. He wasn't willing to let his phone be taken away. For his reluctance he was shot fatally in the head. According to his mother, as he lay dying Little-D asked her to please help his children.

Juan didn't have one of those jail nicknames. Maybe because he was such a quiet fellow, the complete opposite of his fellow inmate and younger brother Four-eyes, who was also in my class. Juan was a very motivated student. He was also one of those students who liked to help out the teacher.

I certainly missed him when he went home. It felt like such a short time he was gone when the school family worker, who kept in touch with released students – and in whose area Juan lived – came to me one morning and asked me, "Did anybody tell you that your right hand student got murdered?" And he pulled out his obituary card from the funeral home and gave it to me.

He told me he had gone to see Juan only recently and he was all happy about starting his new job. Then only yesterday he went back to see how he was making out and his distraught mother, with tears in her eyes, told him that Juan was buried only two days earlier. He had been hanging out with a group of friends when an argument ensued and he was the one stabbed in the chest.

It was especially shocking to me because as quiet as Juan was, I, like the family worker, couldn't picture him getting so involved in an argument that would lead to murder.

They nicknamed him Iron Mike, after Mike Tyson, the former heavyweight champion, who most youngsters still regarded as "the baddest heavyweight on the planet" despite his recent defeats. From my observation of him in my classroom, where he spent three periods a days, I thought he wasn't a bad fellow at all. His one bad habit was often trying to turn a little dispute between two students into a fight. And if it did happen, take himself away and let them face the consequences. I saw it as a childish act from a guy who looked so tough. But I also believed he was older than the soon to be 18 years of age he claimed, making him one of those who had found a way to con the system that he was still an adolescent and therefore wouldn't be saddled with a criminal record. Such guys sometimes actually acted more childish than those 16 years old.

I never actually saw him act out the Iron Mike side of him, but he had such a reputation of knocking out inmates back in the dorm that it was well known on the school floor. His last such act was to break the jaw of a Jamaican fellow, who though on the smallish side, wasn't easy. I was witness to his challenge one day to another student at least six feet tall to "let's go to the washroom for five minutes and settle this rassclaut thing once and for all". I didn't see them settle their feud, either, but the bigger fellow was left to walk around with a black eye and other tell-tale signs of defeat while the Jamaican looked untouched.

In any event, he did go down to defeat at the hands of Iron Mike. But he kept making the vow, "Dat Yankee boy think he really bad, but I know the area where he live and when we go home I gonna show him who is the baddest." I don't think Iron Mike or anyone else took him seriously, because of the many promises made in jail that were not followed through on after release. He and Iron Mike were released within a short time of each other. Not long after making it out of jail, they made it into the newspapers. The Jamaican had pursued a search for him and eventually found him in a park relaxing with his girlfriend. He would do this no more because the Jamaican pulled out a gun and pumped six bullets into him.

Flacko was every bit as quiet as Juan. This very skinny fellow was also one of those who cooperated with the teacher. Clearly, he had a major fault that I called "follower's mentality." He tended to get into trouble with the correction officers, trouble initiated by others which he got the blame for. I sensed that he had this dire need to be wanted. What were the childhood experiences that might have caused this, I couldn't say

On a few occasions when he got into trouble I told Flacko that he had some admirable ways but that his habit of following others was dangerous, especially because they seemed always to let the blame fall on him and he accepted it. It could get him into serious trouble one day though he wouldn't even deserve it. He was a quiet listener, wouldn't even say a word to dispute me. But I doubt if while he was quietly listening that he was giving any thought at all. So sadly, when he went home, I felt sure that everything I said to him was left right there in the classroom.

I was in my classroom one morning when a C.O. came rushing in and slammed the Daily News on my desk before me. "There's your pal," he said, pointing at a photograph of a few Hispanic youngsters. "He finally became a celebrity."

The group had only the day before engaged in a shootout in Manhattan, outside the courthouse of all places, leaving two dead and others hurt. It was a shootout based on love and jealousy. Among the group that caused the damage was Flacko, who not many weeks ago was still attending my class. Following the story in subsequent days it was said that he was the one who had no reason to be there; he went along to show his allegiance to the one who initiated the shooting. The incident didn't result in Flacko's physical demise, but he ended up sentenced to several years in prison.

Damien was another one of those guys who said very little. Also, he perhaps did even less than he said. But he would help out if asked to. We were all shocked when his photo appeared in the New York Post under the heading, "Brooklyn's Most Wanted." Not one person in the school who knew him thought he would rape one girl at gun point and shoot to death another. But according to the law he did just that soon after his release from Rikers.

In the case of Black – not Too Black – it was different. No one who knew him doubt that he had the characteristics that would lead him to commit horrendous crimes. He had a very good reputation as a barbering students. The barbering instructor even made sure he got a set of barbering tools to get started.

    I thought no one saw him in a more negative light than I did. I was turned off from his defiant attitude from the very first day when he joined my class. He always insisted on doing as he pleased, and that no one was to correct him. Our relationship degenerated to its lowest point that day when his very ugly behavior forced me to take an unyielding stand against his continued presence in my class. Not even the principal could get me to stay in the same classroom with him on this day. And when he was removed, he confronted me in the hallway and threatened over and over that I "had to be killed." With his anger at a high, he swore that if he saw me in New York he would murder me, for sure. Threats from students against teachers were not unusual. Generally, we brushed them aside. But I took Black's threat seriously – very seriously. After two correction officers were able to pin him to the floor, huffing, puffing and snorting, I sought out the barbering instructor for information pertaining to his character. He confirmed the students' opinion that Black was very good at barbering, that he was trying hard to help him get started. But he confided in me, "I don't see him ever making it. There's something seriously wrong with that boy."

Black perhaps showed his seriously flawed side sooner than any other inmate did when he went home. He was charged with disrupting the New York City skyline viewing of a visiting out-of-state teacher by raping her at gunpoint – in the presence of her boyfriend. His notoriety was assured. For unlike in the case of Damien who was Black as were his victims, the victim in Black's case was White and all the major newspapers got on the case.

The student artist demonstrates that being incarcerated doesn't mean that one can't have some thought for food.

< 16 >

Temporary Escape from Jailhouse Jeopardy

Just where did the time go? It was now 1998. Eleven years had disappeared since that day I first came to Island Academy fooling myself that I would be gone in six months.

Now, the doctor had handed me down a diagnosis of my suffering with a very bad case of high blood pressure. That I had little awareness about being caught in the grips of this silent killer certainly didn't help the situation. I no longer wondered why as in the past when I used to see people popping pills at a certain time every day. I should have been doing the same maybe since I first came to Island Academy, for it wasn't so long after I started at Island Academy that I started to get those headaches, eye-aches and neck-aches and didn't know what they were symptomatic of. Had I not been ignorant of this it would have been a plus for my health to have been armed with the information that the stress caused by too much confrontation did a lot to push high blood pressure to dangerous levels.

There were times when I had to take more days off than I ever did in the past. Other teachers did the same, referring to the need for a "mental health" day. As for the inmates we mingled with daily, being ill was common among them. It wasn't uncommon for teachers to attribute the constant illness befalling them to viruses existing among the inmates.

Possibly, there could have been used as scapegoats to a certain extent, but our students were constantly coughing, hawking and sneezing. And they didn't normally excuse themselves away from you when doing these things. They unconsciously did so right in your face. The constant reminder to them to "put your hands over your mouth when you sneeze and cough" was generally either ignored or forgotten.

In the summer of 1998 I felt the absolute need to "get away from it all." Getting away in this case meant going somewhere far. My colleague, Mr. Masongo, told me he was going home to Kenya. I made plans to go with him. Since he was leaving a little too early for my plans, he went ahead of me. By the time he sent me back relevant information, I had already concluded that he might have changed his mind and had only recently paid down on my passage to an even more distant place: South Africa. It sounded more interesting than going to Kenya so I decided to stick with it. The fact that I knew no one in South Africa – just one person in neighboring Swaziland which was also on my itenary – and was going on an independent trip was no deterrent.

In August I set out for the unknown. I not only went to South Africa and Swaziland but also Mozambique. It was a most interesting adventure. I labeled it with that popular description "just what the doctor ordered."

I didn't quite get away from it all, though. As I was into my 16-day non-stop sojourn through these southern African nations, thousands of miles away from New York City, I still thought of the students I had left at Island Academy in Rikers Island Jail. I thought of how often I heard them speak – in a manner of bragging – of their recidivist penal experience of being sent to jail upstate, as if being able to have a limited view across the border into Canada from jail was a major accomplishment. I thought of this especially when my sojourn took an especially interesting turn, for instance: looking out at the Indian Ocean from Maputo, Mozambique; going through the sprawling township of Soweto, Johannesburg; traveling to Capetown; traveling from Johannesburg to Mbwane, Swaziland and looking at the beautiful mountains of Swaziland. I knew that I would speak of these things excitedly for years to come. But for years to come many of the students I had taught and tried to change their direction in life would still be speaking, with the same excitement, about their negative inmates' experience. The thought greatly saddened me, for I knew there were those who had the potential to escape from this grip of negativity.

I thought of the just concluded semester at Island Academy. Among others, I had the pleasure of having two Black Nuyoricans in my graphic arts class who did such spectacular art that I said to myself several times, "they were born to be artists."

Because of the on-going publishing program, which had grown to include other publications – notably The Slammer -- to find this kind of artistic talent was always like a blessing. Both these youngsters had Black fathers and Hispanic (White) mothers. What also distinguished them were the extremely huge Afros they wore. Students, teachers and C.O.'s would often ask them why they wouldn't cut their hair. Strangely, they would choose me to give the answer to: "No way." They had even resisted the many suggestions of their mothers that they do so. Of course, this shows a different Black Hispanic from those afore-mentioned as espousing the denial "I ain't Black." So I must mention that I had long observed that many Hispanics such as these two displayed this infatuation with their Afro, regularly giving it the Afro pick treatment to keep it blown out. Ironically, the racial denial seemed to come more so from those undeniably Black.

In any case, both these young artists spent a lot of time with me. One was very forceful, fitted the "tough guy" category very well. The other was very quiet. He obviously had home-related problems. His mother communicated with him regularly. He had no uses for his absentee father. He often told me how fortunate he felt he was to have met me, that it was incredible how much strength he had gained in a few months, how in this time he had done a lot of rethinking of issues and was able to see things differently. One of the things he intended to turn around was his not-so-good relationship with his mother. He was now seeing that much of it was his fault. One thing he set out to do was open up communication between his mother and me. She was quite happy that her son had met me for it seemed to her that he listened to me more that he listened to anyone else. And as much as his being in jail worried her, she had not been as worried since he met me. She was convinced it would help in "saving him from himself." I instilled in her, as I did with him, the belief that with his artistic talent, especially his creation of cartoon-like characters, there were tools small enough – and not so expensive – which could be set up in an apartment room for him to do very well financially putting these characters on T-shirts and selling them to the numerous cartoon-addicted youngsters out there.

I tried to get him to go the positive route by frequently telling him, "It is very easy for even the biggest fool to become a jailbird."

I returned to Island Academy in September 1998 in a very good frame of mind. Having sent postcards to a few of my colleagues while in Southern Africa, the news of my sojourn there preceded me back to school. Since the average person going to distant Southern Africa was still not a regular thing, colleagues sought me out to ask me about it. They found it intriguing that I had actually gone into the home of the internationally famous Nelson Mandela and Winnie Mandela.

By February 1999 the good frame of mind with which I had returned to Island Academy wasn't quite the same. Stress and high blood pressure were giving me quite a beating. As I thought about it, I realized that I had not yet

Journey Through Jailhouse Jeopardy 259

exercised my option of taking a sabbatical leave as had the great majority of those who were in the school system for about the same amount of time. I concluded that I was being a monster to my health, ignoring it through my dedication to teaching. So I filled out the necessary forms to get my well deserved sabbatical.

My sojourn to Southern Africa provided me good escape, but it lasted only 16 days. My body still told me to "get away from it all." I had not paid a visit to my native Barbados for almost 18 years. I simply picked up and went to Barbados.

The student artist shows himself locked down inside, thinking of the nice summer goings-on outside.

< 17 >

Sexual Harassment Set-up in Jailhouse Jeopardy

Then came the ending of June 1999, the end of another school year. I wouldn't be teaching summer classes as I used to do every summer up to about three summers ago. I now turned up for summer school session for only two weeks for the purpose of finishing up projects or doing projects the school needed. I was no longer enthusiastic about teaching summer school or per session in the evenings as did other teachers because of the "good" extra pay, much to the disappointment of the students. Yet there was this anger I felt because I was convinced that the administration was allowing itself to be dictated to by a damn correction officer called Big Ak to cut out my summer classes. He was still covertly engaging in any act he thought would hurt me, such as stigmatizing the class as a contraband hazard.

I wished that I had not elected to do those two weeks in the summer of 1999. Had I not done so, I certainly wouldn't have found myself harmlessly tapping the summer school secretary on her arm and joking, "Hey, look at those biceps." She had done this to me on a few occasions in the past. This morning when I came out of the washroom, hurrying to my classroom, marked the first time I ever did the same to her.

As I exited the classroom to go to the office, there she was complaining to herself, "He ain't got no right to be hittin' on me." As I was returning to the classroom, she was still there and again made the same statement. I went into my classroom not taking any note of what she had said, so convinced was I that she was making a joke as we had done with each other for all the summers she was coming to the school. Every summer she also brought projects she had to have done for herself and others at her regular school.

As I set about my tasks in the classroom, I still heard her voice complaining. I opened the door. This time she was complaining to Big Ak and Rev. I went to her and told her quite honestly, "You know, I thought you were joking, but It seems that you're really tryin' to make an issue out of a simple little thing. If I'm right, I am very, very sorry that I touched you. Please accept my apology. It will never happen again."

She continued with her complaining to Big Ak and Rev, the latter she was regularly seen conversing with. Then I was heading out the door at noon to go home and she approached me in her usual way and said, "Brathwaite, don't pay me no mind, I was just playin' with you." But it didn't matter at this stage. I really didn't like the way she acted and knew there would never be any friendly discourse between us again as far as I was concerned.

Rev came to me the next day carrying all her projects and told me that I should start working on them right away and "I'll make sure she don't get you into a whole lotta trouble."

She always did get her projects a day or two after I had completed my summer obligation. Now I was supposed to stop and give priority to her needs. I was particularly concerned, though, about the man's statement. It sounded to me like what is popularly called blackmail, a term I didn't use. Should I now jump when they wanted me to would make it seem that I was guilty of some transgression and was pleading for mercy. As far as I was concerned, I had done nothing wrong to the woman and therefore had no reason to plead for her mercy.

Rev kept coming to me under the same pretext of coming to my rescue if I would give priority to this woman's need. Each time he did this it strengthened my resolve not to cooperate. Knowing that I wouldn't be coming to school for the full summer program, when I went to the office one morning while she was conversing with Rev, she looked up and commented, "Brathwaite better have my stuff ready before he gets outta here." It sealed my intention not to do her projects at all.

My two-week summer commitment ended. I returned her "stuff" to Rev as he had given them to me – not done – and left for my summer vacation.

A few days later I was contacted by the summer school principal about a complaint made to her that I had physically assaulted the secretary. When I read the complaint I discovered that the secretary had dramatized the incident to make it seem that the harmless tap I gave her on the arm was closer to a knockout punch than a friendly tap.

Two days later I received another mail from the school. I sat down in my backyard and read it. For a long time I couldn't move. There was a major addition to the original complaint. Where the charge of physical assault ended in the original complaint, there was the addition, "And then he rubbed himself up against me." No such thing happened. When I tapped her on the arm I was on the move and had not even slowed down. Moreover, I couldn't recall ever having touched that woman previously.

I was shocked that she had actually added this sexual harassment element. It was even emphasized more than the initial charge. After thinking it over for a long time, I concluded that it was all because it was thought that the original charge wasn't strong enough to "get" me so a more serious charge had to be added.

After regaining my composure – "sort of" – I wondered about this African-American woman who was always professing her Christian values but could so easily play the role of outright liar and hypocrite. I couldn't prove that Big Ak and Rev had urged her on, but in my mind's eye I saw them right in the middle of the situation actually doing more to exacerbate it than she was. The principal, also an African-American woman, felt the secretary was just being mean.

Of course, I was required to respond to the allegations. I did so without hesitation. I told the story exactly as it happened. I detailed the discrepancies in the secretary's account that stood out conspicuously. I called for special attention to be given to the fact that there was no mention – not even an insinuation – of sexual harassment in the original complaint but that it became a major issue in the second complaint. And how was it possible for the major issue to have been overlooked in the original complaint. I implored the committee that would look into the case to read carefully all information supplied. I also explained that the secretary was a close associate of Big Ak and Rev especially and that I could supply proof that these two – of whom there existed at the school a general Board of Education personnel's fear – had committed themselves to creating an atmosphere of hate and hostility in the school for me. True, I couldn't prove their influence over the secretary, but they did have their discussions about it.

It was quite ironic that Big Ak was involved in this kind of accusation.

In spite of knowing deep in my heart that I was innocent, I had a major concern on my way to Manhattan that afternoon for the hearing. America being inundated with special interest groups, and many of them having such unshakeable dedication to strengthening their cause that right and truth didn't matter, what if the women on the committee were women's libbers? Libbers did point out a lot of prejudices against women which I agreed with them for. But in their ranks were those who had a hate-men streak in them. What if the committee was made up of this type?

This obviously was not the case. It was also obvious that they had read the complaints and my response to them carefully, as I had implored. The case against me was dismissed. There was no justification whatsoever for the charge of sexual harassment being made. I was instructed, though, that it was best to not have any physical contact – friendly or otherwise – with anyone on the job.

It would have been a catastrophic experience for me to have been found guilty. I had played the role of father and mother in raising two daughters and had always cautioned them against this habit in America of men touching women on the job. It was supposed to be a well-intentioned, friendly gesture. I always thought it was "tacky," that it was meant for such men to get a cheap thrill, that many women didn't really appreciate it but felt compelled to tolerate it. And having told my daughters not to tolerate this, would I now not look like a damn hypocrite in their eyes to be engaging in the same insensitive lecherous behavior?

I still believed that Big Ak and Rev were instrumental in developing this case against me. But to give Rev his due, though he was always up in the face of female teachers, he wasn't one of whom it could be said was in this category of male-touching-female. Big Ak, on the other hand, was the epitome of this. He consistently hugged and smooched on females. During the time our relationship was good, I told that man on several occasions that he should break this habit or one day he would find himself accused by a woman of perpetrating sexual harassment against her. He never took it seriously; simply laughed it off. Convinced now that he was a major part of the scheme to entrap me as a perpetrator of the same transgression, I thought, what a nasty, vicious son of a bitch.

As for the secretary, I inquired about the location of her church with the intention of going there during a service, while she was in attendance, walking up to the pulpit and telling the congregation what this liar and hypocrite had done to me.

It would have been foolish of me not to think that the

news of the secretary's allegations against me were not known to my colleagues. When I returned to school for the new school year they knew of the allegation, though not of the hearing that had exonerated me.

Surprisingly, it seemed that more than trying to make me look bad, Big Ak and Rev were trying to make themselves look good. They were telling the few teachers they felt would convey the message to me that they knew I thought they had set me up but that it wasn't so. "It was all done by that crazy woman." Yet I felt I saw the guilt parading across their faces.

I gave the principal a copy of the letter stating that I had been found totally innocent. He was happy about this. It was so strongly written in my favor that he encouraged me to make it known to everyone by reading it at the next teachers meeting. He was quite taken aback when I refused. He even volunteered to do the reading for me. I still refused. I told him: "Mister Hines, I gave you a copy because you are the principal and I was instructed to do so. My conscience is clear. I have nothing to prove to anyone else now. People will believe what they want to believe no matter what the evidence tells them to the contrary. Those Jesus freak women especially will support their church-going sister. Let them believe what they want to believe."

I harbored much trepidation about continuing to work at Island Academy. I just couldn't picture Big Ak and Rev not continuing to set me up – unless, of course, I started giving them the impression that I believed they ran Island Academy. I certainly wasn't afraid of these two, but I certainly feared what they could do – behind my back.

Bribing youngsters in jail wasn't at all difficult to do, especially being bribed by an all-powerful correction officer. And students implicating teachers in nefarious acts against them wasn't an unusual thing. And even if eventually found innocent, these teachers never recovered from the stigma the news media cast upon them. Could I ever get over the embarrassment of having my reputation tarnished this way?

I vowed to never be alone with a student again. I cut out that graphic arts class requirement of taking a few students at a time into the darkroom to develop photos and negatives. I suggested to the principal that any time there was no teacher's helper available for my class, it should be cancelled. He didn't agree with me on this one.

I reserved space in the Academy Journal to aim some subtle unflattering comments at big Ak and Rev. It was of great concern to the assistant principal who had very little problem getting the principal to go along with him. It helped down my relationship with Big Ak and Rev. Up to this point they were still making statements as to the effect, "He still thinks we had something to do with helping the secretary to set him up. She did it on her own. And when we didn't go along with her she said how she thought we hated him."

Big Ak started putting pressure on Mr. Hines to "stop the publication of dat propaganda magazine," meaning the Academy Journal. The administration was soon making gestures of appeasement that the autonomy I always exercised in editing and publishing would be curtailed in future. The A.P. had to see the contents and give his approval. I reminded Mr. Hines about the rule against principals having such authority over high school newspapers. I would fight against any such control by them. I also believed that both principal and A.P. might have harbored some concern about what they saw as a little too much power and prestige in the hands of an ordinary teacher, a Black one at that. But I must admit that I never saw their refusal to stand up to Big Ak and Rev in defense of me as their intent to support them over me. On the contrary, I felt sure that they were quite happy when I stood up to them in such a way to remind them that they were not the school's administrators. They just thought it was best for them to take the cowardly approach. Diplomacy, as they no doubt preferred to see it as.

< 18 >

What the Board of Education Needs -- Not A Mayor Like Giuliani

Because Island Academy teachers seemed to somehow see themselves as an extension of the Department of Correction, I didn't doubt that their concerns about the problems confronting them as a result of the problems showered on their agency, the Board of Education, didn't seem as important to them as their colleagues in the mainstream schools saw them.

When the union held rallies to defend teachers against the constant disparaging of them by Mayor Giuliani, the reluctance to raise their pay, the blaming of them for all the shortcomings plaguing the schools, Island Academy teachers showed tremendous apathy. At the same time, teachers were being blamed by parents, who not only thought they were to be able to magically reverse the downward spiraling trend of their children's academic performance as a result of exercising the rights given them by the society to do as they pleased, but should be doing better at baby-sitting them. Beyond a doubt, the mayor made himself the spokesperson for the anti-teachers' movement, consistently berating them. He obviously knew what to do to win a popularity contest. While he berated the group saddled with the underpaid task of dispensing education, he lavished praise on the police as "New York's Finest" and the firemen as "New York's Bravest." So they were known to be by the public – heroes. Teachers had no wonderful description applied to them.

Let it be remembered that while seeking the office of mayor Giuliani had engaged in that very despicable, demagogic act of leading a large number of unruly, drunken police officers onto the steps of City Hall to castigate Mayor David Dinkins, calling him "nigga." When he became mayor he had City Hall cordoned off from the public with steel bars. People could no longer get to the steps.

As the twenty-first century came close, one of the reasons constantly cited for the spiraling downward trend of students' academic performance was that too many teachers were not certified. Being the only city workers who had to possess at least a bachelor's degree to be hired, a master's degree if they wanted to remain hired, also having to regularly go back to college to get extra credits for one reason or another didn't count. Another Giuliani suggestion was that there should be merit pay for the best performing teachers. It was also being advocated that teachers should have their vacation time cut short, that they should be made to teach longer hours. There was on-going feuding between the mayor and the latest of a number of fast-changing schools chancellors.

I always wanted the school newspaper to deal with relevant issues rather than so many of the meaningless issues school newspapers generally dealt with. So Academy Journal dealt with these issues and copies were sent to the mainstream media:

Should a computer teacher who proved his competence in this area on the test and in the classroom be fired from his/her position because he/she failed the science part of the certification test? Did it make him/her less able to teach computer skills? Should a proven competent math teacher be fired from his/her position because he/she did poorly on those questions pertaining to social studies and art? Should a teacher of English who has proven very competent in this subject both on the test and in the classroom but did poorly on the math questions be fired? Should a writing teacher who barely managed to pass all the tests but proved his/her incapability at class control be hired over another writing teacher who passed in this subject area with "flying colors," demonstrated his/her ability in class control, but didn't do well on questions pertaining to science and math? Undoubtedly, the Board of Education would do the idiotic and answer yes to these questions.

True, teachers who demonstrate their incompetence to teach well in their subject areas, irrespective of degrees, shouldn't be allowed to continue teaching. It also makes sense that teachers should have some all-around knowledge of subjects other than the ones they were hired to teach. But it's the knowledge of the subjects they were hired to teach and the ability they demonstrate in doing this that should matter most.

Merit pay for teacher wouldn't produce positive change, either. Certainly, if an impartial survey was carried out to determine the New York City mayor with the greatest propensity for meaning to inflict his views and ideas on this city, Giuliani would easily emerge the undisputed winner. Frightening indeed, because so many of his ideas obviously suddenly fell from out of the dark clouds of his imagination.

Teachers who really want to make a positive difference in the dispensing of education would struggle toward this goal without merit pay. Of course, they should be paid a decent wage to be able to keep up with the constantly rising standard of living. For as much as is expected of them, nobody will give them housing, groceries, or transportation at a reduced rate.

One thing merit pay would surely result in is more of that

societal evil called selfishness, wrapped in nice-sounding euphemisms for acceptability, that inevitably leads to fellow workers tearing down and cutting the throats of one another in the interest of getting that "fistful of dollars" reward. There is also the existing teacher-on-teacher selfishness. Moreover, consideration must be given to the fact that in the society it's not unusual for those who are slick to pass themselves off as the dedicated they are not.

It was thought to be ever so funny, the editorial I wrote implying that chancellors were responsible for much of the problems plaguing the public school system. Obviously, it was thought to be funny because I utilized a lot of humor in writing "the piece," but mostly, I am sure, because I suggested myself as the best choice to be the next chancellor, since almost all who held the position were regarded as failures:

It is understandable that there is so much disillusionment generally regarding the downward trend of education in the public school system. After all, students now have access to psychologists, education evaluators and sociologists, many with the highest degrees in their area, yet their performance and values do not match up to that of students of years earlier who didn't have access to this wealth of purported expertise. The fault is not entirely that of these professionals, though.

The public school system is very badly in need of solid leadership at the very top possessing: sound common sense and perception; observation that is equal to the keenness of an eagle's eyes searching out prey; the strong socio-political consciousness that is not tampered with by the fear to tell it like it is – solid truth.

The problems are many, greatly exacerbated by the tributaries fed from a few major sources, which if only fixed, would significantly weaken the strength of these tributaries' problems.

This is not meant as an ego trip. Other than being employed by the Board of Education of the City of New York, this writer has authored books of creative writing. It is a historical fact that from among such writers have always been found those who are by far more apt to possess the qualities (characteristics) mentioned here than are those whose intelligence is judged only by the possession of degrees. Does this writer possess these qualities (characteristics)? Without an iota of doubt, the answer is yes.

It would be a great thing for the public school system if those with the power would elect this writer its new chancellor.

Flaunting big ideas to cover up the inability to achieve positive things, dodging under, around and stepping over the facts, finding sources on which to blame shortcomings, taking a hefty salary without a conscience attack for knowing that the big promises of positive change have not and will not materialize would no longer be done. Utilizing his obvious vast reservoir of qualities listed here – along with scruples – will either prove so unpalatable to make this writer the shortest term-serving chancellor of them all, or will cure all the major ills befalling the New York City Public School System like no other chancellor has or is likely to ever get done.

Advocating more school time for students, less time off for teachers is a strong case for quantity not quality. What good will more time do in a system where the consensus among youngsters is that the current school time is too long? And if the present teaching time – much of which is spent addressing behavioral problems – has resulted in so much stress among teachers, will they not be more stressed out by this additional teaching time; hence, not really making the extra contribution expected to come out of the additional time?

The best thing extra teaching time will do is help those working parents with baby-sitting problems and those who don't mind having their children out of the house for as long as possible.

Another solution offered by the "experts," whose solutions seldom accomplish anything, was to convince the older "master" teachers to forget about their plans to retire to Florida and continue to teach. Respect is due them for putting in those 25 or 30 years. It is worth reiterating, though, that in these years they learned very well how to manipulate situations in their favor. Notably, they make sure that none of the problem students ever end up in their classes. They have no problem manipulating this situation because when they forego retirement or come out of retirement, they elect to continue teaching at the same schools where they taught for several years and therefore know their way around, so to speak.

How does it help a system of such complexities that the selection of administrators is based primarily on passing courses bearing little relevance to these complexities? The same must be asked of teachers who are required to take courses that are supposed to help them in finding solutions to the daily behavioral problems in the classrooms only to find out that they ultimately must find their own solutions. And if they can't do the latter, but keep resorting to the solutions suggested by the books, they would never be able to control their classes.

It is common knowledge that with the passing of time the problems plaguing the school system have increased and grown worse. Suffice it to say, then, that the solutions offered by the experts are not solutions at all, as the experts are not experts

It doesn't help the situation that after a spate of reports about the very poor academic performance of students, or the worsening of their behavior, that television cameras soon find their way into selected classrooms – undoubtedly staged – to show students being studious and well behaved. It is on these occasions that the issue of schools padding grades is raised. The fact must be faced that the state of academic performance in the public schools is in worse state than it previously was. If teachers would adhere to the official demand that those students not deserving a passing grade should be given a failing grade, the number of failing students would increase phenomenally.

What the Board of Education Needs – Not Giuliani 273

For those who think that the behavioral problem in the schools, for instance, is not deteriorating, they should examine how at the present time (2002) sexual molestation of students by students has joined force with the other behavioral problems. This problem has increased in the last three to four years.

Why the increase in the problematic behavior and the downward spiraling academic performance?

There are many factors to be cited. But there is a major one on which the big shots deliberately turn their backs. Maybe because they are of the same conviction as so many in the society that this is one problem that cannot be turned around. But if it is not turned around, there will be no improvement no matter what other "solutions" are tried. That giant of a wish that American students be able to compete academically on the same level as Japanese and other Asian students will certainly *not* become reality. The problem is rooted in the *don't-give-a-damn, do as I please, have no respect for authority* attitude that is generally recognized by American children as rights given to them by the society – rights they not only exercise in the schools but in the homes.

Student artist hints that being down in jail doesn't mean that one shouldn't reach up.

< 19 >

Ending the Journey Through Jailhouse Jeopardy

It was now well into the 2000-2001 school year. Here I was, in spite of all the inconveniences, still teaching at Island Academy, as though I had not said when I first started at the school in February of 1987 that I would be gone in six months. And believe it or not, but I still had not taken that sabbatical leave, something I was entitled to.

In the years that passed I had seen the implementation of many changes, changes meant to bring about improvement. Maybe a little of this was achieved, but in general there was no doubt about the relevance of that popular paradox, "The more things change, the more they remain the same."

Certainly, the staff changes were many. A few staffers had died: Mr. Brines soon after he was appointed principal of another school; Mrs. Ashe and the tailoring teacher, both within a few months of retiring; Miss Graemes and Mr. Melendez, whose body was found in his apartment after he was missing from school for several days.

Mrs. Straus had left the school system, having decided that putting in those five years more, which would have extended her service to 25 years and guaranteed her a much better retirement check, was not worth the toll on her sanity. We were never that friendly with each other. It certainly came as a surprise to me that a few months before her retirement she approached me in the presence of a few teachers and told me, "You know, Mister Brathwaite, I really owe you an apology for my bad attitude toward you because I eventually got to find out that you wasn't the bad guy I thought you were." I told her not to worry about it. It wasn't that unusual for some people to formulate her kind of initial opinions about me, based mostly on the silence I often exhibited, only to eventually find out that I possess much better human qualities than most of those who struggled to portray these qualities in themselves. I thought it a pity, I told her, as I had intimated to her in the past, that she had allowed a pure Uncle Tom Negro to influence her initial feelings about me. She insisted on denying that such was the case. But I knew very well what was heard by my own ears. I reiterated that she shouldn't worry about it. I knew who I was. And this made me not concerned about how she felt about me before – or after.

The negative attitude of students still prevailed. All the efforts of B.O.E. personnel to get them to think of themselves as students and Island academy as a school on prison grounds were to no avail. They were convinced that they were inmates and the school a part of Rikers Island Jail.

I was disappointed that it was so difficult to get them to think more positively. The government was putting a lot of money into programs to help them to improve their lot. In general, the teachers put in strong efforts.

I understood why many of these students were not enthusiastic about academics; their experience told them that they were "not academic material." But they didn't take advantage of the vocational classes and try to learn a skill at least well enough to get an entry level start in the job market. Take my graphic arts classes, an area of skills very much in demand, skills that could save them from the ranks of recidivism. True, they liked these classes tremendously, but the serious, disciplined attitude that was so necessary wasn't sufficiently there. I would constantly tell them of the importance of having a skill; you took it with you anywhere and gave yourself a very good chance of getting well-paid employment. I even went so far as to get people employed in these skills I was trying to prepare them with to come to the school and have related discussions with them. I showed them videos of these skills in actual operation.

The gangs were still active. The Latin Kings and the Netas, comprised of Hispanics, were perhaps more established than the Bloods and the Crypts, comprised of Blacks. There was a strong religious attachment placed on the Black Muslims, but the D.O.C. didn't quite exempt them from the gang category.

I was a teacher, sent to Rikers to educate, not take on the problems of gangs. I observed, though, that when the Blacks and Hispanics "moved against" one another, the Hispanics tended to have the advantage, primarily because of that old weakness found among Blacks more so than among others: disunity.

The Latin Kings and the Netas were both made up of Hispanics (Latinos) from *all* Spanish backgrounds. And while they had their own skirmishes among themselves, when it came to a major "move against" Blacks, they were united in this move. Blacks, on the other hand, when they "moved against" Hispanics, were fragmented in their efforts. Blacks from America and the Caribbean didn't have the kind of solidarity to move as one. Among Black Americans there were different groups who didn't think they had enough in common to make a unified move: Bloods with Bloods only, Crypts with Crypts only, Black Muslims with Black Muslims only, Five Percenters with Five Percenters only. Among Caribbean Blacks island background was most important

I still saw that shameful habit of many Black youngsters to give white features to human figures they attempted to draw. Youngsters of all other groups naturally gave to such drawings features representing their racial group.

What had not changed, either, was the unprofessional behavior existing among some B.O.E. personnel. There was a significant subtle racial undercurrent. Once that culinary arts class was created and the teacher was White, this is where the White staffers congregated. I wasn't surprised.

Some White teachers needing union help wouldn't follow procedure and come to me, the union rep; they would go over my head. They acted like they wanted to form their own little union group, taking their concerns to a White woman who wasn't a member of the United Federation of Teachers, but acted as if she was the union rep for this group.

I still didn't appreciate the attitude of the culinary arts teacher. I was still convinced that she was the leading one encouraging Big Ak against me. She was also fond of criticizing the Academy Journal. I wondered if this had something to do with her back-biting friend Mr. Jewison.

He had long been dissatisfied over those articles by students about the O.J. Simpson trial and the media treatment of Michael Jackson's marriage to Lisa-Marie Presley. He was wrong that there was a racist twist to the discussions I had with the writing students on these issues, that I was defending Simpson and Jackson because of their race. I told the students of my belief that had Simpson been of any other race, particularly if White, there wouldn't have been the international obsession – and curiosity – over his trial for the murder of his White wife. The students didn't do their jumping and screaming for joy when he was acquitted because of articles in the Academy Journal. They did so because most of them, no matter what their criminal acts, bore a deep resentment against society for putting them in jail; and they saw Simpson as one of them. As for Jackson, I told the students of my belief that if Lisa-Marie was an average White female, White society and its media wouldn't have been so upset over her marriage to Jackson, the media constantly expressing doubts that she was actually having sex with him. Lisa-Marie was the multi-millionaire daughter of the late purported King of Rock 'n' Roll, Elvis Presley, a man so beloved by so many millions of Whites around the world that they refuse to believe he is dead. This meant that Jackson, no matter his being an exceptionally talented musician and entertainer – more so than Elvis was – no matter how white-looking he transformed himself, remained a nigger in their eyes. Hence, the great blemishing of their memories of Elvis by both Jackson and Lisa-Marie. I couldn't possibly have been defending Simpson and Jackson because of their race. I didn't see Simpson as innocent. And I definitely saw him and Jackson – the latter perhaps a bit more so – as two of the foremost self-hating, misguided, clown Negroes of the time; characteristics for which I hold an abysmal abhorrence.

Whatever the case, I wasn't so pleased, either, that the administration seemed to make special efforts to go easy on the culinary arts teacher as far as classroom pressure was concerned. We often had common students and I thought that they, too, perceived of these special efforts and often geared their behavior accordingly, Black ones especially. I would notice that some of them when they came to my class from hers would be in a disruptive rap music mood. I would take it upon myself to investigate their mood while with her and would notice that they didn't display that degree of disruption in their mood. I deplored the double standard, seeing it as a psychological thing whereby they saw it as acceptable to be disruptive when with me. I would reprimand them severely for displaying a slave mentality. It was so natural for them that they were unaware of their double standard. I also recognized something else very important: The culinary arts teacher had the support and protection of Big Ak behind her. When she was faced with any unacceptable behavior from her students and she called him, he would immediately run to her assistance, threatening them.

Mr. Jewison, too, was still constantly "up in" Big Ak's face, whispering. It had taken me a long time to understand why many staff members distrusted him more than they did others, accusing him of being "a wimp" and "a back stabber." Some questioned his sexual preference. I eventually concluded that he was a wimp and a back stabber, a quiet-acting carrier and bringer of divisive gossip. As to that rumor of his refusal to "come out of the closet," it was none of my business. But I did develop a bad attitude against him after we somehow got into a discussion about NAMBLA (North American Man Boy Love Association), an organization which advocated the right of men to have sex with little boys. I told him I thought these men were immoral bastards who should be thrown in jail. He had initially skirted around the issue regarding his feelings about this until I made this statement , then he responded, "If that's what they want to do, why not? What's wrong with it?"

There was a time when Big Ak regularly made some very harsh homophobic statements. Surprising, he was no longer doing so. I wondered about this major change.

There was one thing of which I felt certain, even though for the past few months Big Ak and Rev had not been particularly nasty to me, they had not changed to the point of meaning me any good. I kept in mind the fact that they tended to engage in their "do Brathwaite in" acts when they thought I had to be off guard and they therefore stood a better chance of succeeding. This is precisely how it turned out to be in early 2001.

That evening when the school day ended I was eager to get out of the school and head home to Brooklyn. Mr. Hines came to my classroom and told me he wanted to see me in his office. Thinking it was one of those little things requiring the union rep's signature, I joked with him that he never wanted to see me leave the school and go home, that it was alright for him to stay because he was the one who made all the money, and why not leave the matter until the morning? He told me it was a serious matter.

Mr. Hines handed me a sheet of paper containing a report by Rev accusing me of having "stabbed" one of my students in his buttocks with a sharpened pencil. Supposedly, the student, Jaime, had sought out Rev to report the "attack."

Unlike as in the case of the secretary's complaint, I was not shocked, though somewhat surprised, for there was indeed an occurrence of the sort during the seventh period. I regarded it as a case of the student not being stabbed but "stuck," and accidentally at that.

It had started out with a situation that regularly developed with Jaime: wanting to have his own way and throwing a bad temper tantrum when I didn't give in, and in fact, would do as I did on this day, chide him for being "a seventeen-year-old young man who acts like a little kid." Yet I was never excessively hard on him for this. He wasn't really a bad person. He actually always soon got over his temper tantrum, forgetting that it ever happened. So on this day when he left the classroom and didn't soon return minus his tantrum, I was sure this was the way it would be tomorrow.

But Rev came into contact with him while he was still in his tantrum mood and hearing that his mood was connected to Mr. Brathwaite, set out concocting and encouraging his damaging report. I would also learn later that once he knew that Jaime was about to be released soon, he threatened him with extending his jail time if he refused to help him to get me. He also forced sensationalist statements out of other students. He had them write statements that were not only untrue but about what they had not seen. Some of those writing the statements were not even present when the alleged stabbing took place.

I would later hear their apologies for making these statements:

"They forced me to do dat shit;" "they said they won't let me go to commissary;" "man, you don't understand, we be in jail, we ain't got no choice."

The principal concurred with me that it wasn't about the student being stuck but about who the teacher was that was involved in the incident. Had it been some other teachers in this minor incident, Rev and Big Ak would have ignored the student's complaint and all would have been forgotten. And of course, if it was a case of one of those poundings students got from them, it would have been a normal thing.

It was hinted that maybe having a talk with Rev and Big Ak would put a stop to this rush to make a mountain out of a mole-hill. I made it clear that I wouldn't give them the satisfaction of thinking I was begging them for mercy; let them go ahead and do what they wanted to and I would deal with the consequences.

In no time, so to speak, the school's new A.P. was heard on the phone dramatizing "the stabbing of the student" by the teacher, the sort of kick-my-colleague-ass activity I have already alluded to as being popular among teachers, as opposed to the wall of silence (support) that cops showed for fellow cops and firemen for fellow firemen. But I wouldn't say his was a case of "get Brathwaite," just his big-mouthing, not even thinking of how it could hurt me.

He was one of those who had taken those worthless-ass courses that determined who was capable of becoming leaders in the school system. And I did notice that he immediately set out to be on good terms with Big ak and Rev, two characters with whom he had a few serious arguments while he was still a teacher. In fact, I was sorry when he left the school temporary back then because his occasional standing up to them helped to strengthen my position.

I recalled very well also that he was a teacher who had a very hard time controlling his classes. I had to advise him against struggling to make his voice heard above the voices of his students. Rather, insist on some order in speaking. Put a stop to their bad habit of several speaking at the same time. Implement a system of "you speak now and I'll listen; then I'll speak and you'll listen." It would eliminate the noise and the need to shout to be heard. There used to be so much shouting in his classroom that it disturbed me in my adjoining classroom. And talking to him about his rise to A.P. and his obvious ambition to rise higher, I told him he could avoid many of the common problems if he developed the courage and ethics to treat all staff equally and ignore the propensity of the many to worm themselves into the hearts of administrators for the sake of getting special privileges.

At any rate, by the first period next morning there were more captains than usual on the school floor. So many, in fact, that staffers wondered what was happening. The principal and I sat down with about three of them and we discussed the incident of the student being stuck with a pencil (or stabbed, for those preferring the superlative dramatizing). Lots of notes were taken. In the final analysis, it was concluded that the student was unintentionally stuck in a superficial manner.

It didn't help Rev that he had intimidated students, forced them to give false testimony, and that the student Jaime, after snapping out of his temper tantrum, showed no interest in filing a complaint against me. Also, there were those C.O.'s who worked on the school floor and were not so fond of Big Ak or Rev especially.

Once again, Big Ak tried to distance himself from the issue. But even if students had not informed me of his surreptitious involvement, I would have had serious doubts about Rev pursuing actions against me and not letting Big Ak know. I also would have had serious doubts that Rev would have pursued these actions if Big Ak had suggested that he didn't.

From his home, Jaime sent me a message via one of his homeboys from the 'hood, who was still in jail, saying he was sorry for getting me into trouble. I told his homeboy to tell him not to lose any sleep over it because I knew he wouldn't intentionally try to create problems for me.

News also reached me that in spite of the fact that that very attractive African-American captain from South Carolina approached the issue with problem-solving on her mind and did just that, behind the scene attempts were made by those wanting badly to "get Brathwaite" to resuscitate the issue through contact with Jaime's mother, using the school's psychologist as influence.

Whether true or false, I don't know. I have heard no more of it.

I concluded the school year in June. Working summer was out of the question. It gave me a good chance to think about the past, the present and the future.

In spite of the trials and tribulations, I realized that I had touched so many young lives since February of 1984, more than I ever would have imagined. During my tenure in Rikers Island Jail particularly, I had touched the lives of youngsters of every racial background, and if not every nationality, then not far from it. And I know for a fact that I touched their lives positively – overwhelmingly so.

My reputation as a writer got me saddled with extra responsibility. Seldom was there a time that I was free of two teachers' helpers who were going to college struggling to earn a degree and needed my help with their literature and writing assignments.

The magnanimity of this experience – with the students – being such, only death would erase the memory. And as my retrospective look at this experience continues even now, two years later, this definitely remains a fact:

When the 2002 school year started in September, in spite of the pleading of my principal to change my mind, even suggesting that I would do so if I first went on that sabbatical leave I never took, I had decided to stick with my sudden decision to call an end to this experience through early retirement.

THE END

Publisher's Note

Within a few months after his retirement, the author was medically advised to undergo open-heart surgery. After much self-denial and reluctance, he went through this traumatic experience, which he feels can partly be attributed to all that extra stress that will inevitably befall any teacher in the New York City Public School system who should assume the mammoth task of trying too hard to correct students' behavior.

From Kibo Books

THE MYSTERY MAN by DEREK REECE ...
Convicted Black serial rapist Burke seems so guilty, yet the attitude of London's cops and what transpires in the courts of London beg consideration of his emphatic "not guilty" plea.

JOURNEY FREE: The Eighth House by MAKEELAH AMANI ...
This slim volume of poetry epitomizes so well the adage, "Good things come in little packages."

KEY VISIONS 1.0: The Poetic Ranting of MAKEELHA AMANI...
This CD contains some of her typically hard-driving poems, accompanied by soulful rhythms.

Kibo Books, P.O.Box 021442, Cadman Plaza, Brooklyn, New York 11210
Kibobooks @aol.com